John C. Eccles

The Human Mystery

The GIFFORD Lectures
University of Edinburgh 1977–1978

With 89 Figures

Springer International 1979

Sir John Eccles

CH-6611 Contra (Locarno) TI, Switzerland

Max-Planck-Institut für biophysikalische Chemie
(Karl-Friedrich-Bonnhoeffer-Institut) D-3400 Göttingen, West-Germany

ISBN 3-540-09016-9 Springer-Verlag Berlin Heidelberg New York
ISBN 0-387-09016-9 Springer-Verlag New York Heidelberg Berlin

Library of Congress Cataloging in Publication Data. Eccles, John Carew, Sir. The human mystery. (Gifford lectures; 1978) Bibliography: p. Includes index. 1. Brain. 2. Life-Origin. 3. Human evolution. 4. Anthroposophy. 5. Natural theology. I. Title. II. Series. QP376.E265   573   78-12095

Printed in Germany

The use of registered names, trademarks, etc. in this publication does not imply, even in the absence of a specific statement, that such names are exempt from the relevant protective laws and regulations and therefore free for general use.

Offsetprinting and Binding: Appl, Wemding. 2120/3140–543210

For Helena

who contributed so much

Preface

Under the terms of the endowment by Lord Gifford, the Gifford Lectures have been an annual event in the University of Edinburgh since 1887, and also in three other Scottish universities. According to the will of Lord Gifford they were set up ". . . to promote and diffuse the study of Natural Theology in the widest sense of that term – in other words, the knowledge of God". The assignment is for ten lectures, and I delivered them from 20 February, to 13 March, 1978.

I chose the theme of the Human Mystery because I believe that it is vitally important to emphasize the great mysteries that confront us when, as scientists, we try to understand the natural world including ourselves. There has been a regrettable tendency of many scientists to claim that science is so powerful and all pervasive that in the not too distant future it will provide an explantation in principle of all phenomena in the world of nature including man, even of human consciousness in all its manifestations. When that is accomplished scientific materialism will then be in the position of being an unchallengable dogma accounting for all experience.

In our recent book (Popper and Eccles, 1977) Popper has labelled this claim as promissory materialism, which is extravagant and unfulfillable. Yet, on account of the high regard for science, it has great persuasive power with the intelligent laity because it is advocated unthinkingly by the great mass of scientists who have not cirtically evaluated the dangers of this false and arrogant claim. The danger is already evident in the counterproductive flourishing of anti-science.

In my lectures I built my story upon orthodox science even up to the most recent discoveries and theories in order to reveal in field after field great and mysterious problems, which are beyond present science and may in part be forever beyond science. Such problems arise, for example, when considering the origin of the Universe in the Big Bang, the origin of life, the manner in which biological evolution was constrained through its waywardness to lead eventually to *Homo sapiens,* and finally to the origin of each individual conscious self. These problems are of particular relevance to Natural Theology, which is what the Gifford Lectures are about. But within this almost infinitely wide range of enquiry these lectures will serve to uncover many extraordinary contingencies on the way to the origin of each one of us as a consciously experiencing being. The theme of the contingencies that led to us will keep recurring. It is as if we could have been disembodied observers of the sequential lines of contingencies on which our eventual existence depended. I believe that this dramatic licence will give new perspectives in thought and new meaning to our life, which are desperately needed in this age of disillusionment.

The position I adopt is frankly and unashamedly anthropocentric. I make no apologies because I believe that it conforms with the fact that we are central to all oberservations and to all theories. For example when a description is given of an ant colony by Edward Wilson it is the description by a human investigator with his human wisdom and understanding and not by one of the ant sociobiologists of the colony. This is even the case with man's nearest relative, the chimpanzee. The dedicated and sensitive observer, Jane Goodall, does not write as a chimpanzee, surveying himself and his associates with her as an intruder into his colony.

Throughout I have largely restricted my vision to the scientific story of the way that led to us from the Big Bang. This device has been adopted in order to sustain the dramatic character of my presentation. It is a good exercise in imagination to try comprehending the immense delays and twists of fate in the evolutionary way that led to us after life got started about 3.4 billion years ago (the 'eobacteria'). It took over 2.5 billion years before the appearance of the first multicellular organisms! When the earliest fish, *Agnatha*, appeared, it could not have been predicted that one line of evolution would lead to mammals. And from the earliest mammals, primitive insectivores, no prediction could have been made of the eventual line of primate evolution to hominids and so to *Homo Sapiens* with the transcendent endowment of self-consciousness.

Since the Gifford Lectures are interdepartmental, every effort has been made to present scientific material in a simple form with a minimum of technicality, yet at the same time to tell of the most recent conjectures on the points of major interest to the theme of the lectures. In this endeavour many explanatory diagrams have been presented. However, the last three lectures are on the human brain and the brain-mind problem. It has been important to present the most recent concepts on the way in which our knowledge of the structure and function of the brain leads to hypotheses of the brain-mind interaction in perception, in memory, in voluntary action and in all the manifestations of self-consciousness. There would be no human mystery if the human brain were no more than a chimpanzee brain, or even a hominid brain! It is evident therefore that I have to give a more detailed treatment of the human brain than for any other field of scientific enquiry that is essayed in my lectures. It should be possible for the reader to appreciate the wonders of the human brain particularly in its relationship to the self-conscious mind, even if the text and figures are not fully comprehended in the first reading. I pray the reader's indulgence.

The lectures as printed are genuinely the text that formed the basis of the lectures as delivered, and are not some later compilation that lacks the dramatic quality of a personal affirmation. They were already fully written out, but only in small part were they actually read out to the audience. At the end of each lecture the text was delivered to Mrs. Knight, who very efficiently converted my handwriting into the typescript that was delivered to the publishers fifteen days after the last lecture. There were, however, more illustrations for the lectures than appear in this volume. In the book, for the reader's guidance, each lecture is preceded by the Synopsis that was prepared some two months before the lecture and distributed to the audience. Only in Lecture 10 did the lecture depart seriously from the original plan, so the synopsis has been modified accordingly. Throughout the lectures I was greatly helped by the enthusiasm of the large audience who were faithful to the end of the course of three lectures a week for ten lectures, there being also two discussion meetings. I think we felt the experience to be a conjoint intellectual adventure.

JOHN C. ECCLES

Acknowledgements

I wish to express my thanks to the Gifford Lectureship Committee for the invitation to deliver the Gifford Lectures at the University of Edinburgh during the academic year 1977–1978. My good friend Sir Hugh Robson, the Principal and Vice Chancellor, conveyed the invitation to me, and I was happily looking forward to a renewed association with him. Unfortunately he died unexpectedly a few weeks before the lectures were delivered. These lectures can be regarded as a memorial. I would like to thank especially Professor Tom Torrance who initiated the invitation and Miss Jean Ewan, Secretary of the Gifford Lectureship Committee, for so efficiently and kindly making all arrangements before and during the lectures. I need not name the many friends who made the stay in Edinburgh so memorable for my wife and myself. We greatly look forward to the next Giffords in April and May 1979.

Acknowledgements are given in the text for the many excellent illustrations that form an important part of such a wide-ranging scientifique presentation. My special thanks are due to Professor Rolf Hassler and Dr. Manfred Klee for so kindly arranging for the preparation of the illustrations which was carried out so well by Hedwig Thomas.

Again the staff of Springer-Verlag has given very personal service in the publishing of this book. Dr. Heinz Götze has been a very good friend throughout the whole publishing operation, and I wish particularly to thank Dr. Thomas Thiekötter for his dedication and efficiency and Silvia Osteen who also helped notably.

Contents

Lecture 1

The Theme of Natural Theology:
How the Challenge Will Be Met

Synopsis and Introduction

Lord Gifford founded these lectures for the purpose of having Natural Theology treated as a science just as Astronomy or Chemistry and without reference to revelation. My great master, Sherrington, gave these lectures forty years ago on the theme "Man on his Nature". This introductory lecture will be a survey of the great imaginative insights that Sherrington presented on the nature of man. Throughout he adhered strictly to the evolutionary story of man's origin, hence it was beyond Sherrington's understanding how this materialist mechanism of biological evolution could bring forth beings with self-consciousness and values. Yet he insisted on the pre-eminence of man's non-sensual being, the conscious I, which he contrasted with the matter-energy system composing the body and brain. This theme of frank dualism will be developed further in these lectures.

In the last forty years our scientific knowledge has grown enormously beyond what Sherrington could build upon. There will be a brief survey of some outstanding efforts by scientists to do what Sherrington attempted to do, but with newer knowledge. The insights of Schrödinger, Polanyi, Dobzhansky, Penfield, Thorpe and Lemberg in particular provide thematic material for my presentation, which is dependent so much on the philosophy of my life-long friend and collaborator, Popper.

In considering the human mystery in depth we must retrace the steps whereby we came to be what we are. This story has been essayed countless times in our human history with the myths or stories of origin. Literal interpretations of these stories, as for example the stories of Genesis, have been discredited by the scientific knowledge of the last few centuries. So we have to start anew in the light of this scientific knowledge. But where to start? From our present human situation with our culture and our values we go back to primitive men, then to hominids, then to primate forebears and so on down the great evolutionary tree to the origin of life. Always each backward step leads to the next backward step. So the origin of life leads to the creation of Planet Earth with the chemical and physical conditions conducive to life. But that leads further backwards to the creation of the solar system in our galaxy and eventually to the "Big Bang" some 10 to 12 billion[1] years ago when the whole universe began. It is impossible to go back further in time. So by necessity the next lecture will begin with the Big Bang! We will from the start be raising fundamental issues for Natural Theology.

Lord Gifford founded these lectures for the purpose of having Natural Theology treated as a science just as Astronomy or Chemistry and without

---

[1] Always in these lectures billion is the American billion, a thousand million.

reference to revelation. My great master, Sherrington (1940), gave these lectures forty years ago here in Edinburgh, on the theme "Man on his Nature". In his initial considerations of what was required Sherrington states:

> The Natural Theologist, if we may so address him, in his efforts from consideration of Nature without appeal to revelation, to come to a conclusion about the existence and ways of God has thus to include himself as part of the natural evidence. He then sees himself as a piece of Nature looking around at Nature's rest.

Furthermore:

> Nature in virtue of himself, has now entered on a stage when one at least of its growing points has started thinking in 'values'. This comes before him as part of the evidence to be considered. The province of Natural Theology is surely to weigh from all the evidence derivable from Nature, whether Nature, taken all in all, signifies and implies the existence of what with reverence is called God; and, if so, again with all reverence, what sort of God.

1.1 Sherrington's Gifford Lectures

The general theme of Sherrington's "Man on his Nature" is the dualism of man's nature, body and mind. This philosophical position is completely antipathetic to the established philosophy of this materialistic age. For Sherrington this dualistic nature of man was completely mysterious. Much of his lectures 6–12 is devoted to the great enigma of dualism and the interaction between mind and brain, which he well recognized to be contrary to natural science as it then was. At the time of the lectures the prevailing scientific belief was that man in all his most unique mental characteristics – thoughts, imaginings, memories, decisions, creativities in the arts and in the sciences – would ultimately be explicable in a materialist and determinist mode. There would then be no residue pointing to a mental or non-material component in man's make-up. This promissory triumph of monist materialism was the confidently expected goal of the scientific study of man. The brain-mind problem would then become a non-problem after over 2000 years of fruitless philosophical enquiry, and the principal interest of Natural Theology – the uniqueness of man – would evaporate at the same time. Despite the stress of expounding an unpopular philosophy, Sherrington could have subtle asides, for example:

> I have seen the question asked "why should mind have a body?" The answer may well run "to mediate between it and other mind". It might be objected that such a view is undiluted 'anthropism'. To that we might reply, anthropism seems the present aim of the planet though presumably not its enduring aim.

I shall again raise this question of anthropism in a most striking manner towards the end of Lecture 2.

Always Sherrington was mindful of his assigned task of relating his lectures to Natural Theology. For example at the outset of the tenth lecture he states:

> Our topic of last time asked if and how it is that our thinking is correlated with our brain. If Natural Theology argue from the facts of Nature to a Divine Scheme to which they may point, then that question seems germane to our theme. It lies at the threshold of human approach to the whole Natural Scheme. Unaided human sight will at best compass but a corner of the scheme. There will be much to which man has not access. The distances are immense and he is near-sighted. He peers into a small patch and what he sees there he submits to his reason which after all is very newly hatched. What wonder if his conclusions be meagre and insecure. What wonder they are narrowly anthropomorphic. Such they must be. That to him is perhaps their chiefest value at this present. Without that they would not yield him, we may think, the zest, courage, ambition, altruism, which they do, or to come to our point, the idea of the Divine.

This wonderful and inspiring passage is very close to my own beliefs as I give these lectures. In considering the nature of man, the fundamental concept of dualism keeps on recurring in Sherrington's thoughts:

> No attributes of 'energy' seem findable in the process of mind. That absence hampers explanation of the tie between cerebral and mental. Where the brain correlates with mind, no microscopical, no physical, no chemical means detect any radical difference between it and other nerve that does not correlate with mind. The two for all I can do remain refractorily apart. They seem to me disparate; not mutually convertible; untranslatable the one into the other.

> So our two concepts, space-time energy sensible, and insensible unextended mind, stand in some way coupled together, but theory has nothing to submit, as to how they can be so. Practical life assumes that they are so and on that assumption meets situation after situation; yet has no answer for the basal dilemma of how the two cohere.

So in conclusion Sherrington leaves it as a human mystery:

> Between these two, naked mind and the perceived world, is there then nothing in common? They have this in common – we have already recognized it – they are both concepts; they both of them are parts of knowledge of one mind. They are therefore distinguished, but are not sundered. Nature in evolving us makes them two parts of the knowledge of one mind and that one mind our own. We are the tie between them. Perhaps we exist for that.

I accept and admire this visionary writing by Sherrington, but, in the light of the knowledge that has been won in the four decades since his lectures, I will attempt to define the brain-mind problem more starkly. No longer should we be content with an exposition of the problem in the black box manner. In Lectures 8 to 10 the latest discoveries and the most advanced thinking on the structure and functioning of the cerebral cortex lead on to hypotheses that are essentially scientific and which are justified by their great explanatory power. I am sure that Sherrington would have approved of these imaginative efforts to build coherent theories relating to the brain-mind problem. He also would not have been put off by the criticisms that such theories are not in complete accord with such a basic law of physics as the first law of thermodynamics. As we say in our recent book (Popper and Eccles, 1977), there is need for some revision of physics in order to allow for the interaction of mind and matter in some special regions of the brain. This opinion has already been expressed by the great physicists Schrödinger (1958) and Wigner (1964).

1.2 Subsequent Contributions on the General Theme of Sherrington's Lectures

As could have been forseen, Sherrington's magnificent attempt to face up unflinchingly to the mystery involved in the full range of human experience was subjected to a great barrage of criticism. It is not my task to reply to these critics. There have been effective replies. For example, Gilbert Ryle's (1949) *The Concept of Mind* was answered by Beloff's (1962) *The Existence of Mind* and Feigl's (1967) *The Mental and the Physical* by Polten's (1973) *Critique of the Psycho-Physical Identity Theory*. And recently Popper and I (1977) have published in *The Self and Its Brain* an extensive criticism of the various kinds of parallelism and have further developed the dualist-interactionist hypothesis from Sherrington's formulation in the Gifford lectures of forty years ago. I will briefly present comments by distinguished scientists. This material is of particular importance to me at this juncture because it provides me with valuable support for the developments I will essay in these lectures. It will be recognised that in these last forty years our scientific knowledge has grown enormously beyond what Sherrington could build upon.

The great physicist Erwin Schrödinger (1958) formulated in a forthright manner the dualist problem:

> The world is a construct of our sensations, perceptions, memories. It is convenient to regard it as existing objectively on its own. But certainly it does not become manifest by its mere existence. Its becoming manifest is conditional on very special goings on in very special parts of this very world, namely, on certain events that happen in a brain. That is an inordinately peculiar kind of implication, which prompts the question: what particular properties distinguish these brain processes and enable them to produce the manifestation? Can we guess which material processes have this power, which not? Or simpler: what kind of material process is directly associated with consciousness?

Much of my Lectures 8 and 10 will be devoted to answering these questions. Schrödinger's comments on Sherrington are most laudatory:

> Sir Charles Sherrington published his momentous *Man on his Nature*. The book is pervaded by the honest search for objective evidence of the interaction between matter and

mind. I cannot convey the grandeur of Sherrington's immortal book by quoting sentences; one has to read it oneself.

Moreover Schrödinger analyses the position that has arisen from the scientific method of obtaining a world picture by the restriction of its subject matter to objective phenomena:

> The physical world picture lacks all the sensual qualities that go to make up the Subject of Cognizance. The model is colourless and soundless and unpalpable. In the same way and for the same reason the world of science lacks, or is deprived of, everything that has a meaning only in relation to the consciously contemplating, perceiving and feeling subject. I mean in the first place the ethical and aesthetical values, any values of any kind, everything related to the meaning and scope of the whole display. All this is not only absent but it cannot, from the purely scientific point of view, be inserted organically.

Schrödinger here anticipated the criticisms that I shall make of Monod's book *Chance and Necessity* later it this lecture. He reveals the problem that has to be tackled in considering the nature of man in all its connotations, not only as a scientist, but as a human person with values and emotions, and with deep feelings for personal existence and its meaning, which gives the theme for these lectures on "the human mystery".

The essential dualism of human experience has been well expressed by another great physicist, Eugene Wigner (1964):

> There are two kinds of reality or existence – the existence of my consciousness and the reality or existence of everything else. The latter reality is not absolute but only relative. Excepting immediate sensations, the content of my consciousness, everything is a construct; but some constructs are closer, some further, from the direct sensations.

You will see that Wigner regards the constructs, that is the material world, as having a second order of reality in contrast to the absolute reality of our conscious experiences.

Recognition of the enigma of human experience was well expressed by Thorpe (1961) in a manner completely in accord with Sherrington:

> Every man's world picture is a construct of his mind, yet the conscious mind itself remains a stranger within that construct. For me, the essential fact is that, however much or little I know of the world around me, I know my own mind at first hand, and – in a sense – better than I know anything. It is my mind which experiences and interprets all that my sense organs supply, and the whole of science and every other activity of man is ultimately dependent on this basic assumption that the mind is primary in knowing. From this it follows, I believe, that mind and body are in some sense two things and that there is an external world 'not I' which is a reality, however imperfect my awareness of it may be.

A little later Michael Polanyi (1966) attacked reductionism of biology to physics and chemistry on the grounds that, in a hierarchy of levels,

> the operations of a higher level can never be derived from the laws governing its isolated particulars, it follows that none of these biotic operations can be accounted for by the laws

of physics and chemistry. Yet it is taken for granted today among biologists that all manifestations of life can ultimately be explained by the laws governing inanimate matter. Yet this assumption is patent nonsense.

The reference of Polanyi is of course to a complete explanation of *all* that happens in a living organism. Physical and chemical processes go on in a living organism in a manner that is explicable by physics and chemistry, but are subservient to control by the biological organization of the living cell and this in turn is subservient to control by the whole organism.

Polanyi goes on to state:

> The hierarchic structure of the higher forms of life necessitates the assumption of further processes of emergence. Thus the logical structure of the hierarchy implies that a higher level can come into existence only through a process not manifest in the lower level, a process that thus qualifies as an emergence.

This principle will be invoked in Lecture 4, where we will be considering biological evolution.

In his most thoughtful book *The Biology of Ultimate Concern*, Dobzhansky (1967) presents his views on the human mystery with deep biological wisdom:

> Man can transcend himself, and see himself as an object among other objects. He has attained the status of a person in the existential sense, and with it a poignant experience of freedom, of being able to contrive and to plan actions, and to execute his plans or to leave them in abeyance. Through freedom, he gains a knowledge of good and of evil. This knowledge is a heavy load to carry, of which organisms other than man are free. Man's freedom leads him to ask . . . Big Questions, which no animals can ask. Does my life and the lives of other people have any meaning? Does the world into which I am cast without my consent have any meaning? There are no final answers to these Big Questions, and probably there never will be any, if by answers one means precise, objective, provable certitudes. And yet seek for some sort of answers we must, because it is the highest glory of man's humanity that he is capable of searching for his own meaning and for the meaning of the Cosmos.

These present lectures are attempts to find partial answers to the Big Questions. This is essentially the concern of Natural Theology. Dobzhansky's book is devoted to the Big Questions, and there will be many further references in these lectures to Dobzhansky's *ultimate concern*, a most apt term that he borrowed from Paul Tillich (1959):

> Religion is the aspect of depth in the totality of the human spirit. Religion, in the largest and most basic sense of the word, is ultimate concern. And ultimate concern is manifest in all creative functions of the human spirit.

Finally I will quote from the great biochemist, Rudolph Lemberg, who died in 1976 leaving an unfinished manuscript entitled *Complementarity*, which gave his philosophy of science and of life. Later in these lectures there will be further references to this deeply moving testament, a testament of ultimate concern:

> We are creatures of the earth and part of nature, and also made in God's image in a sense deeper than that, though nature is also God's creation. We are in a special way God's helpmates to whom some creativity has been delegated. We remain part of nature and can as such enjoy its beauty. The knowledge of the really great scientists has not diminished but enhanced their sense of wonder and mystery. Teilhard de Chardin has shown us that, far from being a hindrance to the freedom of our souls, matter is in fact the complement, providing the handholds and footholds on the mountain of our spiritual climb. It appears that some mere scientists of today have forgotten that man is part of nature and therefore nature can never become entirely alien to him.

1.3 Development of the Theme for the Present Lectures

These excerpts from the writings of great scientists since Sherrington's Gifford Lectures reveal that the message he left has not been neglected, but rather has been developed. I have selected authors and quotations that relate specifically to my lectures. I am happy to identify myself with the thoughts of these authors, all of them my friends. I derive assurance that I am not a lone scientist when I am developing the theme in these lectures that are built upon Sherrington's inspired vision. In designing this course of lectures I have been prompted by one of Sherrington's imaginative and poetic asides in his tenth Gifford Lecture:

> Nature has evolved us as compounds of energy and mind. The scene of this operation has been the planet where we are. I would submit with deference that for one of like gift to the historian, here is a theme whose telling would be welcome to humanity. A theme which I would still think of as historical although much of it run back beyond tradition. Even if as fact it be too cloudy for history, it is yet worth telling as an available truth: the planet's story with what it has made and done.
>
> It is a story not remote from us because it is our own. The planet in travail with its children. With the Universe as heroic background for what to us is an intimate and heroic epic. A birth in cataclysm. Aeons of seething and momentous shaping. A triple scum of rock and tide and vapour – the planet's side – swept on through day and night. Then from that side arising shape after shape, past fancy. And latterly among them some imbued with sense and thought. And still more latterly, some with thought eager for 'values'. The planet, furnace of molten rocks and metals, now yielding thoughts and 'values'. Magic furnace. Beside its alchemy and transmutations the most impassioned dreams of Hermes Trismegistus and all his fellowship dwindle to paltry nothing.

In the dramatic context of this challenge by Sherrington, my Lectures 2 to 7 will be concerned with the steps whereby we came to be what we are. This story has been essayed countless times in our human history and prehistory with the myths or stories of origin. Literal interpretations of these stories, as for example the stories of Genesis, have been discredited by the scientific knowledge of the last few centuries. So we have to build up our story of origin in the light of this scientific knowledge. But where can we start? In the search for a beginning we can retrace as far as we are able the sequences of happenings up to the present. From our human situation with our culture and our values we can go back to primitive man, then to hominids, then to the primate forebears and so on down the great evolutionary tree to the origin of life. Always each backward step leads to the next backward step, though with less assurance the further we go. So the origin of life leads to the creation of Planet Earth with the chemical and physical conditions conducive to life. And that leads further backwards to the creation of the solar system in our galaxy, and eventually to the 'Big Bang' some 10–12 billion[1] years ago when the whole universe began. It is impossible to go back further, since time started from that instant, as also did physics. Thus, by necessity, the next lecture will begin with the Big Bang, and will give in outline the principal events that are believed to have happened after that so-momentous occasion. Its scope will be cosmology, not only the history but also the present situation and the future of the universe. We have to realize that our existence here and now is contingent on that initiating cosmic fireball, as it has been called. There is a great chain of contingency from the Big Bang and we will be following the sequences of that chain in lecture after lecture up to our existences here and now.

1.4 Philosophical Basis of the Present Lectures

In these lectures I will endeavour to create an atmosphere of wonder and of humility before the grandeur and immensity of the great cosmos that we can now contemplate in the light of modern cosmology. And superimposed on this material universe we have the creative richness of life in all its wondrous variety with ourselves as participants in life. But we are also able to stand outside the great material world when, as observers and thinkers, we attempt with our creative imagination to understand and to appreciate.

The tremendous successes of science in the last century have led to the expectation that there will be forthcoming in the near future a complete explanation in materialist terms of all the fundamental problems confronting us. These 'great questions', as they are called, have exercised the creative thinkers from Greek times onwards. It has been fashionable to overplay the explanatory power of science and this has led to the regrettable reac-

---

[1] Always in these lectures billion is the American billion, a thousand million, because it gives a much more convenient time scale.

tions of anti-science and of all manner of irrationalistic and magical beliefs. When confronted with the frightening assertion by scientists that we are no more than participants in the materialist happenings of chance and necessity, anti-science is a natural reaction. I believe that this assertion is an arrogant over-statement, as will appear in lecture after lecture. In fact the aim of the whole lecture series is an attack on monist-materialism, which is unfortunately believed in by most scientists with religious-like fervour. You might say that it is the belief of the establishment. During the last century there has been a complete inversion of what may be called the establishment. It must be recognized that monist-materialism leads to a rejection or devaluation of all that matters in life, as has been starkly expressed by Monod (1971) in his book *Chance and Necessity*, where the only value to be recognized as authentic is the truth established by scientific methods. All other values such as beauty, whether of nature or of art, moral values and altruism are regarded as inauthentic. Furthermore those who express beliefs in dualist interactionism, as do Popper and I in our book *The Self and Its Brain*, are labelled by Monod as animists. It is disconcerting, to say the least, to be relegated by Monod to a category that we share with those practising the most primitive superstitions and magic!

As will appear in these lectures I accept all of the discoveries and well-corroborated hypotheses of science – not as absolute truth but as the nearest approach to truth that has yet been attained. But these lectures will reveal in case after case that there is an important residue not explained by science, and even beyond any future explanation by science. This leads on to the theme of Natural Theology with the idea of a Supernatural beyond the explanatory power of science.

If I should be asked to express my philosophical position, I would have to admit that I am an animist on Monod's definition. As a dualist I believe in the reality of the world of mind or spirit as well as in the reality of the material world. Furthermore I am a finalist in the sense of believing that there is some Design in the processes of biological evolution that has eventually led to us self-conscious beings with our unique individuality; and we are able to contemplate and we can attempt to understand the grandeur and wonder of nature, as I will attempt to do in these lectures. But I am not a vitalist in the generally accepted sense of that term. I believe that all of the happenings in living cells will be found to be in accord with physics and chemistry, much of which has yet to be discovered. Yet, as I have already stated, I believe with Polanyi that there is a hierarchic structure with emergence of higher levels that could not have been predicted from the operations going on at a lower level. For example the emergence of life could not have been predicted even with a complete knowledge of all happenings in a prebiotic world, nor could the emergence of self-consciousness have been predicted.

My aim in these lectures is to review the sense of wonder and of mystery in our human existence. We must not claim to be self-sufficient. If we espouse the philosophy of monist-materialism, there is no base on which we can build a meaning for life or for the values. We would be creatures of chance and circumstance. All would be determined by our inheritance and our conditioning. Our feeling of freedom and of responsibility would be but an illusion. As against that I will present my belief that there is a great mystery in our existence and in our experiences in life that is not explicable in materialist terms. This residue is beyond all else the ultimate value of our world. As I shall suggest in the next lexture, the whole cosmos is not just running on and running down with no meaning. Furthermore, I will suggest in later lectures that we are creatures with some supernatural meaning as yet ill defined. We cannot know more than that we are all part of some great design. Each of us can have the belief that we are acting in some great unimaginable supernatural drama. We should give all we can in order to play our part.

It is customary to formulate questions of an existential kind in a general way, for others rather than oneself; and then to put oneself in the picture. My approach is the reverse. My problems arise in attempting to account for my own personal existence with all my most intimate personal experiences. That gives me the advantage of a privileged enquiry into what is uniquely my experience, which is an experience that cannot to even the smallest extent be shared directly by others, for example, at a trivial level, a pain. So in the first instance I of necessity adopt a solipsistic approach. However from the insights gained I am advantageously placed when I extend my enquiry to other selves. It is a game played between objective and subjective epistemologies. My subjective experiences gain an objective status when ranged against the experiences of others, as observed either at first hand or as expressed countless times by the great creative writers of the world. The world literature is the drama of countless selves – of conscious human beings with their sufferings, their joys, their sacrifices, their aspirations, their despairs, their loves, their hates – all aspects of the human mystery.

I conclude this introductory lecture by stating that the theme of the "human mystery" will be explored in such a way as to raise at every stage fundamental issues in Natural Theology.

Origin and Evolution of the Universe

Synopsis and Introduction

The cosmic fireball began about 10 to 12 billion years ago in an immense explosive outburst, the Big Bang. Much can be conjectured about the first 3.5 min, but the origin is completely mysterious. In that time all the matter of the Universe had been created from photons, being almost entirely hydrogen and helium. The expansion of the Universe so initiated accounts for the red shift now observed in the nebulae. These great aggregations of stars resemble our galaxy with its 10^{11} stars, there being about 10^{11} nebulae. So the total number of stars resembling our Sun is about 10^{22}. All nebulae are receding at immense velocities in the expanding Universe, the more remote the faster the recession. Extrapolating backwards from their present velocities of recession they would have been in close proximity about 18 billion years ago. But the rate of recession has been progressively slowed by gravitational attraction, so this value is an over-estimate for the Big Bang some 10–12 billion years ago. Initially great masses of gas were projected from the Big Bang at enormous velocities. Gradually by gravitational attraction these became aggregated into galaxies, but this was a long evolutionary process that is still continuing. Aggregations in primitive galaxies including our own resulted eventually in great stellar masses that within a billion years terminated in supernovae, providing enormous temperatures and pressures in which the heavy elements were 'cooked'. Our Sun came much later, about 4.6 billion years ago along with its planetary system; that will be the theme of lecture 3. Meanwhile we will follow the projected evolution of the Universe into the future. Will it expand on for ever or will it reach a summit and be brought back by gravitational attraction to a catastrophe in the Big Crunch, temporally symmetrical with the 'Big Bang'? From Einstein's General Theory of Relativity, and assuming with Wheeler an actual time of 10 billion years from the Big Bang, and the present recessional speed giving 20 billion years, it can be calculated that the total lifetime of the Universe will be 59 billion years, of which 10 billion have already passed. Here are themes for Natural Theology, as also is the 'anthropic principle' that will be discussed at the end of the lecture.

All peoples have developed myths of origin to satisfy their need for explanations of the world they live in, with the air, water and land, with the Sun, moon and stars, and with the question of some existence after death. The first written accounts of creation myths date from the Sumerians at about 2000 B.C., but this of course is merely our record of what had been orally transmitted for countless generations. The Egyptians also had a mythology dating from about the same time. Greek mythology with stories of creation

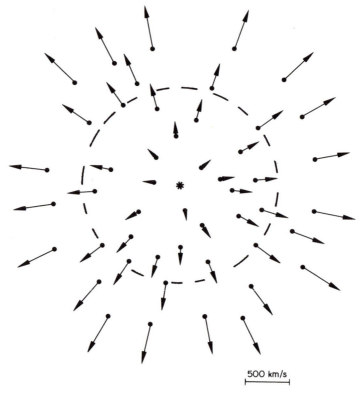

500 km/s

Fig. 2-1. A number of galaxies are shown by dots together with arrows that indicate by their lengths their velocity relative to a given galaxy *G*. Velocity scale is shown below. Note that in accord with Hubble's law the velocities are proportional to the distance from *, the circle indicating a radius of 20 million light years

was first given a coherent form by Hesiod at about 800 B.C. The Biblical account in Genesis, of about 600 B.C., was by far the most intellectually and emotionally satisfying with its wonderful imaginative scope that inspired great painters – for example, Michaelangelo in the Sistine Chapel. In its essentials the Biblical account was accepted by Newton, who even believed in the creation date that was calculated by Bishop Ussher to be 4004 B.C.!

In recent times there have been creation stories in the light of modern science. The rejection of the creation story of Genesis led to the belief that the Universe had always existed and was of infinite extent; hence the question of its origin was meaningless. There was no creation and *a fortiori* no Creator. There is an interesting story of Einstein's derivation in 1915 of an expanding universe from his geometric account of gravitation, the General Theory of Relativity. To him at that time with his belief in a stationary everlasting universe, the idea of an expanding universe was highly distasteful, so he introduced a cosmological term into his equations to counteract the derivation of expansion. Then in 1929 the red shifts observed by Hubble in the spectrograms of galaxies produced empirical evidence for the expanding universe (Fig. 2–1). Forthwith Einstein rejected his cosmological term, calling it "the biggest blunder of my life", and accepting the distasteful expanding universe.

The clear formulation of the expanding universe from an initial great cataclysm was first made by Lemaître in the early 1930s and in 1940 Gamow refined this proposal, and applied the emotive term 'Big Bang' to the cataclysm. However the initial estimates by Hubble for the rate of expansion were too high. They gave a date for the Big Bang of only 2 billion years ago, which was in conflict with other estimates for the age of the Universe. Hence there was then good reason for the alternative hypothesis proposed by Gold, Bondi and Hoyle, the steady-state hypothesis: the Universe had always existed; there was no origin in a Big Bang; the observed expansion was exactly compensated by the continuous creation of atomic particles; these particles in time aggregated to form new nebulae. Hence the composition of space was approximately steady, and it was isotropic, despite the continuous recession of already formed nebulae from each other. In terms of Natural Theology it would appear that, in their efforts to escape from a supernatural creation in the Big Bang by a Transcendent God, they had unwittingly proposed continual creation by an Immanent God!

However, redetermination of the recession rate of nebulae now gives a much earlier dating for the Big Bang, about 19 billion years according to the present best estimates. We shall see that, because of the continuous slowing of the expansion rate by gravitational pull, this figure has to be reduced to 10–12 billion years, which is in good agreement with dates that can be derived for the origin by several methods. Furthermore the evidence for the Big Bang has now become most convincing by the discovery of the predicted faint 'echo' of the Big Bang, as an all-pervasive microwave radiation with a frequency corresponding the average temperature of cosmic space, 3.0 °K (this is the Kelvin scale where zero is at the absolute, -273 °C; thus 3.0 °K $= -270$ °C). So, without further ado, I will from now on talk of the Big Bang as the genesis of our all.

2.1 The Big Bang

It has to be understood that it is only possible to give an account of what happened *after* the moment when the great cosmic fireball exploded in the Big Bang. This fireball was extremely hot and of virtually infinite density, being almost entirely composed of photons (light), which calls to mind the verse in Genesis that the first creation was light: "And God said let there be light". Amazingly, on the basis of theoretical physics it is possible to give a description in some detail of the events that can be assumed to occur in the first few minutes after the explosion. In fact Steven Weinberg (1977) has just published a book called *The First Three Minutes.* The principles of physics make it possible to extrapolate backwards and so define the sequence of events in this almost unbelievable cataclysm of genesis – in the beginning.

It is possible to describe what happened from 0.01 s after the explosion onwards. Up till then it is thought that the temperature was extremely high – greatly in excess of 10^{11} °C – with matter and anti-matter in about equal proportions and an immense excess of photons. Then the temperature rapidly fell because of the expansion. At 0.01 s when it was 10^{11} °C there were already large numbers of electrons, positrons and neutrinos at a density of about 4×10^9. Then protons and neutrons came to exist, but photons, electrons and neutrinos continued to be in enormous excess – 10^9 times more than protons and neutrons. Within 14 s the temperature had dropped to 3×10^9 °C. The electrons and positrons annihilated each other to generate photons. Protons, 83%, were generated in excess of neutrons, 17%. Finally at 3.5 min from the Big Bang the temperature was down to 10^9 °C, the positrons and electrons had almost all been annihilated, photons were 10^9 times more numerous than the nuclear particles and there were 6 times as many protons as neutrons, which accounts for the relative abundance of hydrogen (74%) and helium (26%) in the cosmos ever since. The protons are the nuclei of future hydrogen atoms, and protons plus neutrons combine to form the nuclei of future helium atoms.

So in these few minutes there had been created almost all the matter of the cosmos, which is still about 99% of hydrogen plus helium. The other elements were to be made very much later from the primordial hydrogen plus helium. Moreover the primordially created hydrogen is what fuels the enormous and to us vital output of solar energy that is derived from the nuclear reaction – hydrogen $\rightarrow$ helium. And the hydrogen atoms that form such a large part of the molecules in our bodies and brains were also created in these first 3 min and have been through countless vicissitudes since!

Gamow predicted that the radiation from the Big Bang would still be echoing around the Universe, and, because of the enormous expansion, it would be cooled from its initial extremely high level of hundreds of billions of degrees to an extremely cold level corresponding to radiation at 5 °K. As already mentioned in the Introduction, this prediction has been fulfilled amazingly well in the discovery by Penzias and Wilson that there is a microwave radiation bathing the entire universe in a highly isotropic manner – varying by less than 1 part in 1000 over the entire sky. It has the spectral characteristics of thermal radiation emitted by a black body at 3.0 °K, which is now the average temperature of the universe. This radiation would have been absorbed and re-emitted countless times so that its frequency declined to its present low value (Rees and Silk, 1970). There has in effect been an enormous red shift. The spectrum of this radiation corresponds well with theoretical prediction, so it provides overwhelming evidence for the Big Bang (Gott et al., 1976).

Since time, as we know it, began with the Big Bang, it is not meaningful to ask what came before it. There was no before! Furthermore it is not meaningful to ask where the Big Bang occurred. The Cosmic fireball was the whole Universe. So in retrospect it must be recognized that the Big Bang happened in the whole cosmos – everywhere. As might be expected, scientists have displayed no enthusiasm with respect to the obvious theological implications. One notable exception was the first to develop the concept of the Big Bang, Lemaître, who was a Catholic Monsignor. Since my assignment is to search by scientific means for evidence relating to Natural Theology, I am happy to present the Big Bang story as suggesting the operation of a supernatural Creator. However there has been an alternative proposal, to the effect that the Big Bang creating our Universe was not a unique event, but was just one phase of an unending cyclical expansion and collapse of universe succeeding universe. Consideration of this proposal will be deferred to later in the lecture when the eventual collapse of the Universe is in question.

2.2 Formation of Galaxies and Life Histories of Stars (Calder, 1969)

For at least 100,000 years after the Big Bang the Universe can be pictured as a rapidly expanding and cooling gas of electrons with hydrogen and helium nuclei and with an enormous excess of photons (10^9 times). The temperature was falling rapidly with the expansion, so that by 100,000 years the immensely expanded Universe had cooled to 3000 °K and the

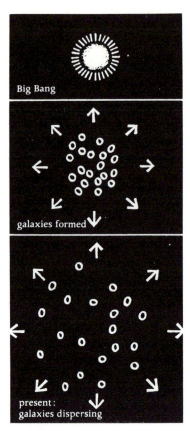

Fig. 2-2. Diagrammatic representation in the upper frame of the Big Bang, then the formation of galaxies with fast outward movement, and in the lowest frame the greater separation of the galaxies which are all still moving outwards. Calder, N.: Violent universe. London: British Broadcasting Corporation 1969

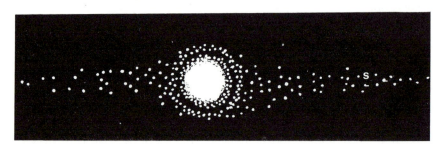

Fig. 2-3. Diagram of section through the disc of our galaxy showing the dense aggregation of stars in the central bulb with a still denser core and with the much more scattered stars in the tapering periphery of spiral arms where our sun is (*cf.* Fig. 2-4 A). Calder, N.: Violent universe. London: British Broadcasting Corporation 1969

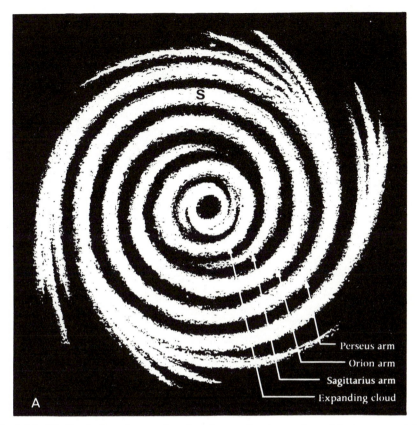

Fig. 2-4 A. Idealized plan of our galaxy based on radio-observations of hydrogen gas lying along the spiral arms. *S* marks the position of our sun. The centre would of course be extremely dense if the picture were for stars as in Figure 2-3, and not for gas. Calder, N.: Violent universe. London: British Broadcasting Corporation 1969

electrons had been captured by the nuclei, so forming hydrogen and helium atoms. From the Big Bang onwards there were primordial turbulences in the gas produced by the forces of radiation pressure and gravitational attraction. It has been shown by calculation that the resulting immense inhomogeneities could be the start of the galaxies (Fig. 2-2). There is evidence (Rees and Silk, 1970) that our galaxy was formed about half a billion years after the Big Bang when the Universe was 1000 times more dense than it is now.

The first components of our galaxy to be formed were the globular clusters of stars (Fig. 2-5), and only later was there organized the principal disc-shaped component that we recognize as the Milky Way. It is about

Fig. 2-4 B. A photograph of a galaxy like our own seen at an angle with arms rich in young stars spiralling out from the bright centre. Reprinted with permission of Hale Observatories, Pasadena, California

100,000 light years in diameter and 3000 light years across and it has an irregular arrangement of spiral arms (Figs. 2-3, 2-4). It revolves slowly around its axis, which is through the dense aggregation of stars in the central bulb of about 10,000 light years in diameter and which has a still denser core. Our galaxy has a total population of about 10^{11} stars. The rotational velocity is much faster towards the centre.

Our Sun is a medium-sized, middle-aged star about half way out along the Orion arm of the galaxy, some 30,000 light years from its centre (S in Fig. 2-4 A). Its rotational time around the galactic centre is 250 million years, which has been called a cosmic year. In fact everything about our Sun is mediocre except that it has a planetary system and that one of these planets has life and ourselves as denizens! There will be more on this in later lectures after we finish cosmology.

As already mentioned, the globular clusters of stars were the first part of our galaxy to be organized. Each of the globular clusters comprises 100,000–1,000,000 stars (suns) (Fig. 2-5) and there are in our galaxy about

Fig. 2-5. A globular cluster, one of the many dense collections of old stars that orbit around the centre of our galaxy on planes making various angles with the plane of our galaxy that is seen in section in Figure 2-4 A. Reprinted with permission of Royal Greenwich Observatory

200 globular clusters travelling in great elliptical orbits around the nucleus of the galaxy and at various angles to its plane of rotation. The globular clusters provide important data on the early composition of the Universe. Spectroscopic examination reveals that the stars are almost entirely hydrogen and helium, more than 99.9%, of which about 29% is helium (Iben, 1970). This composition is different from that of the stars in the galactic disc, showing that these latter must have picked up elements that were formed *after* the globular clusters were assembled.

The globular clusters are also of importance in revealing the life history of stars. It is assumed that the stars of a cluster are of the same age, yet they display a wide range of ageing. It has been shown that the larger the star, the more rapidly it ages. Fortunately our Sun is not prohibitively large and so has a long life cycle. It still has at least 1.5 billion years of steady life before the degenerative processes of ageing supervene.

As illustrated in Figure 2-6, there will be a chain of disastrous consequences when in about 1.5 billion years there is exhaustion of the hydrogen

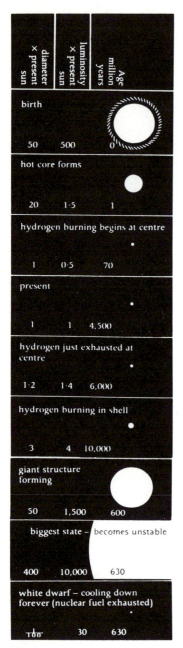

Fig. 2-6

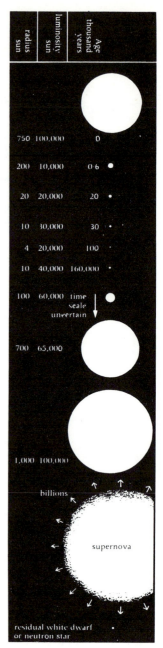

Fig. 2-7

that is now burning to helium at the core of our Sun. For 4 billions of years more it will be burning hydrogen in the shell and will be enlarged so that it will radiate at 4 times its present rate, which would make life very difficult on most of Planet Earth. There is however much worse to come. The burning in the shell increases enormously and the Sun will be 50 times its present diameter with 1500 times its present luminosity. Planet Earth will be scorched beyond imagining. Even still worse follows when the Sun enormously expands to form a red giant star that will encompass all the inner planets including even Mars before its final shrinkage and virtual extinction as a black dwarf. All of these stages are known from observations on other stars that have aged before the Sun. However it has to be recognized that, catastrophic as the eventual fate is, it will be billions of years into the future. There is more than time enough for the cultural achievements that we can anticipate for a glorious future of mankind in the humanities, in the arts, in the sciences and in technology. Furthermore our remote descendants will not be presented with a sudden catastrophe. The time scale of onset will be in hundreds of millions of years. At least we can take comfort that the portended gravitational collapse of the Universe in a Big Crunch (Figs. 2-9, 2-10) will be tens of billions of years later than the actual death of our solar system.

It is known that stellar masses of more than 8 times our Sun's mass have a very short life of 10^8–10^9 years before exploding as a *supernova*. As is diagrammed in Figure 2-7, a very massive star had a lifetime of only 200 million years before its catastrophic finish in a supernova. Supernovae can still be seen occasionally in our galaxy, the last being in 1604 A.D. However several are now observed every year in adjacent galaxies. Our galaxy is long overdue for one, the occurence being once every 50 years on the average. We can hope that it is not one of our nearest stellar neighbours, because the radiation is very intense – up to 10 billion times brighter than the sun, and it could be a biological hazard.

◀ **Fig. 2-6.** Diagrammatic representation of the presumed life history of our sun from its birth to its present middle age (4500 million years) and then its old age and virtual extinction. Note that in the lowest three frames the age is 10,000 million years plus the values of 600 to 630 million years that are indicated. Modified from Calder, N.: Violent universe. London: British Broadcasting Corporation 1969

◀ **Fig. 2-7.** Diagrammatic representation as in Figure 2-6, but for a massive star, 15 times our sun. Its intensely active but short life of about 160 million years terminates in an immensely radiating supernova that collapses either to a very small white dwarf star or to a neutron star. Calder, N.: Violent universe. London: British Broadcasting Corporation 1969

2.3 Cooking of the Elements (Schramm, 1974)

Probably there have been no more than 10^9 supernovae in our galaxy, but they have been very important because the immense temperatures and pressures in and around a supernova are the means for 'cooking' of the other elements besides hydrogen and helium. Even before the supernoval explosion the large stars form elements from carbon up to iron and nickel in the intense temperatures and pressures of their interiors. Elements heavier than iron require more complicated synthetic processes, which are of two kinds. The slow processes can generate elements up to lead and bismuth, because the steps of neutron addition and beta decay are one by one through the stable elements. This slow process appears to occur in the envelope of red giant stars (Fig. 2-6). Because of the steps through unstable elements, the still heavier elements can be generated only by rapid processes of neutron addition and beta decay that seem to have occured just outside the black hole or neutron star remnants of a supernova (Fig. 2-7),

Fig. 2-8. A cluster of galaxies showing many different types of extremely diverse shapes. Reprinted with permission of Hale Observatories, Pasadena, California

where there are intense neutron fluxes. It has to be recognised that the creation of the elements is inefficient at the best. No more than a few percent of the hydrogen and helium is so converted.

The dates of the atomic creations by the rapid process can be assessed from the known relative abundances of radioactive elements with extremely slow decay rates (Schramm, 1974). The times so calculated are 10 billion to 5 billion years ago for the 'cooking' of these elements. This is thus the time range for the great supernovae explosions of our galaxy. So a time of 10 billion years is suggested as a beginning of our galaxy because the lifetimes of the largest stellar masses that give supernovae may be as short as two-tenths of a billion years (Fig. 2-7). Since the globular clusters are extremely deficient in all elements except hydrogen and helium, they must have been formed before the dispersion of the 'cooked' elements through the galaxy.

By contrast our Sun was formed by an immense gaseous aggregation some 4.6 billion years ago, just after the completion of the great cooking period for the elements. Thus the Sun plus its planetary system would be rich in these heavy elements, as will be described in Lecture 3. Planet Earth was particularly fortunate in its material endowment, and hence was prepared for life.

2.4 Galaxies in Space

Our galaxy has a fairly common configuration with a flattened spiral form (Figs. 2-3, 2-4). But there is a wide diversity of galactic configurations (Fig. 2-8) that has not been accounted for. For our present interest it is sufficient to recognise that there is an enormous number of galaxies, about 10^{11}, and on the average they have much the same stellar population as our galaxy, 10^{11}, so the stars of the Universe are inconceivably numerous, 10^{22}. All galaxies participate in the expansion of the Universe, as was first shown by Hubble in 1929 from a study of the red shifts in their spectrograms. Since that time there has been a revision of the expansion rate. This rate is proportional to the distance of the nebula (Fig. 2-1), the proportionality factor being about 17 km/s per million light years of distance. This value indicates that at about 18 billion years ago all nebulae would have been in close apposition.

It is important to recognize that as observers from our galaxy we are not in a privileged position of centrality in the Universe. The same regression relationship would obtain for observers in any other galaxy. This equivalence is called the cosmological principle. However galaxies are not uniformly distributed in space. There are galactic clusters that may have local rotating relationships. In general galaxies were formed by vast aggregations of the gas formed in the primeval outburst of gas from the cosmic fireball, and their velocities of regression were imparted in the initial explosion. In fact the velocity has been continuously slowed from that time by the pull of gravitation. The effectiveness of this gravitational slowing will be considered later. The most remote galaxies are up to 8 billion light years from us.

2.5 Future of the Universe and Gravitational Collapse

The most important questions for the future of the Universe are: will it go on expanding for ever? or, will it collapse into the converse of the Big Bang that has been appropriately called the Big Crunch? There is no doubt that the velocity of expansion has been progressively slowed by gravitational pull right from the start. The problem is to determine the power of this gravitational pull. That power is proportional to the density of matter in the Universe. An approximate estimate of density can be made from the known galaxy population, assuming an average galactic mass and the known dimensions of the Universe. As thus determined, the mass is much less than the least mass for reversal of expansion, perhaps by a factor as large as 25, though it may be as small as 8 (Gott et al. 1976). However there is evidence of a large mass of matter apart from that aggregated in stars, for example in the interstellar gas and dust and even in the black holes (Penrose, 1972; Hawking, 1977) that are now suspected to be not uncommon in the Universe, being formed by the gravitational collapse of a large star (Fig. 2-7).

Black holes are so incredibly dense that the gravitational attraction prevents even photons from escaping, hence the eponym 'black'. That is why we can have no pictures of black holes! The boundary of a black hole is called an event horizon because there are no future events for all matter and radiation crossing that horizon. They are trapped forever by the intense gravitational power. The happening is called a gravitational collapse. There is a wonderful theoretical development in relation to the properties of black holes (Penrose, 1972; Hawking, 1977). Good evidence has been produced that one star of a binary pair has collapsed to form a black hole (Cygnus X-1) (Thorne, 1974). The evidence for a black hole comes from the intensity of its surrounding gravitational field, which arises from its immense mass, and the absence of any other signal from it. The density of a black hole is unbelievable. It has to be in excess of $2 \times 10^{15} \mathrm{g.cm}^{-3}$ in order to exercise this gravitational pull across the event horizon (Thorne, 1974). A cubic millimeter, a small pinhead, would weigh at least 2 million tons, and a star with the mass of the Sun would collapse to a black hole only 6 km across!

Black holes are a final stage in the degeneration of a large star, one of more than eight solar masses (Fig. 2-7), but they are also of interest in that they may be models for the states of affairs at the beginning and at the end of the Universe (Hawking, 1977). The Big Bang may have started from a compression of matter comparable with that in a black hole, and, if there is a final gravitational collapse to the Big Crunch (Figs. 2-9, 2-10), the end will be a gigantic black hole. And that will be really the end. We can think that the gravitational collapse leading to a black hole is the physical counterpart of the theological hell. In 1975 Hawking was awarded the Pius XI Medal of the Pontifical Academy of Science for his great scientific contributions in the field of "Gravitational Collapse". I am sure no one thought of the analogy!

After this brief digression on the theme of black holes, we return to the unresolved problem of the so-called 'missing mass' of the Universe. In fact calculation reveals that with some galactic clusters the total mass must be many times greater than the aggregate galactic masses, otherwise they would not hold together, as they evidently do in some compact galactic clusters such as Virgo or Coma (Rees and Silk, 1970). Recently it has been shown that the outer fringes of galaxies may contain 3–10 times as much matter as that attributed to the visible part of the galaxies (Wheeler, 1977). Moreover it is important to recognize that there are immense aggregations of dust and gas in the spiral arms of our galaxy, where in zones recognized as 'stellar nurseries' star formation is still occurring, apparently by gravitational pull aggregating the dust and gas into a star in exactly the same way as our Sun was formed at about 5 billion years ago. Even individual newly forming stars have been recognized (Bok, 1972).

The future history of the Universe is much debated. As already mentioned there is some doubt as to whether the mass of the Universe is sufficient to generate a gravitational pull that would stop the expansion and bring about a collapse. However an alternative approach has been derived by Wheeler (1974) from Einstein's General Theory of Relativity. Figure 2-10 is so plotted and is normalized in relation to two key times concerning the Big Bang and its aftermath. The present rate of expansion is assumed to give a time (Hubble time) of 20 billion years since the Big Bang. This is close to the best available determination of 19 billion years, which has an uncertainty of at least 10%. But we have seen that because of the gravitational pull there has been a progressive slowing in rate of expansion, so 20

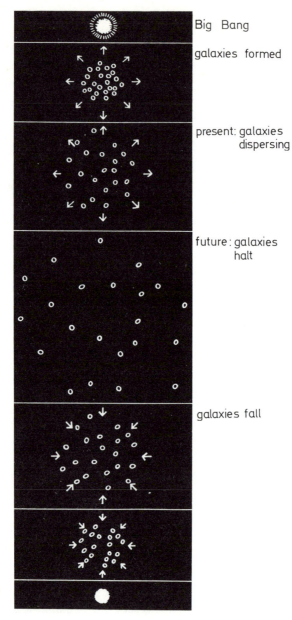

Fig. 2-9. Diagrammatic representation of the Big Bang and the expanding Universe as in Figure 2-2, but with the further history in a cessation of expansion and then the falling together under gravitational attraction to give the eventual collapse in the Big Crunch in the lowest frame (*cf.* Fig. 2-10). Modified from Calder, N.: Violent universe. London: British Broadcasting Corporation 1969

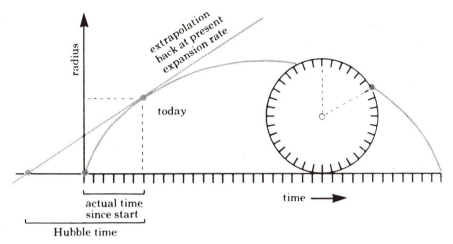

Fig. 2-10. Major features of the Universe according to Einstein's theory, as normalized by two key astrophysical data, each believed uncertain by an amount of the order of 20%: (1) the actual time, $\sim 10 \times 10^9$ years, back to the start of the expansion, as determined from the evolution of the stars and the elements; and (2) the 'Hubble time', or time linearly extrapolated back to the start of the expansion, $\sim 20 \times 10^9$ years; that is, the time needed for galaxies to reach their present distances if they had always been receding from us with their present velocities. In the diagram, as the wheel rolls slowly to the right, the point marks a cycloidal curve for radius of the universe as a function of time. The geometry of the closed model universe is idealized here as a three-dimensional sphere

Illustrative values all derived from

Time from start to now	10	$\times 10^9$ year
Hubble time now	20	$\times 10^9$ year
Hubble expansion rate now	49.0	$\dfrac{\text{km/s}}{\text{megaparsec}}$
Rate of increase of radius now	0.66 lyr	
Radius now	13.19×10^9 lyr	
Radius at maximum	18.94×10^9 lyr	
Time, start to end	59.52×10^9 year	
Density now	14.8×10^{-30} g/cm^3	
Amount of matter	5.68×10^{56} g	
Equivalent number of baryons	3.39×10^{80}	

Wheeler, J. A.: The universe at a home for man. Am. Scientist *62*, 683–691 (1974)

billion years is an over-estimate and the 10 billion years assumed in Figure 2-10 is approximately the best estimate from several ways of determining the actual age of the Universe.

In the diagram the wheel moves slowly to the right, the grey dot on it marking a cycloid curve for the radius of the Universe as a function of time.

This diagram assumes the cosmological principle of homogeneity of the Universe. Our present location is shown some 10 billion years after the Big Bang, and the rolling wheel marks the eventual halting of the expansion at 18.9 billion light years and then the onset of gravitational collapse with increasing velocity to the Big Crunch at 59 billion years from the start. The cycloid curve is symmetrical about the summit. The Big Crunch is temporally symmetrical with the Big Bang. At the gravitational collapse space and time cease to exist, just as they did before the Big Bang and as they do for a black hole. As already mentioned, it has been proposed that the question of genesis could be eliminated if the Big Bang was the immediate and unconditional sequence of the Big Crunch of a preceding universe. There could thus be a cyclic sequence that could go on forever, each Big Bang following the Big Crunch of the immediately preceding Universe. However, Wheeler (1977) states emphatically in respect to this proposed recycling:

> With gravitational collapse we come to the end of time. Never out of the equations of general relativity has one been able to find the slightest argument for a 're-expansion' or a 'cyclic universe' or anything other than an end.

2.6 The Question of Genesis

Einstein once stated prophetically that the greatest mystery is that the Universe exists and is intelligible. Wheeler (1977) asks:

> How did the universe come into being? – realizing full well that how properly to ask the question is also a part of the question. One can even believe that one can only then state the issue in the right words when one knows the answer. Or is there an answer? Is the mystery of genesis forever beyond explanation?"

These are deep questions for Natural Theology. In this context Wheeler (1974), in his Copernican Lecture to the National Academy of Sciences, asks the question: Why has the Universe to be so collossal? It turns out that the time scale of Figure 2-10 as calculated from Einstein's General Theory of Relativity, is extraordinarily dependent on the mass. For example, the mass for 10^{11} galaxies with a total of 10^{22} stars, gives the time scale of Figure 2-10 from Big Bang to Big Crunch of 59 billion years. If we economize and have the Big Bang producing the mass for one galaxy of 10^{11} stars, which is still an immense universe, the time from Big Bang to Big Crunch is reduced to 1 year! As Wheeler (1974) states:

> There would be no opportunity to form new stars, let alone heavy elements, planets and life. The cut-down investment in original matter, far from giving a better return, gives no return at all. From this point of view any purported extravagance in our universe is far from obvious.

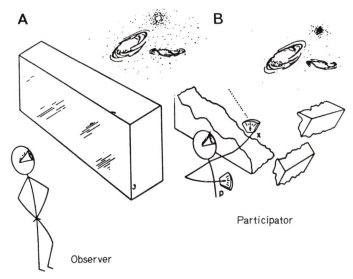

Fig. 2-11. A The observer is viewing phenomena through a slab of glass. **B** The slab is broken and the observer has been transformed into a participator. Wheeler, J. A.: Genesis and observership. In: University of Western Ontario series in the philosophy of science. Butts, R., Hintikka, J. (eds.). Boston (Mass.): Reidel 1977

That is certainly a record in understatement!

It has to be recognized that without many elements much heavier than hydrogen (carbon, oxygen, nitrogen, phosphorus for example) life as we know it is inconceivable. The production of these elements

> requires several billion years of 'cooking' time in the interior of a star. But no Universe can provide several billion years of time, according to general relativity unless it is several billion light years in extent (Wheeler, 1974).

Thus, if there is to be the opportunity for life, the Universe is not extravagantly large.

In developing his thesis of the vital role of 'observership', Wheeler (1977) raises fundamental issues in physics:

> No search has ever disclosed any ultimate underpinning, either of physics or mathematics, that shows the slightest prospect of providing the rationale for the many-storied tower of physical law. One therefore suspects it is wrong to think that as one penetrates deeper and deeper into the structure of physics he will find it terminating at some n^{th} level. One fears it is also wrong to think of the structure going on and on, layer after layer, *ad infinitum*. One finds himself in desperation asking if the structure, rather than terminating in some smallest object or in some most basic field, or going on and on, does not lead back in the end to the observer himself, in some kind of closed circle of interdependences.

In developing this idea Wheeler goes on to say:

> It was long natural to regard the observer as in effect looking at and being protected from contact with existence by a 10 cm. slab of plate glass (Fig. 2-11 A). In contrast, quantum mechanics teaches the direct opposite. It is impossible to observe even so miniscule an object as an electron without in effect smashing that slab and reaching in with the appropriate measuring equipment (Fig. 2-11 B). Moreover, the installation of apparatus to measure the position co-ordinate, x, of the electron automatically prevents the insertion in the same region at the same time of the equipment that would be required to measure its velocity or its momentum, p; and conversely. The act of measurement typically produces an unpredictable change in the state of the electron. This change is different according as one measures the position or the momentum. The choice one makes about what he observes makes an irretrievable difference in what he finds. The observer is elevated from 'observer' to 'participator'. What philosophy suggested in times past, the central feature of quantum mechanics tells us today with impressive force. In some strange sense this is a participatory universe.

Wheeler (1977) then asks:

> If 'participation' is the strangest feature of the Universe, is it possible that it is also the most important clue we have to the genesis of the universe? The position (or momentum) of an object only acquires useful meaning through the participatory act of observation. Does also the object itself only acquire a useful meaning through observership?

Wheeler (1977) then asks the central question:

> Could the universe only then come into being, when it could guarantee to produce 'observership' in some locality and for some period of time in its history-to-be? Is 'observership' the link that closes the circle of interdependences?

And later in the same line of enquiry he asks:

> Could it be that the *observership* of quantum mechanics is the ultimate underpinning of the laws of physics – and therefore of the laws of time and space themselves?

This leads him on to discuss the deep question of observership as a prerequisite for genesis, or what has been called the *'anthropic principle'* as defined by the physicists, Dicke (1961) and Carter (1974). Wheeler paraphrases Dicke:

> Dicke asks what possible sense it could make to speak of the "Universe" unless there was someone around to be aware of it. But awareness demands life. Life in turn, however anyone has imagined it, demands heavy elements. To produce heavy elements out of the primordial hydrogen requires thermonuclear combustion. Thermonuclear combustion in turn needs several times 10^9 years cooking in the interior of a star. But for the universe to provide several times 10^9 years of time, according to general relativity, it must have a reach in space of the order of several times 10^9 light years. Why then is the universe so big as it is? Because we are here!

We have seen already that the genesis of a smaller Universe of 10^{11} stars by a Big Bang leads to a gravitational collapse in 1 year!

Wheeler (1977) defines two contrasting views on the genesis of the Universe:

1. The universe, meaningless or not, would still come into being and run its course even if the constants and initial conditions forever ruled out the development of life and consciousness. Life is accidental and incidental to the machinery of the Universe.
2. Or going beyond the anthropic principle, is the directly opposite view closer to the truth? – that the universe, through some mysterious coupling of future with past, *required the future observer to empower the past genesis?*
Nothing is more astonishing about quantum mechanics than its allowing one to consider seriously on quite other grounds the same view that the universe would be nothing without observership.

Summarising these deep enquiries Wheeler (1977) says:

> Is the very mechanism for the universe to come into being meaningless or unworkable or both unless the universe is guaranteed to produce life, consciousness and observership somewhere and for some little time in its history to be?

There is much in this almost mystical line of reasoning that is of great interest for Natural Theology. I would suggest that there is a vast design in the origin and history of the Universe. We are not mere creatures of chance and necessity, but are central participators in the great cosmic drama. Did not Schrödinger (1958) say that, but for the existence of conscious beings, the whole cosmic performance would be a drama played before empty stalls? A drama presupposes a Dramatist, and we are not only observers but also participants. In a deep sense it is our play. But there is a long and complex chain of contingencies to be traced before we, ourselves, emerge in my seventh lecture! However before then I have to answer a question that many will raise. Is there not life and even intelligent life on countless planets in the universe with its 10^{22} suns? This question will be discussed in the third and fourth lectures, but for now I will say that it is most probable that Planet Earth is unique in having denizens who can participate in the cosmic drama, as we do.

I will close by a light-hearted criticism of observership, removing its necessity. It was composed by my good friend Father Ronald Knox in the 1920s when there was some revival of Berkelianism at Oxford:

There was a young man who said 'God
Must find it exceedingly odd
If that beautiful tree
Just ceases to be
If there's no one about in the Quad.

To which the reply was:

Dear Sir, your astonishment's odd
Because I'm always about in the Quad
And that's why the tree
Continues to be
Since observed by yours faithfully, God.

However, I suspect that the critics of observership would not want to use this weapon to fight with!

Addendum

After this lecture was delivered I received through the kindness of Professor Torrance a xerox copy of a lecture delivered by Sir Bernard Lovell on 13 October 1977 at St. Johns Newfoundland entitled "A contemporary view of man's relation to the Universe". I was delighted to discover that the theme developed by this distinguished cosmologist was so close to the story of my lecture II. I give several quotations with the permission of Sir Bernard:

> When the Universe was one second from the beginning of the expansion *if* the rate of expansion had been reduced by only one part in a thousand billion, then the Universe would have collapsed after a few million years. Can it really be that out of all possible universes the only one which can exist, in the sense that it can be known, is simply the one which satisfies the narrow conditions necessary for the development of intelligent life? The essence of our presence in the Universe today is that *we* require the Universe to have certain properties. Long before we reach the problems of biological evolution on Earth 3 to 4 billion years ago, we face this more fundamental question. At least one essential condition is that the Universe must expand at almost precisely the rate at which we measure it to be expanding. If the rate had been less by an almost insignificant amount in the first second, then the Universe would have collapsed long before any biological evolution could have taken place.
>
> There are several other strange features in those early stages of the expansion, particularly the narrow margin by which all the primeval material failed to vanish into helium that it seems that the chances of the existence of Man on Earth today, or of intelligent life anywhere in the Universe, are vanishingly small. Is the Universe as it is, because it was necessary for the existence of Man? Is there a false logic in the argument, or are the basic axioms of our mathematics and physics wrong? We start from the knowledge of our existence on Earth.
>
> But our measurements narrowly define one such universe which had to be that particular universe if it was ever to be known and comprehended by an intelligent being.
>
> In all the sciences there are hosts of unsolved problems and it is the essence of the faith of the professional scientist that solutions and answers can be found by application of the scientific method and technique. In many cases the faith will be justified but it is a strange feature of our age that in some of the vital investigations concerned with the fundamental issues of the existence of the Universe and of Man's place and comprehension of the cosmos we appear to be penetrating to a greater darkness.
>
> Our hope today resides in the evidences that science is neither materially nor intellectually supreme and that the urgent search for a new synthesis of knowledge and understanding, last achieved by Thomas Aquinas 800 years ago, will succeed.

I share with Sir Bernard the hope that there will be a new synthesis of knowledge and understanding, as expressed in his concluding statement. This Gifford Lecture Series is humbly dedicated to this hope.

Lecture 3

Planetary System and Planet Earth

Synopsis

Two major questions are:
How unique is our planetary system?
How unique is Planet Earth amongst planets?

About 5 billion years ago an immense mass of gas and dust from supranovae coalesced by gravitational attraction to form a great central core with a rotating disc having a mass of less then 1% of the core. Gravitational contraction of the core raised the temperature to at least 10 million degrees so igniting the nuclear reaction, hydrogen to helium, with an immense energy output. The Sun was shining some 4.6 billion years ago as it does still and as it will do for at least 1.5 billion years into the future, when degeneracy will set in.

Meanwhile the rotating disc was broken into fragments, which each aggregated to be a nucleus that attracted gas, dust and particles to form the planets, also at 4.6 billion years ago.

On this so-called nebula hypothesis of planetary creation it would be expected that planetary systems would be common, but none has been observed even in the nearest stars. Most stars are doubles or even triples. There will be discussion of the possible numbers of planetary systems in our galaxy with its 10^{11} stars. The uniqueness of Planet Earth amongst the nine planets of the solar system will become evident from consideration of the latest information delivered by the Viking and Mariner spacecraft. This uniqueness existed before the origin of life and its evolution.

3.1 The Solar System

In the preceding lecture our scope was immense – the whole Universe, its creation, its evolution, its present state and its destiny. Now we come closer to our human theme as we follow the chain of contingency from the origin of our solar system through its evolution and so to Planet Earth in its prebiotic stage. In order to give a critical and coherent account of the solar planetary system, it is necessary to begin with a brief description of its present state (Sagan, 1975).

As shown in the double scale diagram of Figure 3-1, there are eight planets (not counting Pluto) revolving in almost circular orbits around the

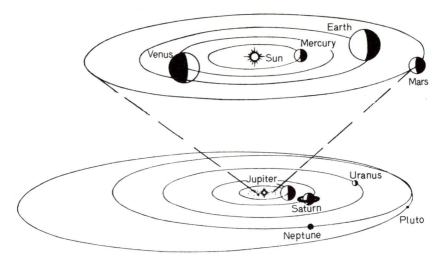

Fig. 3-1. Orbits of the planets about the Sun. Since the dimensions of the other regions of the planetary system are so immense, it has been necessary to explode the scale of the inner regions to make the inner orbits visible. The relative sizes of the planets have been greatly exaggerated in this diagram. Prentice, A. J. R.: Formation of planetary systems. In: In the beginning. Wild, J. P. (ed.), pp. 15–47. Canberra (A. C. T.): Australian Academy of Science 1974

central Sun and in the same plane. The revolution of all planets is in the same direction as the Sun's rotation, which is around the same axis. Furthermore, all planets except Venus and Uranus rotate in the same direction as the Sun. As with Planet Earth, most rotations are inclined at 23 °–28 ° to the plane of revolution, but Venus and Jupiter are very low (3°) and Uranus very high (82 °). Pluto is exceptional in that its orbit is far from circular and is inclined at more than 17 ° to the plane of revolution of the rest of the solar system. These anomalies have been taken to indicate that Pluto's origin was different from that of the rest of the planetary system. Perhaps it was a later addition to the planetary system. It has been suggested that it is an escaped satellite of Neptune. Three of the planets, Jupiter, Saturn and Uranus, have extensive satellite systems that model on a smaller scale the planetary system of the Sun, but there are anomalies.

Table 3-1 indicates that in chemical composition there are three categories of planets: The inner four, labelled rock, have a composition resembling that of Planet Earth, in the middle are Jupiter and Saturn with a composition resembling that of the Sun; the outermost are Uranus and Neptune that present a surface of ices believed to be composed largely of water, ammonia and methane. It is to be noted in Table 3-1 that the rock

Table 3-1. Physical elements of the solar system (Prentice, 1974)

Planet	Semi-major axis of orbit R = 1 $\odot$	Sidereal Period years	Mass $m = 1$ $\oplus$	Density g cm^{-3}	Rotation Period	Major Chemical Constituents	Satellites
Mercury	83	0.24	0.054	5.4	88^d	Rock	–
Venus	155	0.62	0.815	5.1	–	Rock	–
Earth	215	1.00	1.000	5.52	23^{h}56^m	Rock	Moon
Mars	328	1.88	0.108	3.97	24^{h}37^m	Rock	2
(Asteroids)	~600	~4.7	0.0003	~4	~10^h	Rock	–
Jupiter	1120	11.9	318	1.334	9^{h}50^m	H/He	12
Saturn	2050	29.5	95	0.684	10^{h}14^m	H/He	10
Uranus	4120	84	14.5	1.60	10^{h}49^m	Ices	5
Neptune	6460	165	17.2	2.25	15^h	Ices	2
Pluto	~8500	248	0.8?	?	6^{d}39^m	Ice?	–
Sun	–	–	333,000	1.41	25^d	H/He	Planets

planets have a high density of 4–5.5, while Jupiter, Saturn and the Sun have a low density (0.68–1.41) corresponding to their predominantly gaseous composition, hydrogen and helium. A remarkable fact is that in the solar system the Sun has 99.87% of the mass, but only 2% of the rotational energy.

All these features have to be accounted for in our explanations of how the Sun with its planetary system was created from some immense primeval cloud of gas and dust that was gradually coming together about 5 billion years ago. The dust would largely be the output from the supranoval explosions that had been going on for the preceding 5 billion years, as described in Lecture 2.

3.1.1 Origin and Evolution

In this and subsequent sections we will be considering the question: *How unique is our planetary system?* As briefly mentioned in Lecture 2 the Sun was formed, just as other stars, by condensation from an immense aggregation of gas and dust some 4.6 billion years ago. We are now concerned with the special processes that resulted in it having a planetary system (Cameron, 1975). Two suggested modes of creation of planetary systems will be considered.

According to Jeans our planetary system could result from a catastrophic event produced by a near collision of our Sun with another star.

Great tidal waves of gas would be raised on the surface of the Sun and dragged into space, breaking into fragments that eventually condensed to form the planets in orbit around the sun. On this account the creation of a planetary system would be exceedingly rare. Calculation shows that a single occurrence would be most improbable, even in a galaxy where there are about 10^{11} stars. Furthermore, this hypothesis is now abandoned because it seems most probable that the hot gases pulled out from the Sun would disperse into space before they could be aggregated to form planets, and also because it cannot account for the high degree of geometrical order that we have seen to obtain for our planetary system.

The alternative explanation of the creation of our planetary system, the nebula hypothesis, is that now generally accepted. It was originally suggested by Laplace, but severe criticism led to its being abandoned for almost a century. In recent decades the criticisms have been answered. However there is still a considerable variety in the ways that the nebula hypothesis is formulated. Two extreme positions are known as the *equilibrium condensation hypothesis* and the *inhomogeneous accretion hypothesis* (Lewis, 1974). According to the first each planet is formed by a rapid condensation of gas and dust, which will give a different planetary composition depending on the temperature. The more remote from the Sun, the colder will be the temperature (Fig. 3-2 a). According to the other hypothesis the planets are formed by a slow accretion process for a long period of time, even for tens of millions of years, and this would result in the building up of the planet by layer upon layer like an onion. Probably the truth lies between these two extreme formulations in the manner of the account that I now give.

The Sun and the planetary system were created in one continuous operation on a prodigious scale. About 5 billion years ago a great rotating mass of gas and dust began to concentrate under gravitational attraction, which was able to overcome the dispersive tendencies of the gas. As the cloud contracted, gravitational energy would cause an increase in temperature and pressure that would be progressively greater towards the centre. Meanwhile, according to the nebula hypothesis the turbulent movements of the more peripheral gas and dust clouds would become resolved into a revolving movement around the rotating great central mass. This revolution would counterbalance the gravitational attraction that otherwise would pull the outer components of the system in towards the centre. An intermediate stage is shown in section in Figure 3-2a, where there is a large diffuse envelope of hydrogen and helium gas.

Figure 3-2b shows that, as proposed originally by Laplace and as recently shown mathematically by Prentice (1974), the rotating disc would

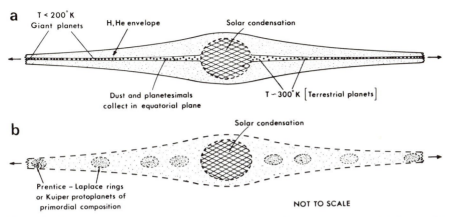

Fig. 3-2 a, b. Cross sections showing central solar condensation surrounded by 'small' (1%–10% of solar mass) nebulae of dust and gas. **a** Parental planetary nebula with discoidal configuration. **b** Parental planetary nebula of Laplacian-Prentice rings or of Kuiper protoplanets. Ringwood, A. E.: The early chemical evolution of planets. In: In the beginning. Wild, J. P. (ed.), pp. 48–84. Canberra (A. C. T.): Australian Academy of Science 1974

fragment into globules. There could be an enormous number at first; but, by gradual coalescence under gravitational attraction, a process we may call *collision accretion*, the planets eventually were formed in their present orbital positions with their characteristic distances from the Sun and with their coplanar revolutions (Fig. 3-1).

Meanwhile the vast central solar mass would have become greatly heated and compressed by the collapse under gravity. When the central temperatures reached 10 million degrees, the nuclear reaction, *hydrogen to helium*, would start and provide the immense energy that would be irradiated. The Sun was beginning to shine, as it has shone for 4.6 billion years, and as it still shines for us. At the most the whole process of solar and planetary formation would take only a few hundred thousand years, so that the solar system, as we know it, was completed about 4.6 billion years ago.

3.1.2 Chemical Composition of the Planets

A complicated problem arises when we try to account for the present chemical composition of the planets. In the first place the nebula hypothesis assumes that the primordial gas-dust cloud was of a uniform composition, and that this composition still obtains for the Sun, except for the continual conversion of hydrogen to helium in its nuclear furnace. On this basis the primordial solar nebula would be composed of 'gases', 98%; 'ices', 1.5%; and 'rocks', 0,5%, as shown in Table 3-2.

Table 3-2. Masses of major components of primordial solar nebula (Ringwood, 1974)

		Wt%
"Gases"	H, He	98
"Ices"	C, N, O, Ne, S, A, Cl	1.5
	(as hydrides, except Ne, A)	
"Rock"	Na, Mg, Al, Si, Ca, Fe, Ni	0.5
	(as silicates and oxides)	

Table 3-3. Composition of type-1 carbonaceous chondrites (Ringwood, 1974)

	Wt%		Wt%
SiO_2	22	NiO	1.2
FeO	23	Cr_2O_3	0.4
MgO	15	H_2O	19
Al_2O_3	1.6	S	5.7
CaO	1.2	Carbonaceous material	9.7

As suggested by Urey (Table 3-3) meteorites known as *carbonaceous chondrites* have a composition that should correspond to that of the dust particles of the primitive nebula from which the solar system was formed (Table 3-3). Apparently these meteorites have come from the asteroid belt and have never been heated above 100 °C; hence they can be regarded as reliable chemical fossils dating from the beginning of the solar system. It is remarkable that such meteorites exhibit, for almost fifty elements, much the same *relative* abundances as the Sun's photosphere (Ringwood, 1974).

Two principal factors are concerned in the attempt to explain how the very different compositions actually attained by the planets were derived from an initial homogeneous mixture of gases, ices and rocks, the latter two being in a finely particulate form. One factor is the temperature at which each planetary assemblage occurred. The other is the mass of the planet being assembled.

The four inner planets (Mercury, Venus, Earth and Mars) have much the same 'rocky' composition, being laid down initially in a temperature of about 300 °K (Fig. 3-2a). So they were too hot for the condensation of the ices. Moreover their relatively small mass was not sufficient to prevent the eventual escape of the gases, H_2 and He. The two outermost planets,

Uranus and Neptune, were laid down in extremely cold conditions so that such substances as methane, ammonia, and water would be frozen into ices that form a large part of the shell around the rocky core of these planets. Moreover their relatively large mass (Table 3-1) would enable them to retain much of the H_2 and He of the primordial nebula that would form the thick outer shell (Hunten, 1975). This gravitational attraction was the dominant factor in the formation of the massive planets, Jupiter and Saturn, that have a composition approximating to that of the Sun except for their rocky core.

If the four inner planets had originally the same composition as the Sun, there must have been an enormous loss of mass when the more volatile components were dispersed into space. For example the 'rock' component is only 0.5% of the total mass of the primordial nebula (Table 3-2), yet it makes up a considerable part of the composition of these inner planets. At least 99% of the mass of the nebula from which one of these planets is formed would have to be lost. According to various authorities the primordial mass of the whole planetary system ranged from 2%–10% of the Sun, whereas now it is just over 0.13%. From Table 3-1 it can be seen that the four inner planets together account for only 6 parts in 1 million of the solar mass (0.0006%).

Following the hypothesis proposed by Ringwood (1974), we can envisage that the terrestrial planets were formed by a single stage of direct accretion of planetesimals with a composition resembling carbonaceous chondrites (Table 3-3). This accretion is assumed to occur fairly rapidly – within a million years for Planet Earth. The impacts of the planetesimals would cause a progressive increase in temperature and this increase would also be produced by radioactive decay (Siever, 1975). When the mass was increased to above 10% of the present earth mass, it is estimated that the surface temperature could rise up to 1500 °C. Actually, if the accretion was very rapid, Earth's temperature could rise to 10,000 °C. The estimate of 1500 °C assumes a relatively slow accretion, up to a million years, with the consequent opportunity for continual cooling by irradiation.

At 1500 °C there would be melting and evaporation of some of the rocks. The molten metallic iron would be able to force its way down through the rock structure because of its higher density and so would reach the core of the earth where it still is, while the lighter silicate rocky material would ascend towards the surface. This immense gravitational movement within the Earth would raise its temperature by a further 2000 °C, an effect that has been called 'the iron catastrophe'. That intense heating gave opportunity for a distribution in depth within the earth to its present density gradients.

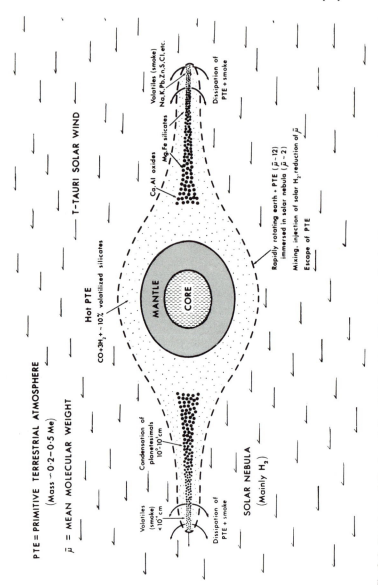

Fig. 3-3. Structure of Earth and its primitive atmosphere immediately after accretion according to the 'precipitation' hypothesis. After Ringwood, A. E.: The early chemical evolution of planets. In: In the beginning. Wild, J. P. (ed.), pp. 48–84. Canberra (A. C. T.): Australian Academy of Science 1974

Furthermore, because of this great increase of temperature, the outer layers of the earth would be vapourized to form a massive hot primitive atmosphere amounting to one quarter of the mass of the Earth and composed largely of CO, H_2 and volatilized silicates. The hypothesis requires that this atmosphere escaped from the Earth after accretion (Ringwood, 1974). Figure 3-3 shows in section the equatorial aggregation of this atmosphere around the rapidly rotating Earth. On cooling the silicates of this atmosphere would condense to form planetesimals, giving a ring much as Saturn has, but much more massive, while the gases, CO, H_2, He, would escape into space. Eventually, aggregation of the silicate planetesimals would form the Moon. This theory of the Moon's formation accounts for its present composition, with silicates resembling those of the Earth's crust, but with a deficiency of the iron in the Earth's core.

The satellite systems of other planets are assumed also to have developed from *protosatellite* systems such as that shown in a simplified form in Figure 3-3 as an equatorial disc of planetesimals, dust and gases. The five inner satellites of Jupiter can be accounted for in this way, but the outer satellites have various disorders of motion, even retrograde for the outermost four. It seems that these disorders are relics of catastrophic collisions early in the planetary history. There are many signs of such catastrophes in the motions of the Planets and their satellite systems, for example, the extraordinarily large tilt in the rotation of Uranus and in the orbits of its attendant moons, the retrograde rotations of Venus and Uranus, and the asteroid system.

In Table 3-1 there is an entry labelled 'asteroids'. These are usually very small bodies and they travel in an asteroid belt with a planetary revolution that lies between Mars and Jupiter. It can be seen to fill in a large gap in what otherwise is an approximately logarithmic sequence of planetary orbits, column 1 of Table 3-1. The largest asteroid is Ceres, 955 km in diameter, and there are several others large enough to be graced by names of Roman Goddesses (Hartman, 1975). However the total mass of the asteroids is far below that of Mercury, the smallest planet. A more recent estimate (Hartman, 1975) would raise the total mass to about 0.0001, which is still no more than 2% of Mercury. I think we can regard the asteroids as resulting from a failure of assemblage to form a planet, a failure that would appear to be ascribable to its too-small mass. However in this planetary drama there is doubtless Jupiter that with its enormous mass stole much of the material from the asteroid belt. For our present interest, I think the asteroid belt represents, as it were, a frozen exemplar of a planetary formation that aborted at an early stage.

One major problem in our story of the creation of Planet Earth has been to dispose of the immense gaseous envelope that it would have on the assumption that it was created out of the same nebula composition as the Sun. At the time of this formation the Sun would have been in an early stage of its development, in what is called the *T-Tauri phase*, where it would be emitting immense quantities of its mass in the so-called *solar wind*, made up largely of protons. In this way the Sun could lose up to half its mass. This wind is indicated in Figure 3-3. It would sweep away all the outer envelope of the embryonic Earth, which would thus be reduced to its present 'rocky' composition. The same phenomenon would occur for the other three terrestrial planets and also for the Moon. Incidentally, it should be noted that the emission of the solar wind can account for the large reduction of the rotational energy of the Sun so that now it only amounts to 2% of that of the whole planetary system, whereas its mass is 99.87%. The solar wind is still blowing but much less than in the T-Tauri phase.

The recent intense study of the Moon has given most important information on the early history of the inner planets of the solar system. Firstly, the isotopic ratios, e. g. of *Strontium-87 to Strontium-86* give an age of 4.6 billion years for the formation of the Moon (Brown, 1977), which is the age given to the Planet Earth also by isotopic ratios.

Secondly, it has revealed the intensity of the bombardment by planetesimals for the period of 4.6–3.9 billion years ago. The lunar crust was repeatedly fractured and the whole moonscape today is densely covered by meteorite craters (Wood, 1975; Brown, 1977). Some 3.9 billion years ago the meteorite bombardment declined. It must be assumed that Planet Earth had a similarly violent bombardment for the same period, and then a decline. However, almost all traces of this violent youth have been effaced on Planet Earth by the intense weathering that has occurred by water and wind. The Moon gives a model of the cumulative bombardments that Planet Earth suffered until the environment of the planetary orbit had been swept clean of planetesimals. Now we mostly have meteorites that have strayed from the asteroid belt. It must be appreciated that at last we mercifully have an almost immaculately cleaned space for our planetary revolution!

On any explanation of the origin of a planetary system, there would be a messy environment requiring billions of years of planetary sweeping! Carbonaceous Chondrites form only a small fraction of meteorites that fall on Planet Earth, which are mostly stones, though there are also 'stony-irons' and 'irons'. All of these date from the time of the creation of the solar system or soon after (Atkins, 1977).

3.2 Frequency of Planetary Systems

The nebula hypothesis of creation of a planetary system is very plausible and appealing. One might expect that planetary formation would be very common so that there would be immense numbers of such systems in our galaxy with its 10^{12} stars. In this connection we have three miniature models of a planetary system in the satellite systems of Jupiter, Saturn and Uranus. As yet, however, no other planetary system has been detected for any star. It must first be recognized that direct observation of a planet as large as Jupiter would be far beyond the most powerful telescopes even for our nearest stellar neighbour. The glare of the central star is so brilliant that any planetary companions are masked. The only hope would be to have massive telescopes in space above the distortions of the Earth's atmosphere. However there are alternative procedures.

Firstly, there is evidence that some of the nearest stars exhibit small perturbations that indicate a gravitational pull by a revolving dark companion. There are of course many telescopic and even unaided visual observations of two or more stars forming a closely linked rotating family, but the separating distances are enormously greater than for our planetary system. In some the companion star may be very small and faint. All of these examples are called visual doubles. Possibly all transitions exist to the dark companions that in extremely favourable cases may be recognized by the small perturbations. For example, Barnard's star, one of our nearest neighbours at 6 light years distance, appears to exhibit small perturbations and Kumar (1972) lists six others. In these cases the dark companions may be burt-out stars, or they may be bodies too small to reach an interior temperature sufficient to generate the hydrogen to helium combustion. The critical size for this is 0.07 times the Sun's mass, and they could be faintly luminous (Kumar, 1972).

Secondly, there is a powerful spectrographic method of differentiating stars that are too closely apposed for separation by optical astronomy (Abt, 1977). It turns out that most of the bright stars tested have 1, 2 or even 3 companions. For example of the 123 bright stars there were 57 with 1 companion, 11 with 2, and 3 with 3. It is suggested by Abt that the remaining stars have either black dwarf companions or planetary systems, but these estimates depend on dubious extrapolations. Abt therefore proposes that there is a need for more discriminative techniques or for space telescopes.

Thus it can be concluded that there is still no convincing evidence even of another planetary system that is at all like ours. This conclusion becomes of great interest when we will be considering in Lecture 4 the possibility of life elsewhere in the Universe. A study of our planetary system and of the conditions for stability of such a system has led Kumar (1972) to define the conditions necessary for a dynamic balance that would ensure stability in the orbit of a planet over long periods. Also because of instability there are unlikely to be planetary systems for double stars, and single stars are relatively uncommon. Thus Kumar arrives at the conclusion that planetary systems are much rarer than is customarily claimed. In our galactic system with 10^{11} stars, there are probably not more than 10^6 planetary systems, and there may be only one!

3.3 Fitness of Other Planets for Supporting Life

This topic raises the second major question of this lecture: *How unique is Planet Earth amongst planets?*

As our attention focusses on our planetary system, the centre of interest moves to the physical and chemical conditions obtaining for the eight planets with respect to their suitability for the creation and fostering of life. In this context we have to compare with the other planets, Planet Earth before the origin of Life. The earliest evidence for life in the most primitive form, eobacterium, is about 3.4 billion years ago. So after its creation there was a long period of over a billion years when Planet Earth was as lifeless as the other planets. Let us simplify the comparison by eliminating the outer Jovian planets, Jupiter, Saturn, Uranus and Neptune, which we have seen to be completely different from the four innermost planets, Mercury, Venus, Earth and Mars, and to be quite impossible as a venue for life as we know it. So we will start with Mars.

We have an immense wealth of information about Mars (Pollack 1975) that was delivered by the Mariner probes and the Viking landings (Leovy, 1977; Margulis and Lovelock 1977). The terrain has been beautifully photographed (Fig. 3-4) to display a desert with rocks, rubble and fine sandy material, much like the regolith on the surface of the moon. It has also enormous volcanoes, deep valleys and high mountains. Everywhere there is evidence of erosion by the sand and dust storms. At the poles there are ice-caps which probably are a mixture of frozen CO_2 and H_2O. The surface temperature may rise almost to 0 °C during the day, but goes down to $-$ 80 °C at night. The atmospheric pressure is very low, less than 1% of the Earth's atmosphere. Moreover its composition is very different (Leovy, 1977) with CO_2, 96%; N_2, 2.5%; Argon, 1.5%. Oxygen is less than 0.1%.

Fig. 3-4. Photograph from the Viking spacecraft showing the rocks and wind-blown dust on the surface of Mars. Margulis, L., Lovelock, J. E.: The view from Mars and Venus. The Sciences *17,* No. 2, 10–13 (1977)

The water vapour is extremely low, and, if it were all precipitated, it would give a depth of only 10^{-3}–10^{-4} cm. With Earth this precipitation usually gives 2–3 cm, which is many thousand times more. Actually the Martian water vapour almost is at saturation because of the very low temperature and pressure. Some of the H_2O may be held in the crust as permafrost or chemically bound, but there is a tremendous difference from Planet Earth with its two-thirds coverage by oceans.

It has been calculated that the great differences between the atmospheres of Mars and Earth are attributable to the total out-gassing from volcanoes in Mars being hundreds of times less than that of Planet Earth (Leovy, 1977). Leovy also makes the important suggestion that oxygen and nitrogen molecules can be ionized by ultraviolet radiation in the upper atmosphere and in that state can escape from the Martian gravitational field. Planet Earth's much stronger gravitational attraction with almost 10 times the mass (Table 3-1) prevents this loss. It is calculated that in Mars the out-gassing of N_2 would have resulted in 100 times the present atmospheric concentration but for this loss. Ultraviolet dissociation of water vapour would also lead to loss of water because of the eventual loss of hydrogen. However this loss would account for a layer of water 1 m deep during the whole life history of the planet (Leovy, 1977), which is far from accounting for the water deficiency of Mars relative to Planet Earth.

Most ingenious testing of Martian soil has failed to discover any organic chemical substances or any chemical reactions that could be related to biological processes. Positive results would have been given by even the most barren soil of Planet Earth. The gas chromatograph mass spectrometer reported no organic carbon or organic nitrogen compounds in Martian soil (Margoulis and Lovelock, 1977). Yet we must believe that carbonaceous chondrites (Table 3-3) fall on Mars just as on Planet Earth and these would distribute organic chemical compounds to the Martian regolith. Presumably some of this meteoric material may be encountered in other sampling sites.

Venus is in great contrast to Mars in that its surface temperature is extremely high, 470 °C. Also the atmospheric pressure is very great, about 90 times that of Planet Earth. Its atmosphere is almost entirely CO_2 (97%) with some CO, but O_2 and H_2O are extremely low. The thick cloud cover seems to be largely sulphuric acid with perhaps some hydrofluoric acid, and these clouds could deposit a rain that would be fantastically corrosive. The limited information on the surface constitution indicates that it is rocky, much like Mars, Mercury and the Moon. The general composition of Venus is supposed to resemble that of Planet Earth (A. and L. Young, 1975) because both were formed at the same time in close proximity in the solar nebula (Fig. 3-2B), and both are of about the same size and with a similar density (Table 3-1). Yet there are two great differences that have not been accounted for. The first is the aridity of Venus and the second is the enormous atmospheric pressure on Venus. Other differences can be explained. For example, the very high temperature is attributable to the greenhouse effect of the atmosphere. Certainly Venus would be a most inhospitable planet for life with its impossibly high temperature, its corrosive atmosphere, and with its shortage of water and oxygen.

Mariner 10 has flown past Mercury and has contributed wonderful pictures of its barren crater-marked surface (Murray, 1975). There is at the most a very minute atmosphere of helium and the temperature range is extreme, from 430 °C during the long days (88×12) h to -170 °C during the equally long nights. There is no trace of water. It is inconceivable that life could ever have started on Mercury.

So far as the internal constitution can be assessed, Mars, Earth, Venus and Mercury have much the same composition, as is indicated by their similar densities 4, 5.5, 5.1, and 5.4 (Table 3-1), which contrast with the values for the Jovian planets. The surface and rock formations seem to be similar, granite and basalt for Mars and Earth and possibly for Venus. With all there appears to be a mantle probably composed of silicon, magnesium, iron and aluminium, and a core predominantly of iron. The surface features of Mars, Mercury and the Moon are similar with widespread cratering as already described. With Mars there is also the disturbance of the great dust storms, and there are apparently water courses meandering across the surface. Possibly they were cut in the remote past when the surface temperature was warmer and water more plentiful. Now there can be no water in the liquid state and the surface temperature is so low with deep permafrost that no deep water could reach the surface. There is no sign on Mars of the layered sediments that have been deposited under water on Planet Earth.

Before it was significantly affected by life Planet Earth was remarkably different from the other inner planets despite the rather similar general composition that was derived from the accretion of dust and particulate matter circling around the primitive Sun (Fig. 3-2 B). *The great differences are in the abundance of water and in the atmosphere.* There has been much controversy about the primitive atmosphere of Planet Earth. The original idea of a reducing atmosphere of NH_3, CH_4 and H_2O is now challenged (Ringwood, 1974) on the grounds that NH_3 and CH_4 would not be stable in the high-temperature phase of planetary formation. The atmosphere must have been produced later by volcanic out-gassing of H_2O, CO_2 and N_2. These out-gassings were enormously greater than for Mars. So the primitive atmosphere of Planet Earth would have been CO_2 and N_2 with the H_2O condensing to form the oceans as the temperature cooled. The immense production of H_2O is thought to have come from hydrous silicate minerals such as serpentine, amphibole and mica (Parmentier, 1977).

Certainly we have much to learn with respect to this unique feature of Planet Earth. It is important to recognize that there was virtually no oxygen in the primitive atmosphere of Earth. It was created much later by photosynthetic activity of living organisms. Under the influence of water, sedimentary rocks were formed on Planet Earth at least as early as 3.8–3.7 billion years ago, as shown by radioactive dating. Much later, as we shall describe in Lecture 4, the first organisms appeared and Planet Earth was to become greatly changed thereby. We can regard the story revealed in this lecture as being preparatory to the wonderful events described in Lecture 4 and in subsequent lectures. But the story of this lecture has been focussed on the chain of contingency whereby one planet came to be formed with special features conducive to life, while all the other planets failed abysmally on the test – *the fitness of the environment for life.* So the chain of contingency passes unambiguously to Planet Earth, as in some great design in the manner of Natural Theology.

3.4 Conclusions

At the conclusion of this cosmological part of my lectures it can be said that the Universe is fantastically large with its 10^{11} galaxies and about 10^{11} stars in each. In this overwhelming display of immensity our galaxy is not distinguished by any special features. It is just an ordinary spiral galaxy. And our Sun is not distinguished in the galaxy. It is of mediocre size and has a nondescript position (Fig. 2-4). Also Planet Earth is fifth in size and is not distinguished by its position in the planetary system (Table 3-1, Fig. 3-1). As we have seen, its special features only appear on close examination. In his many lecture assignments the astronomer Harlow Shapley was superb in his presentation of the immensity and grandeur of the cosmos, and eventually at the end of his lecture he would condescend to mention this pathetic little planet that was so insignificant that his audience were expected to be humiliated. However, after an intimate lecture in this manner to the Australian Academy of Science, I raised an objection on the grounds that "our planet is exalted above all heavenly bodies because it harbours Harlow Shapley". Touché. Let us treasure and love this beautiful salubrious Planet Earth – our home in the immense loneliness of cosmic space.

We have already seen that grandiose stars soon burn out. Our Sun's mediocrity in size is our salvation. Also of tremendous importance was the long waiting period of 5 billion years from the creation of our galaxy to the assemblage of the dust and gas that made our solar system (Lecture 2). In that 5 billion years there had been built up in the galaxy immense quantities of dust and particles containing the whole spectrum of elements that had been cooked in the supernovae. Moreover Planet Earth's size and position in the planetary system were well chosen. The temperature is just right for the macromolecules that are the essential basis of life. And the size was adequate to retain such essential gases as H_2O, O_2, N_2 and CO_2 and yet to allow dispersion of the immense load of H_2 and He which had to be accepted originally in order to secure an adequate rocky core. The Jovian planets show the disastrous consequences of being too large, while Mars and Mercury illustrate the extremely tenuous atmosphere that remains, if too small. So the atmosphere of Planet Earth can be built up to an ideal state for life, though for this the oxygen produced by primitive organisms is essential, as we shall see in Lecture 4. But the most wonderful endowment of Planet Earth is the immense supply of water, which is in great contrast to the other planets. So on the basis of "The fitness of the Environment" for life one is tempted to assert that Planet Earth is "the best of all possible worlds", in the manner of Voltaire's Candide!

Lecture 4

Origin of Life and Biological Evolution

Synopsis

When formed 4.6 billion years ago Earth would have been very hot, but by 4 billion years it would have cooled to present temperatures with a hard crust of land, oceans and atmosphere. In the prebiotic stage before the existence of life there probably was synthesis of organic molecules by electric discharges or ultraviolet light acting on the atmosphere of ammonia, methane and water. These molecules could have polymerized to form macromolecules such as primitive proteins or nucleic acids, and by interaction aggregates of these molecules could have formed self-organizing systems, which were concentrated on surfaces of clays or in shallow pools. It is however still a long way from such conjectured systems to the first primitive living cells.

The earliest fossil remains of living organisms possibly are the eobacteria of 3.4 billion years ago, but the earliest fossil remains of algae dated only from 2 billion years ago. Thus there are enormous time spans for the most improbable events that led up to the creation of the first primitive single-cell organisms. So life continued for 1.4 billion years. The first multicellular organisms appeared about 700 million years ago, and then biological evolution as we know it commenced. A brief treatment of the genetic code and mutations leads up to the process of biological evolution. Emphasis is placed on natural selection as being an interaction between the organism and the 'fitness' of the environment. There is no predictable line of evolutionary development. On the contrary there is maximization of diversity, natural selection giving ruthless testing of what is fit to survive. In following the line of evolution that led to us, vertebrates appeared in the ocean as primitive fish 440 million years ago, and 30 million years later vertebrates moved onto land – amphibians and then reptiles. But the evolution of mammals was a very uncertain process, and could have terminated when the mammal-like reptiles after 100 million years of existence were nearly extinguished 200 million years ago. They fortunately survived to evolve into mammals. These were insignificant relative to the giant dinosaurs of that period. But the dinosaurs mysteriously died out and the mammals eventually flourished with wide diversification. And so the primates, our forebears, came to exist 50 million years ago and from them came the apes, which diversified further to give the primitive ancestors of man, *Ramapithecus* to *Australopithecus*. Finally there will be critical discussion of the much debated question of the frequency with which life originated in other planetary systems of our galaxy, Planet Earth being the only example in our solar system. Much more debatable is the possibility of intelligent life. There is much in this evolutionary story that relates to Natural Theology. Particularly so if, as I will argue, Planet Earth is probably unique in harbouring intelligent self-conscious beings.

4.1 What is Known to Have Happened: The Fossil Record
(Planet Earth, 1977; Biology Today, 1975)

Because the theme of these lectures is "The Human Mystery", the attempt
will be made to limit the account of the fossil record to the organisms that
lie close to that part of the evolutionary tree that leads on to man. For
example, plants and fungi are neglected, as also are great regions of the
invertebrata and vertebrata. Table 4-1 shows the time scale of the geological ages since the formation of the earth.

In the last lecture I mentioned that there was a long period between the
formation of Planet Earth at 4.6 billion years ago and the first fossil records
of living organisms. The oldest known rocks are a series of volcanic and
sedimentary rocks with a radioactive dating of 3.8–3.7 billion years ago
(Siever, 1975). So by that time Planet Earth had cooled sufficiently to have

Table 4-1. The geological ages, shown from the bottom up, but not in a uniform time scale

		Millions of years ago	
CENOZOIC	Holocene	0.01	Early civilizations
	Pleistocene	2	
	Pliocene	7	Emergence of hominids
	Miocene	26	
	Oligocene	38	
	Eocene	54	
	Paleocene	65	
MESOZOIC	Cretaceous	135	Main fragmentation of Pangaea: transgression of sea over land
	Jurassic	190	Start of fragmentation of Pangaea
	Triassic	225	Worldwide regression of sea from land
PALEOZOIC	Permian	285	Formation of Pangaea
	Carboniferous	345	
	Devonian	395	Animal life takes to the land
	Silurian	440	First land plants
	Ordovician	500	Major transgression of sea over continents
	Cambrian	570	
PRECAMBRIAN	Proterozoic		First multicellular organisms
		2500	
	Archaean		
		3500	First unicellular organisms
		3780	Age of oldest known terrestrial rocks
		4600	Formation of Earth
		10000	'Big Bang'

a solid crust and liquid water in excess in the oceans, beneath which sedimentary rocks were being laid down. During the cooling there probably had been torrential rains for millions of years, as evidenced by the build-up of the great oceans. The land masses were less extensive than now, as in the earliest reconstructions some 600 million years ago, and have since then drifted over the surface of the Earth.

The search for the earliest fossil remains of living organisms is a very exacting task because these would be the mineralised remains of single cells of microscopic dimensions. Thousands of specimens of sedimentary rocks have to be prepared as ultrathin polished sections for examination by light microscopy and electron microscopy. In this search the first successes were fossils of algae in a dense silicon rock, Gunflint chert, with a radioactive dating of 2 billion years ago (Fig. 4-1). More recently fossils of presumed organisms, *'Eobacterium'*, have been found in the Fig-tree cherts of Swaziland, which are dated up to 3.4 billion years ago (Fig. 4-1 a, b). This his-

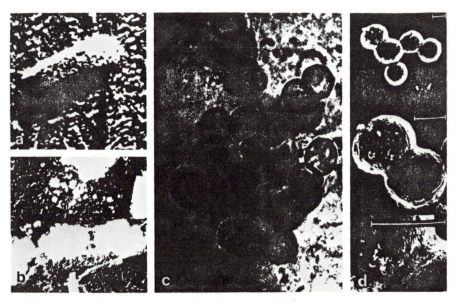

Fig. 4-1 a–d. Fossils of some of the earliest known organisms
a Fossil of a bacteria-like organism that lived 3.1 billion years ago (Figtree Formation in South Africa). **b** Fossilized bacteria found in sedimentary rock in Canada, dating about 2 billion years ago. **c** A fossilized clump of algal cells dating from about 900 million years ago (Bitter Springs Formation of Central Australia). **d** Scanning electron micrographs of a sample of the Bitter Springs algae in the process of mitotic division. Two higher magnifications of one of the dividing algal cells are also shown here. Reprinted from *Biology today,* 2nd ed. with permission of CRM Books, a Division of Random House, Inc. and Dr. J. William Schopf

tological record is supported by the organic carbon content of the rock. A much earlier dating for blue-green algae than 2 billion years has been given by the *Stromatolites,* which are columnar structures believed to be built around clumps of blue-green algae. They have been called blue-green algae reefs. They are found embedded in limestone and may be up to 1 m in diameter, which suggests an enormous mass of algae. The earliest stromatolites, in the Bullawayan Formation, are dated at 2.9 billion years ago (Sylvester Bradley, 1977). Figures 1 c and d are remarkable pictures of algae.

The concentration of oxygen in the primitive atmosphere is believed to have been extremely low, perhaps no more than one ten-thousandth of the present concentration. So the earliest living organisms would be existing under practically anaerobic conditions. From 3 billion years ago the oxygen was increasing and probably had reached a concentration of up to 10% of the present atmospheric oxygen some 600 million years ago. Then there was a rapid increase, the present level being attained in the last 100 or 200 million years, with a concentration of just over 20% of the atmosphere. In those 2 billion years an enormous amount of molecular oxygen had to be created – enough to cover the whole surface of our planet with a depth of 2 m liquid oxygen! It is assumed that this essential change in the atmosphere was due in the first place to the blue-green algae, and later all green plants would have contributed enormously, but the first land plants date only from 440 million years ago.

The simplest chemical formula of the photosynthetic process by chlorophyll and related pigments shows that CO_2 and H_2O are combined to form a carbohydrate with the liberation of O_2.

$$6 CO_2 + 6 H_2O = C_6 H_{12} O_6 + 6 O_2.$$

However, this formula conceals most complicated cyclic chemical reactions involving organic phosphates. As a consequence of this most remarkable evolutionary development, the Earth's atmosphere was changed from reducing to oxidizing about 1 billion years ago. The development of multicellular aerobic organisms had to await the building up of a sufficient concentration of oxygen in the atmosphere. Hence the long waiting period of nearly 3 billion years from the earliest evidence of life to the beginning of the Cambrian age 600 million years ago. However, very important developments were occurring in the change from the primitive *prokaryotes* to *eukaryotes* which will be described in the second part of the lecture.

With the Cambrian era (570–500 million years ago), there begins the rich fossil record that continues right through to the present age. There were many species with hard body parts, in the first place an exoskeleton but later on an endoskeletal system, both excellent for fossils. However, in

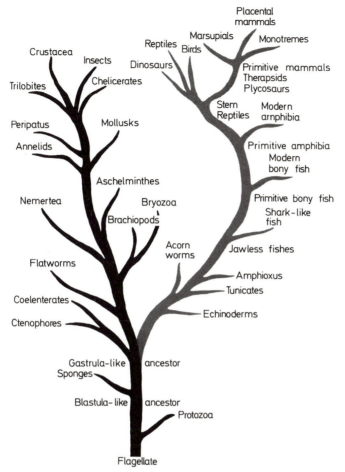

Fig. 4-2. A diagram illustrating current theories of the evolutionary relationship in the animal kingdom. The branch including the Protostomia is indicated in black and the branch including the Deuterostomia is in grey. Villee, C. A.: Biology. Philadelphia: Saunders 1972

the preceding Precambrian era there are fossil records of multicellular organisms, but these were small and soft, so the fossil record is meagre (Brasier, 1977). It must not be assumed that such organisms were rare. The first fossil records are of soft multicellular organisms resembling jelly-fish and worms some 700 million years ago. So the great developments of the Cambrian era were built upon considerable Precambrian breakthroughs from unicellular to complex multicellular organisms. Almost all the invertebrate phyla were created by the evolutionary process before the end of the

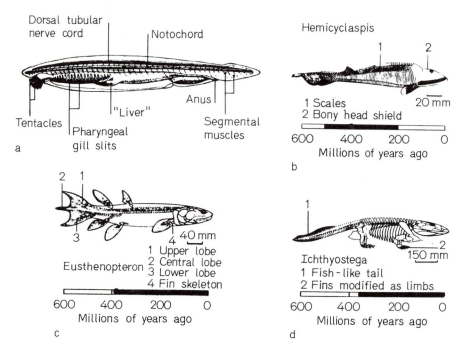

Fig. 4-3a–d. Chordates to early vertebrates
a A primitive chordate (Lancelet) with gill slits, a dorsal nerve cord and a notocord. Reprinted from *Biology today,* 2nd ed. with permission of CRM Books, a Division of Random House, Inc. **b** *Hemicyclaspis,* a jawless fish (*Agnatha*). **c** *Eusthenopteron,* a fossil Crossopterygian. **d** *Ichthyostega,* the earliest amphibian. **b,c,** and **d**, reprinted from *Planet earth* with permission of Elsevier Publishing Projects (U. K.) Limited

Cambrian era. Most of these early organisms have become extinct. Notable were the Trilobites, most complex arthropods with well-developed eyes. They left a great fossil record during their success period for 200 million years, but they died out about 300 million years ago. The diversity of Cambrian life is illustrated by the wide variety of feeding strategies – herbivores, carnivores and predators, scavengers and filter-feeders.

In the late Cambrian there developed the Tunicata (Fig. 4-2), which are the earliest members of the Phylum to which we belong – Chordata. The fossil record is as yet unclear, but there is no doubt about the present constitution of the phylum Chordata (Fig. 4-2). It has a large subphylum, Vertebrata, and two other very small subphyla, Urochordata (Tunicates) and Cephalochordata (Amphioxus). These two primitive subphyla point to the organism from which the phylum Chordata evolved, which is a primitive echinoderm, called Hemichordata. Echinoderms have a fossil record from

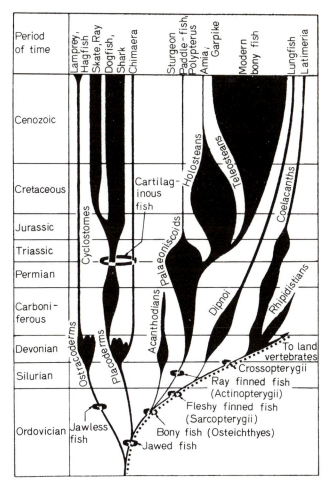

Fig. 4-4. A presumed pattern of evolutionary relationships of the fishes. Note tenuous line to *Crossopterygii* and thence to land vertebrates, indicated by dots. (By courtesy of the late Prof. A. S. Romer)

the early Cambrian. So the evolutionary sequence would be: a primitive echinoderm evolving to a primitive chordate. This chordate would be characterized by an internal skeleton, the notocord, running the length of the animal with a nerve cord dorsal thereto; and ventrally, a complete gut with gill clefts; and laterally, segmental muscles (Fig. 4-3a).

The first clear fossil record of vertebrates is in the Ordovician era, about 450 million years ago. Primitive jawless fishes (Fig. 4-3b), like the lamprey, had evolved from the primitive chordata (Forey, 1977). These fish of class

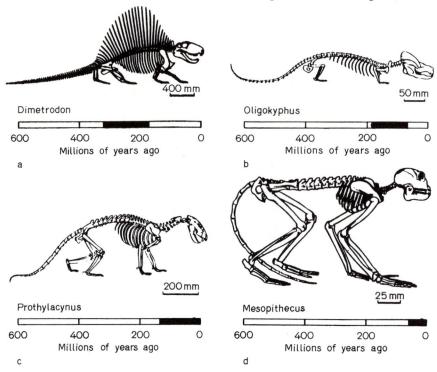

Fig. 4-5 a–d. Specimens in mammalian evolution. **a** *Dimetrodon,* a mammal-like reptile, by far the largest of this type. **b** *Oligokyphus,* a primitive mammalian insectivore. **c** *Prothylacynus,* an advanced insectivore. **d** *Mesopithecus,* a primate (see Fig. 4-7). Reprinted from *Planet Earth* with permission of Elsevier Publishing Projects (U. K.) Limited

Agnatha were poorly formed for swimming and feeding. Nevertheless they flourished in Silurian and Devonian seas and even invaded rivers and lakes. But after some 100 million years they were largely extinct except for the hagfish and lamprey that still survive (Fig. 4-4).

Fortunately, our evolutionary line was not dependent for too long on the uncertainties of survival of jawless fishes. About 400 million years ago, there evolved from the Agnatha the much more efficient jawed fishes, which constitute the great diversity of fishes up to this time (Fig. 4-4). It is essential for our purpose to single out one unique family because they provide the evolutionary link to amphibians. The *Crossopterygians* are nearly extinct, the recently discovered Coelacanth being the sole survivor (Fig. 4-4). These fish were remarkable because their four fins were really four legs (Fig. 4-3c) and also they had nostrils and lungs for air breathing. From the arrangements of the bones and muscles it is recognized that these

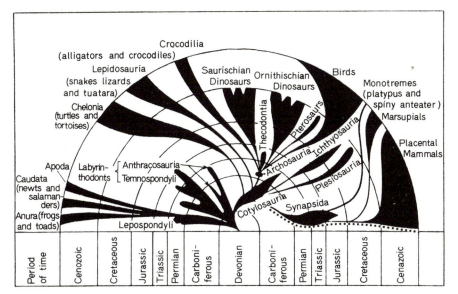

Fig. 4-6. A presumed pattern of evolutionary relationships of the land vertebrates. Note tenuous line to Synapsida and thence to placental mammals, indicated by dots. By courtesy of the late Prof. A. S. Romer

fish could use their fin-limbs for walking on land. In fact, the Coelacanth is called 'old four legs'.

In the Silurian era and later there were invertebrates such as worms and insects burrowing in the sands and mudflats along the seashore, so it was not surprising that fish-like amphibians struggled out of the sea to forage on these flats where there was not the severe competition from the teeming fish in the sea. This invasion of the land by amphibians occurred in the Devonian era. They had evolved from the Crossopterygian fish by further development of the limbs that now had digits (Fig. 4-3 d). However, the invasion of the land was not completed as they preferred a watery habitat. At this same time the land was also invaded by plants, so it became a much more attractive environment for survival. There was much diversification of amphibians, and one major group, the *Anthracosaurs* (Fig. 4-6), became completely adapted to terrestrial life, though their young still lived in water. Otherwise they resembled reptiles, and it is assumed that reptiles evolved from this group.

This evolution of reptiles was accomplished in the Carboniferous era by the change to a hard or leathery-shelled egg that hatched out on land. The reptiles were more fitted to survive on land than amphibians and greatly benefitted from the drier conditions of the next age, the Permian. The continents had drifted together to form the great continental assemblage, *Panagea*. The land in close relationship to the oceans was greatly reduced in area, but the reptiles flourished because they had developed a complete independence from a watery existence. So our evolutionary line was apparently secure, and it now becomes more clear, because in the late Carboniferous era with the great diversification of the reptiles, there were developed reptiles with mammalian features (Fig. 4-5 a). They are known as the subclass *Synapsida* (Fig. 4-6) and were the first animals to adapt fully to a terrestrial life. However after initial successes they nearly all became extinct by 200 million years ago. But the mammalian line was being established about 200 million years ago by evolution from the only surviving group, the *Cynodonts,* who were active insectivores that had already developed mammalian features such as a secondary palate so that they could breathe while chewing (Fig. 4-5 a).

Meanwhile, the reptiles had scored an immense success of a quite different kind – in the *Dinosaurs*. From 225 million to 65 million years ago, (the Mesozoic) Earth was dominated by these massive creatures with their monstrous bodies and their formidable jaws. The small mammal-like reptiles and the small mammals must have been hard put to survive this great display of reptilian power. The fossil record indicates that there was near-extinction about 190 million years ago. But in the end the great reptiles perished, all being gone by 65 million years ago in a quite mysterious way (Fig. 4-6). One likes to think that the harsh conditions in the terrible struggle for survival had been a strong force for natural selection with even an enhanced cerebral capacity in these primitive mammals. Maybe they had brought about the dinosaurs' downfall by preying on their eggs!

Our evolutionary line would have looked most unsure in the great dinosaur age when the primitive mammals were so insignificant, rather like present-day shrews (Fig. 4-5 b). Yet the dinosaurs perished and the humble mammals survived to found the next age of dominance, the Age of Mammals, in the Cenozoic era from 65 million years ago to the present.

The first mammals in our evolutionary line were the *Insectivores* (Fig. 4-5 c), which evolved from the reptilian insectivores. Distinguishing features presumably would be their care of the young by lactation and their control of body temperature. The Monotremes and Marsupials were evolutionary side branches and not in the main line (Fig. 4-6). The *Primates* can first be recognized at 70 million years ago in the type strangely known as Purgatorius, the first Prosimian. In the Eocene era (54–38 million years ago)

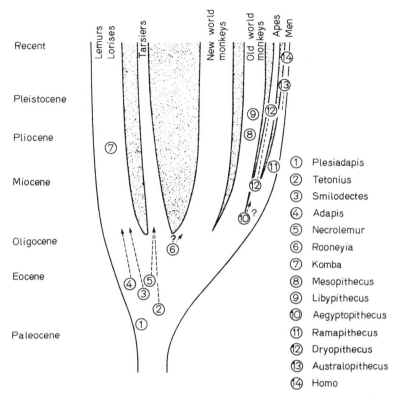

Fig. 4-7. Phylogeny of the primates related to the Cenozoic geological ages (4cf. Table 4-1). The list of species is indicated by the numbered circles. Jerison, H. J.: Evolution of the brain and intelligence, p. 482. New York, London: Academic Press 1973

the Primates became largely tree-dwellers, possibly because of rodent competition on the ground. Their well-formed digits were of great advantage, and were further developed to give the opposable thumb with flattened nails instead of claws. Furthermore, the eyes were directed forward in order to give the stereoscopic vision so important in an arboreal existence. Probably the complex interaction between vision and movement in trees gave selective advantage to the development of the brain (Fig. 4-5 d).

Unfortunately the fossil record of primate evolution is defective (Fig. 4-7). Probably the total population was never large, as can be recognized in the anthropoid population today.

In the Oligocene (38–26 million years ago), there was evolved a genus *Propliopithecus* with facial features and dentition showing hominid characteristics. This genus could be on the evolutionary line to hominids, but the fossil record from 30 million years ago is most inadequate. A small primate *Rooneyia* (Fig. 4-7 [6]) with a fossil skull of 35 million years ago is most interesting because it is the first primate to exhibit a greatly enlarged brain (Jerison, 1973). When allowance is made for its small size (b. w. 200 g), its brain of over 7 g was three to four times that of the mammals at that time. *Rooneyia* is thus important in indicating the propensity of the primate stock to evolve larger brains, but it is not clear if it is on our evolutionary line (see 6 in Fig. 4-7). The first good fossil record of prehominids is for *Ramapithecus* (11 in Fig. 4-7), which in the last few years has been identified in three widely scattered sites in Asia, Africa and Europe (Simons, 1977). It seems clearly to be on the hominid line rather than on the pongid line to the anthropoid apes. We shall be returning to the theme of the fossil record of the hominids in Lecture 5.

4.2 Explanations of Fossil Records by Evolutionary Theories

We now come to consider the theories that have been developed to explain the evolutionary history leading from a prebiotic world to the present.

4.2.1 Prebiotic Organic Chemistry

Two classes of substances are of supreme importance to living organisms, the proteins and the nucleotide assemblages in deoxyribonucleic acid (DNA) and in ribonucleic acid (RNA). In prebiotic organic chemistry we have to concentrate attention on the constituents of these substances, which are respectively the amino acids and the purine and pyrimidine bases.

There are two theories about the presumed prebiotic accumulation of organic chemicals on Planet Earth.

The first is that they were seeded from space. In recent years this theory has received strong support from the discovery by radio-astronomers that there is a wide range of molecules in space. The identifications are quite precise. There are many organic molecules, some with as many as seven atoms. The constituent atoms are H, O, N, C, S and Si. Important molecules identified are formaldehyde, hydrogen cyanide, cyanoacetylene and isocyanate (Brown, 1974). No amino acids were identified in the early investigations, and also no ring compounds. These interstellar molecules undoubtedly will be moving into Earth's atmosphere, and they could have contributed importantly to its prebiotic organic chemistry.

Another interesting input of organic chemicals from interstellar space is via the carbonaceous chondrites, which contain a considerable proportion of carbonaceous material (Table 3-3), including amino acids, purines and pyrimidines. Unfortunately, none of the fundamental DNA bases was amongst those identified (Ringwood, 1974). It is suggested that, during condensation from the solar nebula, these substances were formed from CO, H_2 and NH_3. Judging from the moon's history there must have been an enormous meteoric bombardment in the early history of the Earth, so a great quantity of carbonaceous material could have been accumulated.

However it is doubted how much this prebiotic seeding of organic molecules contributed to the build-up of organic materials on Planet Earth, so special importance attaches to the alternative that these molecules were made locally. There have been most comprehensive investigations (Miller, 1955, 1957; Calvin, 1961, 1969) on the generation of organic molecules when gas mixtures that are assumed to resemble the primitive atmosphere (CH_4, NH_3, H_2O and H_2) are subjected to spark discharges. Such conditions would occur with lightning discharges and also it is assumed that high-energy radiation by cosmic rays and ultraviolet would have acted similarly. A wide range of organic substances was detected by Miller in the earliest experiments, even the amino acids glycine, alanine and aspartic acid, and the list has grown with later investigations. Recently Miller substituted N_2 for NH_3, and the range of organic chemicals produced closely resembled that in a carbonaceous chondrite.

An important addition to this prebiotic story was made by Oro, who synthesized the highly significant purine base, adenine, from NH_3 and HCN. Adenine can easily be converted into the other essential purine of DNA, guanidine. Orgel (1974) has demonstrated the formation of the other essential constituents of DNA, the pyrimidine bases. Electric discharge through an N_2, CH_4 mixture gave cyanoacetylene and hydrogen cyanide, which have also been identified in interstellar space. Cyanoacetylene plus water and cyanogen generates pyrimidine bases by simple chemistry. Finally the other essential component of DNA, ribose, is formed when formaldehyde acts on lime or chalk. Thus we have generated in this prebiotic stage all the components for building up proteins and DNA.

Unfortunately there has been some criticism of the composition assumed for the primitive atmosphere, which is alleged to have been slightly oxidizing rather than reducing (Ringwood, 1974). The out-gassing from the earth, by volcanoes and otherwise, is likely to have been largely H_2O, CO_2 and N_2, but there could also have been some CO and H_2. It is interesting that Abelson got very similar organic products when he applied electric discharges to a minimally reducing atmosphere with CO_2, N_2 and H_2O. In conclusion it seems that in the prebiotic stage there could have been a supply of all the organic molecules required for synthesizing the macromolecules essential for life, namely, proteins and DNA. However, the quantities formed are problematic. The proposal that the primitive oceans were converted into a hot soup is surely absurd. The problem is to develop ideas about the way in which these molecules could be sufficiently concentrated for effective interaction.

4.2.2 Steps in the Building of Proteins and Nucleic Acids

This is the second stage in the creation of a living organism. It is important to realize that concentrations are important, so it is an attractive proposal by Fox (1964) and others that solutions of prebiotic chemicals were concentrated by evaporation from pools. Another important suggestion is that of Paecht-Horowitz, Berger and Katchalsky (1970) that effective concentrations were achieved by adsorption on clays, which in this way acted as catalysts. Such means of concentration lead to the events with which we are now concerned, namely, the self-organization of macromolecules that has been specially studied by Eigen (1971), Eigen and Winkler (1975), Orgel (1974) and Schuster (1977). It should be mentioned that Fox (1964) has shown that solutions of amino acids evaporated on a bed of hot lava (about 130 °C) are polymerized and can be induced to form cell-like structures that have been called 'proteinoid microspheres'. They may even grow and divide. However, their appearance is deceptive. They are not related at all to true cells because they lack nucleic acids.

Orgel (1974) has had remarkable success in the early stage of self-organization of amino acids and nucleotides. The necessary source of energy is supplied by hydrolysis of the pyrophosphate bonds of ATP (adenosine triphosphate), which in turn could be produced in the primitive earth along with many other types of polyphosphates. In this way he has synthesized oligonucleotides of 3 or 4 subunits and polypeptides of 6 or 7 units. Of course this is far from the hundreds of units of even the simplest proteins or DNA, but it points the way.

Eigen (1971) has developed important theoretical treatments based on chemical kinetics. He has concluded that nucleic acids cannot organize themselves for a correlated function, as in the double helix of DNA, without catalytic help. This is provided by the complex enzyme systems (proteins) in a living cell. Eigen has also concluded that it is improbable that biologically useful proteins can be formed by self-assemblage of amino acids. The really important conclusion of these studies of theoretical models is that biologically meaningful self-assemblage does occur when there are concurrent syntheses of proteins and nucleic acids. Various model systems are analysed in order to investigate the manner of this co-operation between nucleic acids and proteins so that there is effective self-assemblage.

From these kinetic studies Eigen (1971), Eigen and Winkler (1975) and Schuster (1977) have proposed that, given a continuous supply of energy, catalytic hypercycles will lead to biochemical systems, undergoing evolution to the level of complexity of primitive organisms. The system of amino acids must be simplified in order to set up a system of organizational hypercycles, and Schuster (1977) has suggested starting with 4 amino acids instead of the 20 now used in protein manufacture. They could have different properties, one hydrophobic, one hydrophilic, one positively charged, one negatively charged. The hypercycle is defined as a model system involving catalysis and autocatalysis of a higher order (Schuster, 1977). That is, it operates from simple cyclic catalysis to highly organized networks involving proteins and polynucleotides. However, it is evident that a great gulf still separates these prebiotic chemical systems and the biochemistry of a living cell.

4.2.3 The Living Cell

Despite the predictions based on prebiotic organic chemistry it has to be recognized that the simplest living cell (Fig. 4-8) is an enormously complicated organism that would require four major developments from macromolecular organic chemistry. *Firstly,* there must be organization of a cell encapsulated by a surrounding membrane. *Secondly,* there must be some chemical processes within the cell providing the mechanism for building up and utilizing an organization of energy-rich substances. *Thirdly,* the membrane surrounding the cell must be permeable to substances so as to allow exchange with the environment and the building up of its contents by metabolically operated pumps. *Fourthly,* there must be some mechanism in the cell for storing and utilizing the information that controls its biological processes and that is necessary for the duplication of this information when the cell subdivides in the reproductive process.

There is still a chasm between prebiotic organic chemistry and the simplest living organism. It has been a great achievement to build up prebiotic chemistry in the attempt to bridge this chasm, and conceptually Eigen has made a notable advance by his postulated hypercycles. But this great pre-

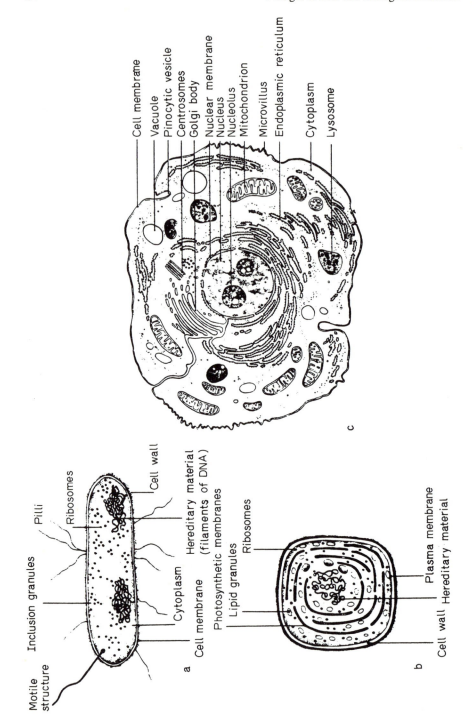

biotic structure has hardly yet begun to arch across the chasm to the simplest cell. It is particularly disappointing that on the biotic side there seems no way to construct or discover more simple living organisms that could help in the arching towards the prebiotic side. Viruses are not helpful because they are examples not of a very primitive life, but rather of a degenerated parasitic life.

One of the simplest living cells is a bacterium, and Eobacteria are the earliest living organisms to be identified. The bacterium illustrated in Figure 4-8a exemplifies the above four requirements. It is encapsulated by a membrane and contains various structures in its cytoplasm that are concerned in metabolism. The membrane is permeable to nutritive substances entering and to metabolic waste products leaving, and it also is equipped with metabolically driven pumps. The information for the working of the cell is encoded in the two coiled filaments of DNA. Before the cell divides these filaments are duplicated by an accurate copying process so that the two daughter cells are each provided with the full code. This precious genetic material, the DNA, is suspended freely in the cytoplasm. This is the most primitive arrangement and such cells are called *prokaryotes*. As shown in Figure 4-8b the other earliest identified cells, the blue-green algae also are prokaryotes and in general resemble the bacterial cell.

An advantageous evolutionary development was to have the DNA filaments enclosed by a membrane that separated them from the cytoplasm, so forming the nucleus of the cell (Fig. 4-8c). These cells are called *eukaryotes* and are the standard arrangement for the cells of all organisms except bacteria and the most primitive algae. The segregation of the precious genetic material in a nucleus was a very important evolutionary development because it protected the complex machinery that is required for transcription from the information encoded on the DNA. Furthermore, it simplified the process of the duplication of the DNA before subdivision of the cell, and in addition it opened the way to a fully developed process of sexual reproduction.

By a highly technical comparative study of the sequence of nucleotides in a special type of ribonucleic acid and of the amino acid sequences in cytochrome C, Kimura (1977) has discovered that the eukaryotes deviated

◄ **Fig. 4-8a–c.** Prokaryotes and eukaryotes. **a** Structure of a typical bacterial cell. **b** Structure of a typical blue-green alga. a and b reprinted from *Biology today,* 2nd ed. with permission of CMR Books, a Division of Random House, Inc. **c** Structure of a typical animal cell, a eukaryote with the genetic material enclosed in a nucleus. Villee, C. A.: Biology. Philadelphia: Saunders 1972

from the prokaryotes 1.8 billion years ago. This marks the first profound evolutionary development from the prokaryotes, which had existed from the times of the Eobacterium at 3.4 billion and of the blue-green algae at 2.9 billion years ago. The importance of this development will be appreciated when it is realized that the DNA filament coiled in the bacterium of Figure 4-8a is 1.0 mm in length, which is almost 1000 times longer than the cell. One cannot imagine the trickiness involved when this long tangle of the double helix (Fig. 4-9) is being duplicated into the two tangles which separate in the subdivision of the cell. In favourable cases this duplication may take place every 20 min! The situation is very much worse in any one of our cells, where the total length of the DNA is about 2 m, more than 100000 times longer than the usual size of the cell! However, the problem is much less tricky in eukaryotes because the DNA is subdivided into many fragments in the chromosomes of the nucleus. There are 23 pairs of chromosomes in humans.

4.2.4 Biological Evolution (Villee, 1972; Simpson and Beck, 1969)

In order to be able to present an intelligible account of the essentials of the evolutionary process, it is necessary firstly to give a much simplified account of the genetic material of the cell, DNA, and of the mode of action via its genetic code. DNA is an extremely long double helix (Fig. 4-9), each strand having a 'backbone' made of alternate phosphate and sugar (ribose). To each sugar there is attached one of the following four molecules: the purine bases, adenine (A) and guanine (G) and the pyrimidines, thymine (T) and cytosine (C). The linkages of the two helices are effected by the cross-linkages that occur every 3.4 Å (Fig. 4-9). A in one links to T in the other or G in one to C of the other. So a sequence could be:

    G   T   A   G   C   A   T
    C   A   T   C   G   T   A

for the linkage pairs of a very short segment of the two helices. The code is thus written linearly along each strand. For a bacterium the code of each strand has about 1.5 million letters. With us there are about 3.5 billion letters in each strand, which gives the preliminary information for building all of the cells of a human being. Before the cell divides the two strands of the double helix separate and an enzyme system makes for each the complementary strand. The two double helices that are thus reconstituted are

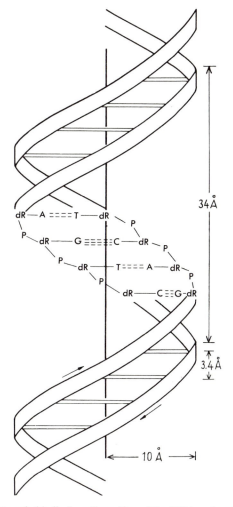

Fig. 4-9. The double-stranded helical configuration of the DNA molecule. The two nucleotide strands are held together by hydrogen bonds forming between the complementary purine (*A* or *G*) and pyrimidine (*T* or *C*) pairs. Note the dimensions given for the spacing, and for width and length of one helical configuration. (Modified from Simpson and Beck, 1969) From LIFE: AN INTRODUCTION TO BIOLOGY, Shorter Edition, by George Gaylord Simpson and William S. Beck, (c) 1969 by Harcourt Brace Jovanovich, Inc. Reproduced by permission of the publishers

identical copies of the original. The genetic information that builds and controls the cell is coded in the nucleotide sequences, the A T G C letters, along the DNA strands.

It is beyond the scope of this lecture to go into the detailed manner in which, by the precise processes of transcription and translation, this DNA code is read out in the building of the amino acid sequences of a protein, and so is effective in building the structure of the cell and in the enzymatically controlled metabolism of the cell. Enzymes are proteins. The code for any such action is carried in linear array on the DNA strands, not by a short sequence of letters as illustrated above, but by some thousands of letter sequences, called a *gene*. Genes carry the precise instructions for building the amino acid sequences of particular proteins. It will be recognized that, for building the many species of proteins required for the living processes of a bacterial cell, its DNA chain of about 3 million letter sequences is not extravagant. With our cells the number is more than 1000 times greater, 3.5 billion. Again, this is not extravagant for coding the information required to build the proteins of our cells. It has been estimated by Dobzhansky that the number of human genes is at least 30,000. For an average protein of 500 amino acid sequences, there are required 1500 nucleotide pairs, for 3 pairs are required for each sequence. So 30,000 genes require 4.5×10^7 nucleotide pairs. But with redundancies the number could be many times larger.

Normally in reproduction there is an accurate copying of the linear code written in the DNA, and hence there is stability in the genes from generation to generation. However, changes called *gene mutations* do occur in the DNA code. There may be mistakes in copying with the replacement of one nucleotide for another, such as G for A, or there may be more radical changes with deletion or inversion of one or more nucleotide base pairs or even inversion of larger DNA segments. These copying errors may lead to the substitution of one amino acid for another in a protein. The effect of this may be negligible in the functioning of the protein. However, in the great majority these exchanges are deleterious to the survival and reproduction of the individual. Only on rare occasions is a mutation beneficial for survival and reproduction. Such a mutation will be transmitted to successive generations and will result in enhanced survival of the biological group sharing this mutation. So in time by *natural selection* this favourable mutation may come to be incorporated in all members of that species, which consequently reflect a slight change in genotype. Later another mutational selection may be added, and so on.

This is the essential basis of Darwin's theory of *natural selection* or *survival of the fittest*. Favourable gene mutations are selected, whereas the unfavourable are eliminated. Hence by an initial process of pure chance, the gene mutation, there can be wrought by natural selection all the marvellous structural and functional features of living organisms with their amazing adaptiveness and inventiveness. As so formulated, the evolutionary theory is purely a biological process involving mechanisms of operations that are now well understood in principle, and it has deservedly won acceptance as providing a satisfactory explanation of the development of all living forms from some single extremely simple primordial form of life. This theory stemming from Darwin and Wallace must rank as one of the grandest conceptual achievements of man.

A recent development has been the recognition that many mistakes in DNA copying are virtually neutral. For example the mutation may result in a changed amino acid sequence in a part of the protein that is not vital for its functioning. Or, again, the mutation may be in a part of the DNA that is not concerned in building protein, so it will be selectively neutral. In time there can be a large accumulation of such neutral mutations that have changed considerably the original DNA of a population. With a changed evironment these mutations may no longer be neutral.

4.2.5 Evolution and Environment

In the competition for some favourable environment, an *eco-niche*, the most fitted organisms survived and left more progeny for producing the next generation, and so on, while those less fitted failed to prosper. Furthermore, the process was not static. In the larger environment the most successful organisms were those that also 'explored' other potential eco-niches and so had many chances of selection. Thus biological evolution is a process of interaction of organism with environment. This was stressed by Lawrence Henderson (1913) in his classic book *The Fitness of the Environment*.

There is no predictable line of evolutionary development. On the contrary, there is maximization of diversity, natural selection giving ruthless testing of what is fit to survive. A consideration of all the environmental factors that contributed to and moulded biological evolution led Blum (1968) to recognize the apparently unique and accidental character of many of the factors that contributed essentially to the environment. Evolution is thus a process of trial and error.

Let us now return to the life of the primordial bacterium. It is dependent on an environment of nutritive material from which it derives the energy for its living processes, including growth and reproduction. Thus it is a *heterotroph* in contrast to an *autotroph*. This latter type is endowed with metabolic machinery which makes it independent of environmental nutrients. It is generally believed that the first bacteria, being heterotrophs, may eventually have run into difficulties from exhaustion of the environmental nutrients that were built up by prebiotic chemistry. Fortunately mutations provided some living organisms with alternative energy sources. The most notable is of course the use of pigments for photosynthetic metabolism, as was done by the blue-green algae with chlorophyll (Fig. 4-8b). Bacteria also developed pigments for photosynthesis.

If we consider the time scale of the existence of living organisms, what seems beyond imagining is the enormous duration of the simplest prokaryotic phase, which was some 1.6 billion years before the re-arrangement of the genetic material into the nucleus resulted in eukaryotes. We can be concerned at the terribly slow rate of progresses, especially when we realize that this was the progress that eventually led to our appearance on the stage of the cosmic drama!

We may ask how effective was natural selection in those primitive conditions. The primordial unicellular type of life had immense stability, and innovation seems to have been at a low level. Thus the process of biological evolution was inordinately slow compared with the happenings with multicellular organisms. But it must be realized that even single-cell prokaryotes of today are immensely complicated organisms with subtly balanced enzyme systems operating on instructions from the genetic material DNA via RNA, the processes of transcription and translation, and these instructions are controlled by feed-back. It may be that a billion years was spent in improving the design of the DNA and of the transcription and translation processes. Perhaps the rationale of this was to minimize copying errors. It seems as if time-wise this initial stage of Eobacteria at 3.4 billion years ago came relatively soon, being only 0.4 billion years after the cooling of Earth, the formation of the oceans and the beginnings of prebiotic chemistry, at 3.8 billion years. The long drag in evolutionary development came after that time. To evolve the eukaryotes 1.6 billion years were required, and subsequently it was 1 billion years before the first multicellular organisms appeared. A plausible suggestion is that multicellular organisms could flourish only when there had been a large increase in the atmospheric oxygen – perhaps up to 10% of its present level.

In retrospect the amazing phenomenon is that some 700 million years ago multicellular organisms came to exist, and with them the fantastic innovative powers of biological evolution were revealed. Its occurrence could never have been predicted after almost 3 billion years of unicellular existence.

4.3 General Considerations

We traced our evolutionary line in the fossil record. There seem to be two over-riding rules, namely, to avoid the immediate successes that come by profound adaptations, and to cherish plasticity. In that way dead ends have been avoided though they were most successful in their limited and temporary ways. For example, in invertebrata the insects developed eyes and a related brain that are marvels of design and precision, never to be approached in any later biological design. Yet insects were critically limited in size by their encasing exoskeletons and by their respiratory mechanisms. The molluscs also made great evolutionary progress with their respiratory pigments and with a motor system and a central nervous system that were very highly developed in the octopus and the squid; yet they were left far behind the advanced vertebrates. By contrast the primitive echinoderm, Hemichordata, had the evolutionary line to Chordata and so on to Vertebrata.

The fish on the evolutionary line that led to us (Fig. 4-4) were poor swimmers with fins partly fitted as limbs for crawling. Apparently they could not survive in the strong competition from the superbly swimming fish in the ocean, so from rivers and lakes they crawled up on land to evolve as the first amphibians. Amphibians made a seemingly miraculous innovation that has not been sufficiently acclaimed, namely to add five digits to each of the primitive limbs of the Crossopterygian fish (cf. Fig. 4-3d). In this way we have come to the wonderful endowment of fingers and toes. Try to imagine life with only the limb stumps that amphibians inherited. There was the tragic reversion to this state in some thalidomide babies. It was remarkable that the next advance on our evolutionary line was through the humble reptiles, Synapsida, that barely survived in the devastating competition with the much more impressive reptiles, notably the dinosaurs. Yet an insignificant insect-eating reptile with some mammalian characteristics (Fig. 4-6a) was to be the originator of the great mammalian classes. The first step was to the simplest mammals, the insectivores, from which there evolved such impressive mammals as the carnivores, the herbivores and the cetacea. But our evolutionary line avoided these lines that led to the sacrificing of the digits of the limbs for paws or hoofs or flippers, and led instead to the unimpressive early primates (Fig. 4-6d) that adopted an arboreal existence, apparently as an escape from the strong competition on land. So the digits were preserved and even developed in the line that led to us; and vision triumphed over smell.

We can see repeatedly how plasticity was cherished though at the cost of immediate success and at the risk of extinction of our evolutionary line. It has to be recognized how tenuous was that line of evolution that led to us (Figs. 4-4, 4-6) As Kimura (1977) so aptly states:

> the human species represents an unbelievably lucky outcome in the game of evolution; we are like a gambler that has been kept winning all the time in the past.

Is this not of great interest to Natural Theology? In his characteristic poetic manner Sherrington (1940) states in his Gifford Lectures also a theme for Natural Theology:

> Does it not seem strange that an unreasoning planet, without set purpose and not knowing how to set about it has done this thing to an extent surpassingly more than man has? It is to be remembered that Earth's periods of time have been of a different order from man's and her scale of operations of a different order, and that man's cunning in this respect dates but from yesterday. Yet, we agree, it does seem strange. It is enough that evolution by rearranging old parts is constructing new harmonies, chemical and biological. It is composing new melodies from some of the same old notes.

4.4 Extraterrestrial Life?

There has been much speculation about the possibility of life on other planets of the galactic system. The Viking mission to Mars has failed to find any trace of chemical processes that could be attributed to living organisms. But the environment of Mars is most unsuitable for life as we know it because of the negligible supply of water and oxygen. As we saw in Lecture 3, any other planet of our solar system is quite impossible for life. The fitness of the environment provided by Planet Earth has been ably discussed by Blum (1968) following the pioneer considerations by Henderson (1913, 1917). The first essential is a plentitude of water. Also carbon must be readily available, as in CO_2. In this way there are provided the three most common constituent elements of cells: hydrogen, oxygen and carbon. Other essential elements are: nitrogen, phosphorus and sulphur for nucleotides and proteins; sodium, potassium, calcium and chlorine for the ionic constitution of living organisms and their environment; magnesium and iron for the essential pigments, chlorophyll and haem respectively. All these elements are essential for life as we know it and are in plentiful supply on Planet Earth, which also has the temperature range that is essential for the existence of the organic constituents of living cells.

Given this fitness of the environment for life as we know it, it is remarkable that life seems to have arisen only once on Planet Earth during the billions of years of this fitness! The unity of life is exhibited most strikingly by the fact that all living organisms without exception have the same highly complex chemical systems, DNA and RNA for the genetic coding of information, and the proteins are composed of the same 20 amino acids for substantiating the genetically coded information. We can conclude that the origination of life is a very rare event, indeed even in the most salubrious conditions. And once life has started there was much travail and incredible delay in its early stages, as witness the time of over 2 billion years to win through to the simplest multicellular organisms.

The number of planetary systems is still unknown, but even if there are billions in our galaxy, life as we know it may be a rare phenomenon, even at the most primitive level. Some astronomers have the strange and biologically untenable idea that evolution, once it gets started, will lead to intelligent beings like humans, or more interestingly, superhumans. Such ideas can be entertained only by those who are ignorant of the extraordinary hazards of evolution. It is sufficient to recall the extremely tenuous and unpredictable evolutionary line that led to us. Dobzhansky (1967) states:

> It is because of this predestination that I am inclined to question the belief that, if life exists in different parts of the universe, it is bound to result in formation of man-like, or perhaps even of superman-like rational beings. Together with Simpson (1964), I consider this not merely questionable, but improbable to a degree which would usually mean rejection of a scientific hypothesis.

Blum (1968) expresses a similar reason for rejection. Despite this strongly negative opinion of evolutionary biologists, some astronomers, for example Sagan and Drake (1975), advocate the attempt to communicate with super-intelligent humanoids in our galactic system. The problem arises – should we broadcast or should we simply listen? Actually, the search is now being conducted by listening, and several advanced techniques are being used or advocated. There has even been one exciting false alarm – otherwise just cosmic silence! I think it highly likely that this romantic project will ultimately be killed by boredom.

Lecture 5

Human Evolution:
The Story of Cerebral Development

Synopsis and Introduction

The sequences of primate evolution towards hominids will be outlined. *Dryopithecus* to *Ramapithecus* to *Australopithecus africanus* were in the prehominid phase from 15 to 12 million, 8 and 5 to 1.0 million years ago, respectively. There is a worrying gap between 8 and 5 million years with no fossils. During this long period there had been changes in life style as shown by the dentition and by a fully erect striding existence, but the brain was not greatly enlarged above that of apes. *H. habilis* at 2.8 to 1.0 million years was distinguished by a considerable increase in brain size (about 1.5 times) and had a matching performance in tool culture. *H. erectus,* with brains almost up to 1000 cc, carried on this development from 1.0 to 0.5 million years ago and spread widely over Eurasia. Finally at 400,000 to 100,000 years ago *H. sapiens* appears in some isolated fossils in Europe and Ethiopia with brain sizes of 1100 to 1400 cc.

Neanderthal man continued on the *H. sapiens* line from 100,000 to 40,000 years ago and then was replaced by Cromagnon man, though possibly there was fusion. The Neanderthals had brains slightly larger than modern man and had an advanced stone culture with evidence of the first ideas of spirituality.

It will be shown that brain size is a very imperfect measure of brain development. Using the brain of existing anthropoid apes as some criterion of the brains of the primates from which man evolved (*Australopithecus,* for example), it will be shown that there were large qualitative changes in the brain, not only in the proportion occupied by the highest level, the neocortex, but also in the proportions of neocortex devoted to special functions such as speech, memory, cognition etc. It is believed that this long operation of human evolution was accomplished by the same processes of mutation and natural selection that characterized the Darwinian story of lower forms as described in the preceding lecture. However, when the stage of *Homo* was reached, a new process progressively assumed dominance. It is cultural evolution and today it is ascendent, biological evolution having almost ceased. The selection pressures are now derived from culture.

As in Lecture 4, I will present the factual record from fossils and then proceed to consider the factors responsible for the evolutionary changes wrought by natural selection. However, we now have a new orientation because we have to concentrate on the cerebral development, which in the last million years resulted in an unprecedented evolutionary advance. There will be a special treatment of the allowance for body size in making comparative assessments of brain size. This adjustment of total brain weight neglects the fact that the brain is a composite organ with many large components differentially responding in evolution. So there will have to be consideration of the much more discriminative evaluation of regions of the brain.

5.1 What is Known to Have Happened: The Fossil Record

In Lecture 4 we traced our evolutionary line up to our primate ancestors. The primate evolutionary tree is illustrated in its general features from the Eocene period onwards in Figure 4-7 (Jerison, 1973). From 30 million to 10 million years ago a cosmopolitan genus, *Dryopithecus*, flourished over large parts of central and northern Europe, Asia and East Africa. It may have originated from the oligocene primate *Aegyptopithecus* (see 10 and 12 in Fig. 4-7). Despite the inadequacy of the fossil evidence it has been suggested that from *Dryopithecus* there arose about 12 million years ago some three branches: *Ramapithecus*, which was clearly distinguished by the hominid features of its jaws and teeth; and two other branches with pongid characteristics, possibly the precursors of the anthropoid apes (Simons, 1977). *Ramapithecus* had the same wide distribution as *Dryopithecus*, but there are no fossil remains after 8 million years ago. This leaves an unfortunate gap of about 3 million years before our evolutionary line can be recognized again in the *Australopithecines*, which have very similar jaws and teeth (Simons, 1977), but the lack of any fossil skulls makes it uncertain how far Ramapithecus is on the hominid line.

In the next evolutionary stage there is some confusion with at least two Australopithecine species co-existing in Africa, often in the same regions, the slender *A. africanus* and the more massive *A. boisei*. There is general agreement that this latter species was not on the line to *Homo*, but to a dead-end, becoming extinct some million years ago after evolving into an even heavier species, *A. robustus*, as indicated in Figure 5-1. One specimen from Swartkrans had a body larger than the largest gorilla.

In Figure 5-1 there are alternative trees with branches at 3 to 6 million years ago, one with the *A. africanus* line leading to *Homo* and the other with it leading to the dead-end. A more complete fossil record is needed. Another controversial issue is the question: Where was the evolutionary line to *Homo* established? We have seen that *Ramapithecus* was very widely distributed over Europe, Asia and Africa, and there was a similar wide distribution for *H. erectus*, a later stage on the way to *H. sapiens*. Nevertheless, the transition presumably occurred in Africa because that is the only

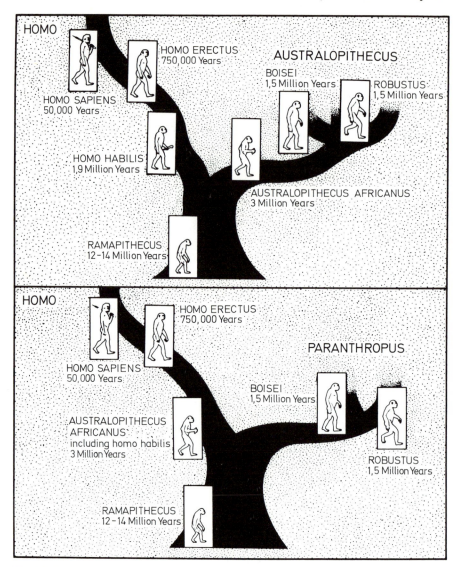

Fig. 5-1. Diagrams of alternative views of man's evolution. In the lower one *Australopithecus Africanus* is on the evolutionary line that led to *Homo sapiens,* in the other it was on a side branch that died out. Libassi, P. T.: Early man, nearly man. The Sciences July 1975. Copyright 1975 by The New York Academy of Sciences

location so far recognized for the intermediary stages, the Australopithecines and *H. habilis* (Simons, 1977).

Table 5-1. Evolution of man: body and brain weights

Species	Body wt. (kg)	Brain wt. (g)	Millions years ago
Homo sapiens	~ 50	1150–1550	0.5 to present
Homo erectus	~ 50	900–1070	0.75–0.5
Homo habilis	~ 50	590–700	3.0 –1.3
ER 1470	–	770	2.8
Australopithecines:			
A. boisei	~ 50	av. 530	5.0–1.0
A. africanus	~ 30	av. 450	5.0–1.0

A. africanus had a pelvis and leg bones which indicated that he walked upright, though imperfectly so, as also is indicated by the poise of the skull on the vertebral column (Tobias, 1973). This postural change is a remarkable advance, being the first time that a primate had a bipedal striding locomotion. Even today the anthropoid apes, chimpanzee, gorilla and orangutan, are quadripedal in locomotion. However the *A. africanus* had a disappointingly small brain, averaging 450 g[1], which is only about the size of the brains of the present anthropoid apes; but with allowance for the smaller body weight the brain is relatively somewhat larger, as indicated in Table 5-1 and Figure 5-7 (*A*). The brains of *A. boisei* and *A. robustus* are rather larger, averaging 530 g, but this is attributable to their much larger size, as is indicated in Table 5-1 and Figure 5-7 (*Z*). There has been some dispute about the possibility that these several Australopithecines were living together in the same general area, as suggested by Richard Leakey. This seems likely from the fossil record, and possibly there may have been interbreeding. No doubt there was also competition for food. Eventually the more advanced hominid, *H. habilis,* may have contributed to the extinction of all Australopithecines about 1 million years ago.

We now come to the greatest drama of the whole evolutionary story. Probably, as shown in the lower frame of Figure 5-1, from this unremarkable primate, *A. africanus,* there evolved our predecessors in the genus *Homo,* firstly *H. habilis* with an increase of 50% in the brain weight (Tobias, 1973). In other respects *H. habilis* had not acquired any strikingly new characters, having the same jaws, teeth and upright striding posture as *A. africans.* As Mayr (1973) convincingly states the increment in the brain is paramount in indicating that a new genus, *Homo,* had been initiated. The

---

[1] All the measurements of brain weight are derived from the volume of endocranial casts and the assumption of a specific gravity of 1.0 for brain.

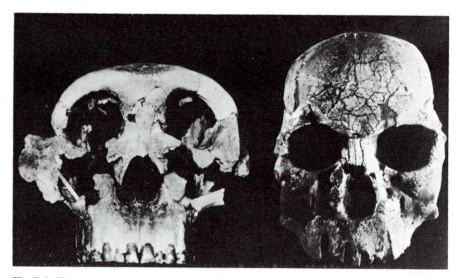

Fig. 5-2. The skull to the left is *Australopiithecus boisei* (see Fig. 5-1) with small cranial capacity and massive jaw. The skull to the right is the famous ER 1470 from East Rudolph. It has a much larger cranial capacity (780 cc). Further description in text. *Left:* Reprinted with permission from J. and D. Bartlett/Bruce Coleman Ltd. *Right:* Libassi, P. T.: Early man, nearly man. The Sciences July 1975. Copyright 1975 by The New York Academy of Sciences

recent discovery by Richard Leakey of a remarkable series of fossils with larger brains and even earlier dating than the first discovered specimens of *H. habilis* has complicated the evolutionary story. The first discovery, labelled ER 1470, had a brain of 780 g and a dating of 2.8 million years ago, though critics have attempted to reduce this to 2 million years. The remarkable change from *A. boisei* is illustrated by the skulls of Figure 5-2, which reveal the great increase in brain size.

In Figure 5-3, the brain size is plotted against the dating for the whole fossil record that leads on to *H. sapiens*. Six *A. africanus*, (*AF*), four *A. robustus* (*AB*) and three *H. habilis* (*HH*) are plotted as averaged values distributed along the approximate time range of these species. ER 1470 *(filled circle)* is seen to be far above the line drawn for the evolutionary advance, and it would be so even with a 2 million dating *(open circle)*. It seems simplest to regard it and the later discoveries of large-brained primates in the same fossil beds as advanced members of the species *H. habilis*.

After the fossil records of *H. habilis* there is a considerable gap in time until about 750,000 years ago, when there are the first fossils of the much more advanced hominid, *H. erectus*. It seems desirable to use this simple generic term rather than the many specialized names that have been used

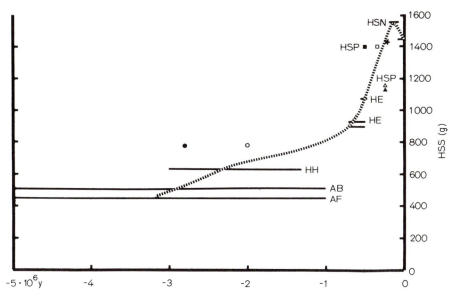

Fig. 5-3. Calculated sizes of brains of hominids in grams are plotted against the time in millions of years before the present age. The *dotted line* shows the approximate time course of the growth in brain size. Further description in text

for the *H. erectus* fossils discovered in different countries, Java, China, East Africa and Europe. The brain size has been now much increased even to above 1000 g (Holloway, 1974) and the skeletal fossils show that members of this species were erect striding individuals considerably taller than the Australopithecines (Fig. 5-1). The average brain sizes are plotted in Figure 5-3 (*HE*) as horizontal lines corresponding to the period of existence. The Chinese variety had an average brain of 1075 g, dated at 500,000 years ago (Villee, 1972). The Javanese variety averaged 930 g, and the East African, 900 g. *H. erectus* used his larger brain for considerably advancing culture as we shall see in the next lecture. However the several varieties of *H. erectus* were but staging stations on the evolutionary journey to *H. sapiens*.

Some 500,000 years ago there began a rapid evolution of the brain to the size of present *H. sapiens*. There are relatively few fossils in this transitional period from *H. erectus* to *H. sapiens Neanderthalis* and the five single specimens are plotted by points in Figure 5-3 for the mean values of dating and size in grams. The brain size is within normal limits for *H. sapiens*, so they deserve their classification as *H. sapiens preneanderthalis* (*HSP* in Fig. 5-3), particularly as they were associated with quite a sophisticated tool culture. There are several other fossil skulls from areas as widely dispersed as Rhodesia (1300 g) and Java (Solo) (1300 g), but they have not been accurately dated. These earliest members of *H. sapiens* existed right through the severe Riss glaciation (200,000–125,000 years ago) but they pulled back from the areas of severe cold.

These scattered fossils in the period after *H. erectus* fill in the gap until the appearance of Neanderthal man (HSN) at about 100,000 years ago. The distinguishing features were the large brain, the average, 1550 g, being distinctly higher than the average for present *H. sapiens* (HSS), about 1450 g. This large brain was packaged in an old skull that was long and low with a big face and a receding forehead. The skeletal remains show a height of 150–165 cm with a powerful frame. A false reconstruction on the basis of an arthritic skeleton gave a misconception about the Neanderthal's posture and gait. He had an upright posture and great agility. Furthermore his large brain gave him a more intelligent performance than any of his predecessors, for example in his tool culture, which was highly sophisticated. The fossil record comprises more than 100 specimens and shows a wide dispersal over the habitable world: Europe; across Africa north of the Sahara and finally to the Congo; across Asia to China and even to southern Siberia. He endured the extreme cold of the Wurm glaciation from 75,000 years ago, being better adapted than his predecessors. But the fossil record comes to an end about 40,000 years ago, and with it the characteristic Neanderthal flaking tool culture. There seems no mystery about the origin of Neanderthal man. He evolved from the very similar preneanderthal *H. sapiens*, perhaps in some favourable breeding community. But there is mystery in his sudden disappearance about 40,000 years ago.

The usual story is that modern man, *H. sapiens sapiens,* appeared on the scene as Cro-Magnon man about 40,000 years ago. The name comes from the location of the first skeletons at Cro-Magnon in southern France. However, there is no good evidence about the origin of this new variety of *H. sapiens*, which is of course very similar to modern man. It has been suggested that the location was western Asia in the region of the Caspian Sea. Then again it is unsure how much interbreeding there was between the Neanderthals and the Cro-Magnons. For example, the celebrated caves, Tabun and Skhul, on Mt. Carmel in Israel provide evidence of cohabitation (Mayr, 1973). On the other hand, there are caves showing a distinct deposit between the lower Neanderthal remains, tools etc. and the upper Cro-Magnon remains, which indicates a considerable interval between the respective occupations.

After the tenacious following of our evolutionary line that we have been doing from the first origin of life, it is something of an anticlimax to find so much unknown, and such diversity of opinions just at the final stage of the appearance of our own kind on Planet Earth. The present fossil record suggests that *H. sapiens sapiens* evolved independently in widely separated breeding communities of *H. sapiens*, either the Neanderthals or the Pre-neanderthals. The attractive view would be that all races diverged from an initial pure Cro-Magnon stock and then migrated over the accessible world and diversified by cladogenesis to give origin to the diverse races of mankind. However it seems more likely that the actual origin of the races of mankind occurred in widely dispersed areas in Asia (China and Java), in Africa, as well as in Europe. A much more adequate fossil record is needed.

It is important to recognize that in the time spans we are considering, say 50,000 years, enormous distances can be covered by the operation known as *budding*. From a breeding community some members move out to exploit an adjacent hunting area, perhaps 20 km away. In the next generation there could be a similar budding with a further 20-km migration. A movement of 20 km in a generation of say 20 years would give 10,000 km in 10,000 years. It is, of course, not envisaged that there was any planned migration. There was just an invasion of new hunting areas, perhaps displacing or eliminating weaker occupants. The movement would not be linear, but rather opportunistic in a wandering way, a kind of random walk.

Nevertheless, Africa, Asia and Europe could easily be populated in 50,000 years by some new efficient race such as Neanderthal man.

5.2 Evaluation of Human Cerebral Development

5.2.1 Allowance for Body Weight

So far we have assessed the cerebral development simply by the criterion of brain weights. As Jerison (1973) has pointed out, the brain size must be evaluated with an adjustment to body weight. Figure 5-4 is derived from a double logarithmic plotting of brain weight against body weight for the largest specimens of 198 vertebrate species (Jerison, 1973). The individual points lie within two sloping polygons that include all members of the categories of lower vertebrates (fish and reptiles) and of higher vertebrates (birds and mammals). Each polygon has an axis approximating to the lines drawn according to the formula

$$E = k P^{2/3},$$

where E and P represent brain and body weight respectively, and $k = 0.007$ and 0.07 for the two classes. The exponent $^2/_3$ is in accord with a surface-to-

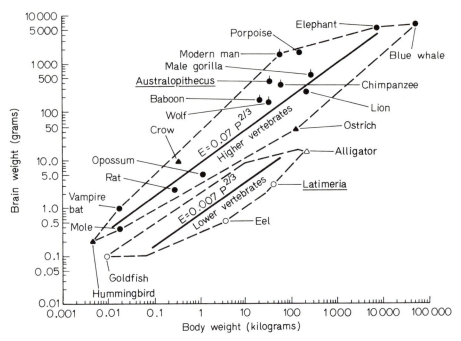

Fig. 5-4. Selected data to illustrate brain-body relations in familiar vertebrate species. Data on the fossil hominid *Australopithecus* and on the living coelacanth *Latimeria* are added. Minimum convex polygons are shown by *dashed lines,* enclosing visually fitted lines with slopes of two-thirds. Jerison, H. J.: Evolution of the brain and intelligence. New York, London, Academic Press 1973

volume relationship, and no doubt is partly indicative of the neuronal size, smaller animals having smaller neurones and hence more in a given brain weight.

In the more primitive primates, both fossil and living, the double logarithmic plotting (Fig. 5-5) reveals that the brain size does not depart far from the relationship of brain to body weight for average living mammals, drawn as the sloping line with $k = 0.12$. It may be noted that the very early fossil prosimian, *Rooneyia*, already mentioned in Lecture 4, had a high position, the square located on the upper side of the polygon. In contrast, in Figure 5-6 the higher primates all lie within a sloping polygon above the line for average living mammals. A small polygon, *B*, encloses all the Baboon points, and likewise all the anthropoid points lie in the triangle *P*. The rectangle *A* includes all *A. africanus* points and the circle *Z* the *A. boisei* points. *H* indicates the high position of *H. sapiens*. Below and to the left are the many species of simians.

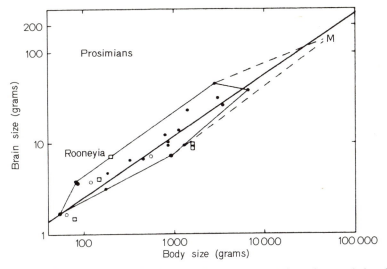

Fig. 5-5. Brain size as a function of body size in the prosimians. Polygon is extended as *dashed line* to include *Megaladapis edwardsi (M)*, the giant Pleistocene fossil lemur. Small squares are Eocene and Oligocene fossils. Note that prosimiams are 'average' mammals, since the line is nicely centred through the polygon. Three of the fossil prosimians are below the polygon. Jerison, H. J.: Evolution of the brain and intelligence. New York, London: Academic Press 1973

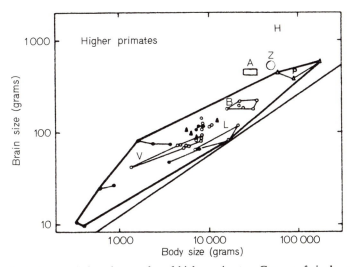

Fig. 5-6. Brain-body relations in samples of higher primates. Groups of single genera indicated: *V,* Vervets (*Cercopithecus*); *L,* Langurs (*Presbytis*); *B,* baboons (*Papio* and *Mandrillus*); *P,* great apes (*Pongo, Pan, Gorilla*); *A, Z,* Australopithecines as in Figure 5-7; *H, Homo sapiens,* Jerison, H. J.: Evolution of the brain and intelligence. New York, London: Academic Press 1973

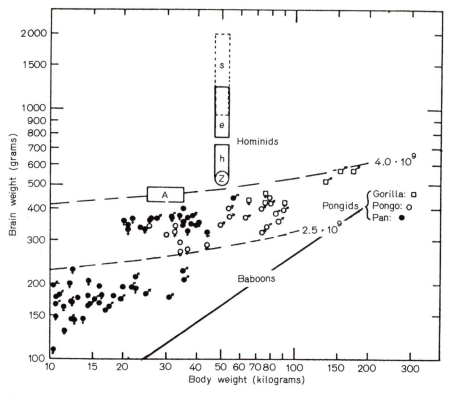

Fig. 5-7. Brain-body relations of populations of baboons, apes, and hominids to indicate pattern of increase in relative brain size among these groups. Hominids indicated are *Australopithecus africanus* (Gracile) (*A*), *Australopithecus boisei* (Robustus) (*Z*), '*Homo habilis*' (*h*), *Homo erectus* (*e*) and *Homo sapiens* (*s*). The straight line gives the linear relationship on the double log scale for the average living mammals. Jerison, H. J.: Evolution of the brain and intelligence. New York, London: Academic Press 1973

Figure 5-7 gives a similar but more detailed plotting for individual primate specimens. It reveals that baboons and anthropoid apes have a lower brain/body ratio than even the most primitive hominids, the Australopithecines *A* and *Z*. The brains of *A. boisei (Z)*, *H. habilis (h)*, *H. erectus (e)* and *H. sapiens (s)* are plotted on the assumption of a common body weight of about 50 kg. Again the sloping line gives the relationship for average living mammals. The enlarged brains of the higher primates are clearly demonstrated. The curved broken lines in Figure 5-7 relate to a calculation by Jerison (1973), of 'extra neurones' above the values for average living mammals, and show clear separations between baboons and pongids and between pongids and hominids.

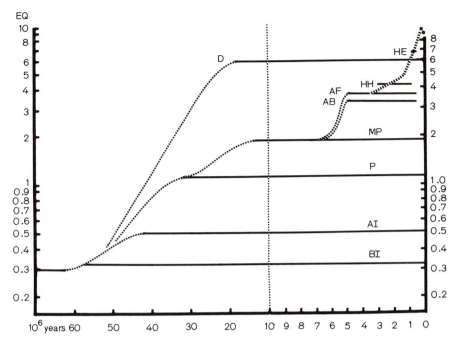

Fig. 5-8. Calculated encephalization quotients (*EQ*) are plotted against the time in millions of years before the present age. Note change in time scale at 10 million years. *BI,* basal insectivores; *AI,* advanced insectivores; *P,* prosimians; *AF, Australopithecus africanus; HE, H. erectus.* The *solid square* and *circle* are *H. neanderthalis* and *H. sapiens* respectively

Useful calculations from the plottings in Figure 5-4 to 5-7 give values called *encephalization quotients* (EQ) for different mammals. Jerison (1973) defines the EQ as the ratio of the actual brain size to the expected brain size as given by the average for living mammals, which is expressed by the formula $E = 0.12\ P^{2/3}$. The EQs as so derived are given in Table 5-2.

In Figure 5-8 there is an approximate plotting of the time scales for the development of the EQs in the Cenozoic age, the so-called Age of Mammals. The EQs are calculated relative to that for average living mammals, and Figure 5-8 is based on the data published by Jerison (1973) in his carefully documented monograph. Mammals entered the Cenozoic age 65 million years ago with an average EQ of 0.3, and this low value has continued to the present time almost unaltered for the basal insectivores (BI) as defined by Stephan and Andy (1969), which now have an average EQ of 0.31 (Jerison, 1973). Early separations of more advanced insectivores (AI) are shown. Primates originated at the beginning of the Cenozoic age, but the fossil record is inadequate, hence the broken line plot. However by 30 million years ago the fossil prosimians (P) show much the same EQ as prosimians today (Fig. 5-5). Monkeys and apes (MP) diverged from prosimians about 30 million years ago (Fig. 4-7), but the fossil record is inadequate until about 10 million years ago. The mean EQ of 1.9 is shown unchanged for the last 10 million years. The evolution of the Australopithecines comes later at about 5 million years ago. The high EQ for *A. africanus* (AF) is a distinct advance, but the Australopithecines did not further advance as a genus and died out about 1 million years ago. Meanwhile *H. habilis* (HH) probably evolved from *A. africanus* at about 3 million years ago, and is shown evolving to H. Erectus (HE) and *H. sapiens*, as in the previous figure on an expanded time scale (Fig. 5-3). It is to be noted in Figure 5-8 that the time scale is compressed by a factor of 4 beyond 10 million years ago.

An entirely different time scale for EQ increase is shown for the porpoise (dolphin, D), that reached its full development 15 to 20 million years ago, in contrast to the EQ development for our evolutionary line, which did not begin its rapid rise to its present summit until 1 million years ago, and did not surpass the porpoise until about 500,000 years ago. The large size of the porpoise brain with a rich convolution resembling the human brain in its general features has given rise to the suggestion by Lilly and others, that the

Table 5-2. Encephalization quotients (EQ)

(Primates)	EQ
Prosimians	Average 1.1
	Highest 1.8 (Rooneyia and 2 others) Lowest 0.62
Baboons	Average 1.9
Pongoids	Average 1.9 (Pan, 2.3)
Australopithecines	
A. africanus	Average 3.8
A. boisei	Average 3.3
homo habilis	Average 4.2
homo erectus	Average 6.5
homo sapiens	Average 8.5
From Figure 5-4, some other interesting EQs are:	
Dolphin (porpoise)	6
Elephant	1.0
Blue whale	0.37

Other values for the elephant average 1.3. It is possible that with very massive bodies the formula does not hold and that the EQs of the elephant and whale may be considerably underestimated.

porpoises may have an advanced intellectual life if only we could communicate appropriately! These suggestions have been severely criticized by Wilson (1975) in his authoritative book *Sociobiology*. It has to be recognized that there is a very highly developed auditory system in Cetacea (Jansen, 1973). Much of the cerebral cortex is concerned in a very sophisticated processing operation on the auditory data which is used as an echolocation device. The information so derived could be used in building up from moment to moment a three-dimensional spatial representation of the surround, which would be of vital importance in navigation, in hunting shoals of fish and in social life (*cf.* Wilson, 1975).

5.2.2 Progression Indices of Cerebral Components

It will be recognized that brain weight is a very crude criterion of brain performance at any level. We need far more discriminative comparisons. An important advance in this respect has been made by Stephan and associates who have measured the volumes of many component structures of brains from serial sections at equal intervals (*cf.* Stephan and Andy [1969]). The base line for comparison was derived from measurements on basal insectivores, the most primitive mammals. On a double logarithmic plot, brain weight is linearly related to body weight with a slope of 0.65, which is in good agreement with the exponential of $^2/_3$ in Jerison's plottings (1973). Comparisons between different species of mammals were made for specific brain structures on the basis of *progression indices*, which express how many times larger a brain structure is than the same brain structure in an average basal insectivore of the same body weight. The power factor of 0.65 is employed for extrapolation to conjectured insectivores of body weights beyond those actually obtaining.

In Figure 5-9 the progression indices for neocortex show that *Homo* (156) is far ahead of *Pan* (58) and other primates. Similarly in Figure 5-9, for the hippocampus, *Homo* (4.2) is far above *Pan* (1.75). Some other simians are higher than *Pan* but the gorilla is very low. By contrast, in Figure 5-9 for the olfactory bulb, *Homo* (0.023) is the lowest of all simians, and all simians are very low relative to basal insectivores. These comparative figures clearly show that with *Homo* there is a dominance of the neocortex and also of the hippocampus, while there is an extreme deficiency in olfaction. In relation to Lecture 9 on learning it is of special interest that the structures associated with the hippocampus (regio entorhinalis, subiculum and septum) correlate well with the hippocampus (Stephan and

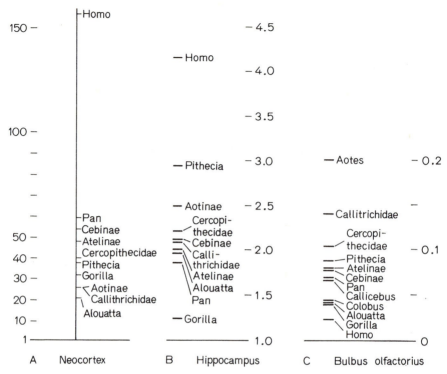

Fig. 5-9. A Progression indices for the neocortex. They express how many times larger the neocortex is than that of a typical basal insectivore of equal body weight. The scale is for simians, average indices are given for each species, and 1 on the scale is the average value for basal insectivores. **B** Progression indices for the hippocampus expressed as in **A**. **C** Progression indices for the bulbus olfactorius expressed as in **A,** but note that all simians are far below an index of 1 for the average insectivore. Eccles, J. C.: Evolution and lateralization of the brain. Vol. 299, p. 161. Copyright 1977 by The New York Academy of Sciences

Andy, 1969), whereas the primary center for olfaction (Fig. 9-5) is completely different. Stephan has carried out this precise quantitative correlation with several other brain structures, but they are not related to the theme of these lectures.

5.2.3 Qualitative Comparison

The next stage of comparison will concern the detailed topography of the neocortex. The brain weights (Fig. 5-3) and progression indices for neocortex (Fig. 5-9) show a remarkable development with *Homo,* but our enquiry

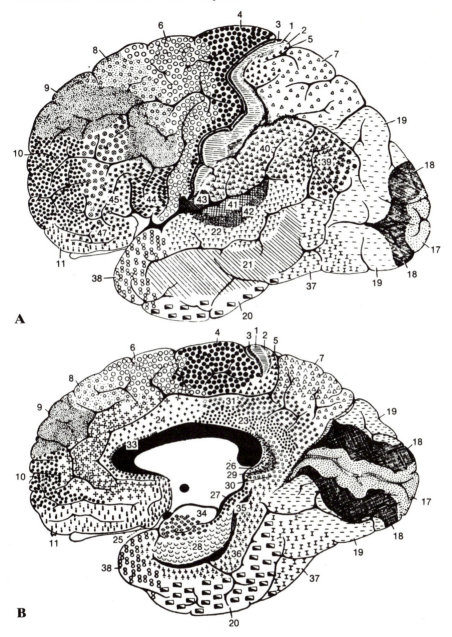

Fig. 5-10. Brodmann's cytoarchitectural map of the human brain. The various areas are labelled with different symbols and their numbers indicated by figures. **A** Lateral view of left hemisphere. **B** Medial view of right hemisphere. Brodmann, K.: Vergleichende Lokalisationslehre der Großhirnrinde. Leipzig: J. A. Barth 1909

must be pressed beyond quantitative considerations because it is generally agreed that there are qualitative differences between different areas of the neocortex. In part these differences can be recognized by a comparison of the areas of the frontal, parietal, temporal and occipital lobes, but this is unsatisfactory because of the subdivision of each lobe into primary receiving or transmitting areas on the one hand and the association areas on the other (*cf.* Fig. 8-1). The only comparison for the prefrontal areas (frontal lobe excluding areas 4 and 6) of man and other primates is that by Brodmann (1912), who found as percentages of the total neocortex 29% for man, 16.9% for chimpanzee and 11.3% for the macaque. There has been a remarkable increase in human evolution.

Still more discriminative information is given by a detailed study of the cortical laminated structure (Fig. 8-3). On this basis it has been possible to construct fine topographic maps, that of Brodmann (1909) for the human brain (Fig. 5-10) being now generally accepted. Figure 5-10 becomes of particular interest when it is compared with maps of other primates that were constructed by Mauss (1908, 1911) with Brodmann's approval, namely the monkey Cercopithecus (Fig. 5-11), and the anthropoid ape, *Pongo* (Fig. 5-12). A particularly striking difference between Figures 5-11 and 5-12 on the one hand and Figure 5-10 on the other is displayed by areas 39 and 40 that form a considerable part of the Wernicke speech area (Fig. 8-1). In Figure 5-12, these areas are small, barely protruding from the fissure of Sylvius. The relationship of these areas to linguistic ability stands revealed. The Wernicke area of the human left hemisphere (Fig. 8-1) is generally depicted (Penfield and Roberts, 1959) as extending over Brodmann areas 41, 22, 21, 40, 39 and 37 and as also being specially related to the planum temporale concealed in the fissure of Sylvius (Geschwind, 1974). It is noteworthy that the large temporal lobe area 37 in Figure 5-10 was not recognizable in Figures 5-11 and 5-12. In general it seems that the inferior parietal and superior temporal areas (Wernicke speech area) are hypertrophied in the human hemisphere relative to any corresponding areas in Figures 5-11 and 5-12. A general indication of this hypertrophy is shown by the location of the primary visual area, 17, which in the human brain (Fig. 5-10) is largely displaced from the convex surface of the occipital lobe to a medial situation. Likewise there seems to be a relative hypertrophy of the human prefrontal area in conformity with the percentages quoted above. The Broca (motor) speech area (Brodmann's areas 44 and 45 in Fig. 5-10) is not recognized in the maps of Figures 5-11 and 5-12. Also in Figure 5-10 the extreme prefrontal areas 9, 10 and 11 are much larger than in Figures 5-11 and 5-12. It should be noted that much of areas 9 and 10 in

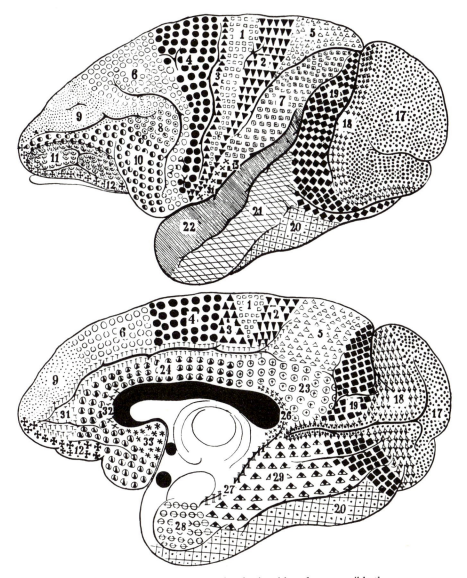

Fig. 5-11. Cytoarchitectonic map for a monkey brain with as far as possible the same connections of numbering as in Figure 5-10. Mauss, T.: Die faserarchitektonische Gliederung der Großhirnrinde bei den niederen Affen. J. Psychol. Neurol. *13*, 263-325 (1908)

these figures should be homologized with area 46 in Figure 5-10 (*cf.* Walker, 1940).

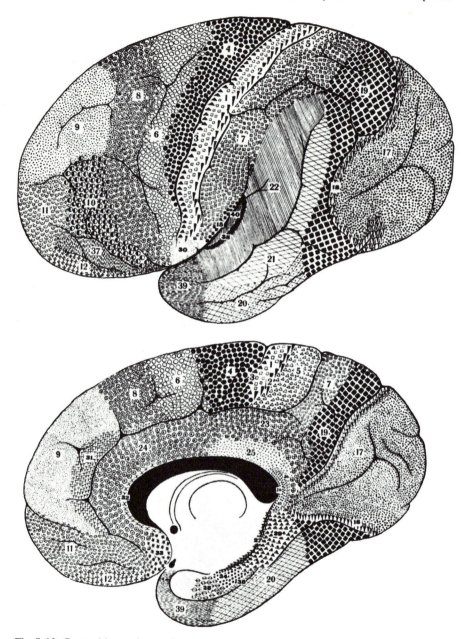

Fig. 5-12. Cytoarchitectonic map for the brain of an orangutan with much the same conventions as in Figure 5-10. However, as pointed out by Beck, the symbols 38 and 39 are misplaced relative to Figure 5-10. Mauss, T.: Die faserarchitektonische Gliederung des Cortex cerebri der anthropomorphen Affen. J. Psychol. Neurol. *18*, [Suppl. 3] 410–467 (1911)

Unfortunately there are no cerebral maps of the chimpanzee (*Pan*) brain corresponding to those of Figures 5-10 to 5-12. In the extensive study by Bailey et al. (1950), there are many maps of the *Pan* cortex, but they cannot be related to the areal numbers of the Brodmann maps (1909). Until there is a further rigorous study, it is uncertain whether the *Pan* brain is a considerable advance over the brain of the other anthropoid ape, *Pongo*, in Figure 5-12, in respect of development of Brodmann areas 37, 39 and 40 of the Wernicke speech area and also of areas 44 and 45 of the Broca speech area. The simplest demonstration of a qualitative difference between the brains of *Pongo* and *Homo* derives from a large difference in those areas of the human brain that appear to have come late in the evolutionary development.

From endocranial casts of fossil skulls (Holloway, 1974) it has been possible to gain some information about the changes in form of the brain at the various stages of its evolution. Necessarily this information is very imprecise, but it does indicate that with the increasing size of the brain there were special developments of the parietal, temporal and prefrontal lobes. It is important to recognize that the potential performance of the brain is not to be assessed simply by its size with due allowance for body size. Some qualitative change was already evident in the manner of life of the Australopithecines (Hawkes, 1965; Jerison, 1973).

5.3 Selection Pressures and the Pre-Eminence of Linguistic Development

In the evolution of the human brain there are two remarkable features to be explained, as can be seen by reference to Table 5-1. Firstly, the Australopithecines existed in a relatively unchanged form for about 4 million years, which indicates a very stable ecological niche to which they had become well adapted. It is believed to be open grassland of savannah country much like that inhabited by baboons today. They were partly carnivorous, taking advantage of a bipedal locomotion for ease of movement and survey in long grass. Furthermore it is presumed that their successful survival depended on their relatively enlarged brains, which gave them the ability to imagine and to plan so that they could hunt more resourcefully in a much wider terrain than other mammals, including other primates. Presumably their cerebral endowment would give them more effective communication within the troop for hunting or organization against enemies. In this long stable period of up to 4 million years the Australopithecines paralleled the pongids, which apparently have not advanced in brain size for over 10 million years (Fig. 5-8). The recently discovered much larger brain dated at 2.8 million years (ER 1470 in Table 5-1 and Fig. 5-2) does, however, indicate that there were at least isolated instances of remarkable advances in brain size. Thus the concept of the long stable Australopithecine era may have to be revised to admit evolutionary novelties that eventually resulted in the amazingly rapid brain increase through the various stages of *Homo* (*cf.* Fig. 5-3), the Australopithecines meanwhile becoming extinct by 1 million years ago.

As Jerison (1973, 1976) points out, the most significant period in the evolution of the human brain came after the long stable Australopithecine period. The successive prolonged ice ages resulted in destruction of the easy ecological niches. Survival depended now on the ability to face the environmental challenge and adapt to new niches characterized by protection from cold in confined and crowded shelters and with the invention of protective clothing and the use of fire. It can be conjectured that extreme selection pressures were provided by the harsh conditions. The challenge of these conditions provided a premium to highly intelligent planning and communication within the confined social groups. Communication by gestures and sounds became developed to carry more information by elaboration of vocal signals. The primitive animal language of expletives and warning signals was transformed with the introduction of names for things and for actions so that primitive verbal description became possible. Thus imagery could be triggered by verbal symbols. This much improved communication was of great value in organization of the tribe in social cohesion, in hunting and in warfare.

Thus, in the last million years from the times of *H. habilis* through *H. erectus* to *H. sapiens,* increasing brain size and performance was ensured by natural selection. This success story would seem to suggest an indefinitely continued brain growth, but in the last 100,000 years this has not occurred. Perhaps further enlargement of the brain would have resulted in difficulties in birth, or perhaps further enlargement did not result in an improved performance. Be that as it may, our human inheritance of brains averaging about 1400 g, is the end of the evolutionary story. And now in any case biological evolution for man is at an end because selection pressure has been eliminated by the welfare state. Natural selection is no longer permitted to happen.

With the evolution of *Homo*, emphasis will be placed on the dominant role of language and the associated imagery and conceptual abilities in bringing about the extraordinarily rapid expansion of the neocortex. The linguistic areas indicated in Figure 8-1 give only in part the neocortical areas concerned in language. For example it is now recognized that lesions of the minor hemisphere result in linguistic disabilities. Also, when destruction of the linguistic area in early life leads to transfer of linguistic performance to the minor hemisphere (Milner, 1974), there is grave deficiency of the normal functions of the minor hemisphere because of the extravagant demands made on cortical space. There is an alternative explanation that cerebral development was associated with the increased demand for fine motor control in the construction and use of tools. Undoubtedly this is a contributory factor, particularly in relation to the imagery and planning necessary for good performances, but in the human cerebral cortex the linguistic areas are much larger than those concerned in movement control.

The most challenging finding in this whole story of human evolution is the extraordinarily rapid brain growth in the last 3 million years or so (Fig. 5-3). Mayr (1973) states that:

> . . . the increase in brain size in such a short period from an average of 460 g to more than three times as much is almost unbelievably fast.

However, even more remarkable is the change in the quality of cerebral performance made possible by the development of new regions of the cerebral cortex. In searching for an explanation we have to look for extraordinarily strong selection pressures that could induce such amazing developments. We shall be considering this further in Lecture 6, but a big factor must have been the growing importance of linguistic communication in hunting, in warfare and in social organization. We have already mentioned the great demands that speech makes on brain resources. Another factor would be the continual improvement in tool culture, with its demand for skilled movement control, both in the manufacture of stone tools and in their use. In addition Mayr (1973) has made the interesting suggestion:

> that the breeding structure of the primitive hominid groups was such that it gave the leaders of each band an enormous reproductive advantage. Polygamy is widespread even among existing primitive human tribes and it is the individual with leadership qualities who has the greatest chance to have several wives . . .

and Neel et al. as quoted by Mayr (1973) have suggested:

> that the single most dysgenic event in the history of mankind was departure from a pattern of polygamy based on leadership, ability and initiative.

5.4 Theory of Biological Evolution

The unprecedented speed of cerebral development in the last evolutionary stages to *H. sapiens sapiens* must be assessed relative to the two essential components of biological evolution.

Firstly, there are mutations that arise purely by chance:

> When applied to evolutionary change, chance means that the nature of the change is not determined by an existing need. For instance, the occurrence of a particular mutation is not induced by the need for the adaptive change which this mutation would make possible. (Mayr, 1973)

Secondly:

> Natural selection is anything but accident. Natural selection is a process that quite directly adapts; it is creative by always putting together the gene combinations which have the greatest chance of having greatest survival. (Mayr, 1973)

> The beauty of natural selection is that in every single generation it makes a new decision as to what is now the thing to be selected for and . . . this is made possible by the numerous mechanisms that exist to produce tremendous genetic diversity. (Mayr, 1973)

These succint statements by Mayr make it clear that the official theory of biological evolution gives no opportunity for any guidance of the evolutionary development by long-range goals. Any belief in finalism is rejected. It is essentially opportunistic, natural selection being concerned only with the survival and propagation of a particular generation, and then again opportunistically for the next, and so on. In these lectures we will be considering critically whether the stark official theory of biological evolution can plausibly account for the whole amazing story of how we come to be.

It is of the greatest importance to science that there be from time to time a critical examination of established theories, particularly when they tend to harden into dogmas. The amazing success of the theory of evolution has protected it from significant critical evaluation in recent times. However it fails in a most important respect. It cannot account for the existence of each one of us as unique self-conscious beings. I will be raising this criticism in later lectures. For the present we should realize that the denial of long-term goals renders meaningless the belief that one has in the drama of the providential escapes of our evolutionary line, as for example at the stage of the mammal-like reptiles. Let us return now to the anthropic principle which links the coming-to-be of the cosmos with the eventual appearance of observership (Lecture 2). But this observership requirement is tied in to the origin of life and to the eventual appearance of conscious, intelligent beings. Can the evolutionary line that we have been considering in the last two lectures be understood as part of the same mysterious process that links cosmic existence to observership? The strange waywardness of the biological evolutionary process seems to match that of the cosmic evolution. Yet we are here! It is the human mystery.

Dobzhansky (1967) stresses the unpredictability of evolution:

> The gene combinations which now compose the genetic endowment of the human species did not exist in, say, Eocene or Cretaceous time. Could a biologist, if one had lived in those remote times, have predicted that the human species would eventually evolve? This is not as difficult a question as it might seem – if the ancient biologist had only a knowledge comparable to our present one, he could not have made such a prediction.

I will quote from Tobias (1971) in a remarkable passage that fittingly concludes this lecture and leads on to Lecture 6.

> Nothing is more striking and more sustained in the whole of human evolution than the twofold trend towards increase in brain size on the one hand, and, on the other, towards cultural activities, cultural mastery, and indeed utter dependence on culture for survival. These two sets of changes are indissolubly linked. The chain between them may be set forth simply as follows: increase in brain size $\rightleftharpoons$ gain in intricacy of neuronal organization $\rightleftharpoons$ rise in complexity of the nervous function $\rightleftharpoons$ ever more diversified and complicated behaviour responses $\rightleftharpoons$ progressively amplified and enhanced cultural manifestations.

Lecture 6

Cultural Evolution With Language and Values: The Human Person

Synopsis

This lecture will have strong philosophical implications, hence it is necessary to preface it by a statement of Popper's theories of three Worlds: World 1, the matter-energy of the cosmos; World 2 of all subjective experiences; and World 3, which is the cultural heritage of mankind.

There will be a brief survey of cultural evolution from the tool culture of the earliest Paleolithic times some million years ago through to the great advances of the Upper Paleolithic with the wonderful achievements of the cave paintings. But the most important creations of primitive man were language at the uniquely human levels of description and argument. It will be argued that effective communication by language provided the strong selection pressure that caused the amazingly rapid increase in the brain, threefold in 3 million years. It is known that a large fraction of the cerebrum is concerned in linguistic performance in its widest sense. The size of the brain and the linguistic performance may increase *pari passu*. It is surprising that the fossil remains indicate a primitive life even when *H. sapiens* had a brain matching ours in size some 100,000 years ago.

Then came the first evidence of self-consciousness and values. Ceremonial burial customs at 80,000 years ago, and compassionate treatment of the incapacitated at 60,000 years along with floral burials. There will be a consideration of how values could be derived in what had hitherto been a biological world controlled by 'survival of the fittest'. The mystery of their origin challenges our imagination as we recognize that values demand the rejection of the processes of biological evolution as a norm for civilized human beings. Sherrington regarded altruism as the noblest of all values, and the one absolutely essential for the future well-being of humanity. There is always the threat of domination by '*H. praedatorius*', unscrupulous and ambitious creatures operating by the maxims of biological evolution – survival of the fittest. If they succeed there will be regression to barbarism after the brief transcendental era enlightened by values in a cosmos that otherwise knows no values. A brief glimpse of the first great civilization, the Sumerian, lights up the way by which we have come to our heritage of the World 3 that has made us.

6.1 The World of Culture (World 3)

Lectures 4 and 5 were devoted to the biological story of our origin and of our coming to man's estate entirely by the process of biological evolution. In contrast to biological evolution, my thesis is that cultural evolution is exclusively human. Culture is man made. Man alone has the potentiality to participate in culture both as an experiencer and as a creator. Animals have no culture and are blind to culture. Behaviour that is learned uncritically or automatically by imitation as a result of some conditioning procedure is not cultural, although it is not, as such, inherited. But it is at the highest level of performance of the animal nervous system, being part of the conditioning process. It represents the summit of the studies of the behaviourists and the physicalists. I am aware that my extreme position will invite attack. It will be attacked on the grounds that in many of their behavioural patterns animals exhibit a sense of beauty or of design. For example, there are the structures made by animals, such as spiders' webs, or nests built by wasps or ants, or by birds. But as against this I raise two objections.

In the first place it is remarkable that animals building some of the most elegant structures with geometrical design have relatively simple nervous systems – as for example the social insects: ants, bees, wasps and the spiders. Other constructional animals such as birds and lower orders of mammals, the badgers and the beavers, also have nervous systems less highly developed than the higher orders of mammals, e. g. the anthropoid apes, which have virtually no constructional propensities.

Secondly, we have the amazing story of the immense time lag between man's development of a full-sized brain (Fig. 5-3) and his significant progress in cultural evolution, as I shall outline after introductory sections on the nature of culture.

Since this lecture will have strong philosophical implications in respect to culture, it is necessary to preface it by giving an account of the recent contributions of Popper (1972) and Popper and Eccles (1977). As against the commonly held monistic belief in materialism or the belief in a dualist world (matter-energy on the one hand and the subjective world of conscious experience on the other), Popper (1972) has developed a three-world philosophy. This is illustrated in Figure 6-1.

World 1 is the whole material world of the cosmos, both inorganic and organic, and including machines and all of biology – even human bodies and brains.

World 2 is the world of conscious experiences, not only of our immediate perceptual – visual, auditory, tactile, pain, hunger, anger, joy, fear, etc. but also our memories, imaginings, thoughts, and planned actions that he refers to as our 'dispositional intentions'.

World 3 is the world of objective knowledge, which would include the objective contents of thoughts underlying scientific and artistic and poetic expression. In particular, Popper stresses the World 3 status of all theoretical systems and of problems and problem situations and critical arguments.

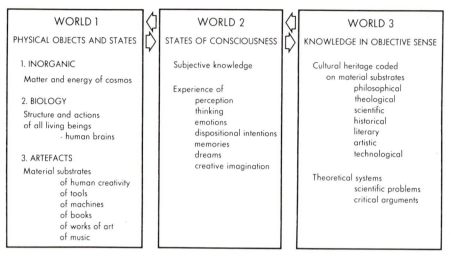

Fig. 6-1. Tabular representation of the contents of the three worlds that comprise everything in existence and in experience. Popper, K. R., Eccles, J. C.: The Self and Its Brain. Berlin, Heidelberg, New York: Springer 1977

The importance of World 3 will be readily appreciated when we come to consider its relationship to Worlds 1 and 2.

In fact we can state that in World 3 are all linguistic expressions and all arguments and discussions and all records of human intellectual efforts; and in particular there are the records preserved in libraries and museums either as written records or as paintings, sculptures, ceramics, ornaments, tools, machines, etc. However, it is important to recognize that in World 3 there is only the objective knowledge that is coded symbolically in the actual structures that serve as vehicles for this knowledge. The material structures carrying the codes such as books, pictures, plastic art forms, films and even computer memories would be of course in World 1.

World 3 is the world of culture and is essentially a world of storage. It has been the genius of man through the whole story of his civilization to have left in enduring form his imagination and understanding as well as his sense of design and purpose, which was initially in the style and form of his fashioning of clay, of stone, of flint and of pottery, or in the delineation of his cave paintings. The surviving fragments give insight into the creativity of primitive man, and reveal the slow emergence of more sophisticated forms of symbolic expression. All of these enduring records of human creativity belong to World 3, and give us insight into the thoughts and imaginings of human beings of the remote past, that is of the contents of their World 2.

6.2 Evolution of Culture

As we survey the cultural story of mankind the most remarkable discovery is that there were eons of incredibly slow development (*cf.* Dobzhansky, 1962; Hawkes, 1965).

6.2.1 The Paleolithic and Mesolithic Ages

For the earliest records of hominid development we are dependent on stone tools. It is doubtful if the Australopithecines can be credited with any paleolithic culture even of the most primitive kind (Tobias, 1973). Presumably they had advanced beyond the present pongid level as hunters and aggressors by operating in some haphazard manner with weapons of bone, horn and wood. It is disappointing that the considerable cerebral development with an EQ of about 3.8 (Fig. 5-8) resulted in no systematic stone culture through the enormously long existence of Australopithecines – some 4 million years. Probably they had a secure ecological niche as hunters in open grass lands, where their erect running ability would be of great advantage in hunting. They may have formed wood into weapons with some skill, but nothing of that would survive in the fossil record. Presumably Australopithecines existed for so long because they were efficient hunters despite the inadequacy of their tools. Their cerebral capacity could be effective in the better co-operation of groups in planning and in hunting.

With the evolution of *H. habilis* some 2.8 million years ago we have the beginning of the *Paleolithic age*, as is revealed by the simple pebble tools or choppers found in the oldest Oldowan culture in Kenya and the adjacent region of Ethiopia. Such tools were made with a rough bashing of small stones to get an edge for cutting, chopping or scraping (Fig. 6-2 C).

At a much later stage there was improvement in stone tools in the Acheulian and Abbevillian hand axes (Fig. 6-2 A and B). From their location and dating they seem to be the products of *H. erectus* and *H. sapiens preneanderthalis* some 500,000–200,000 years ago. From then on there was progressive improvement and diversification of stone tools through the Lower Paleolithic age, which is conveniently dated to end with the coming of Neanderthal man some 100,000 years ago.

The *Middle Paleolithic age* corresponds to the Neanderthal age from 100,000 to 40,000 years ago. There was a great improvement in tool manufacture by the *flaking technique* that gave a good range of tools with finer cutting edges. Their manufacture required skill and a good understanding of the way to obtain the desired cleavage plane from the block of flint.

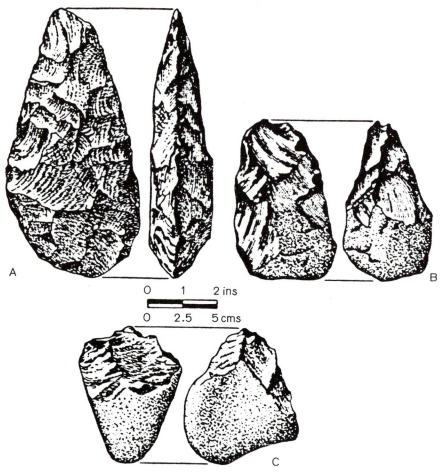

Fig. 6-2 A–C. Pebble tool to hand-axe. **A** Acheulian tool. **B** Abbevillian tool. **C** Oldowan pebble tools. By permission of the Trustees of the British Museum (Natural History)

The *Upper Paleolithic age* corresponds to the Cro-Magnon culture from 40,000 to 10,000 years ago. Their *blade technique* resulted in still finer blade tools and in an amazing variety of specialized tools for working bone and wood and even sewing needles so that skins could be made into good clothing.

For our present story the tool cultures provide the best evidence of the improved technical performance that went with larger brains from *H. habilis,* to *H. erectus,* to *H. sapiens* (Fig. 5-3). We can regard the best hand axes of the Lower Paleolithic, the Acheulian (Fig. 6-2 A) as already works of art with their attractive regular form. The later 'laurel leaf' blades are fine works of art of Cro-Magnon manufacture in the Upper Paleolithic.

Jacquetta Hawkes (1965) has expressed with remarkable insight the relation of primitive man to his activities:

> It is not until the sudden appearance of art and ritual burial towards the end of the Paleolithic Age that we have anything beyond the faintest hint of man's inner, unifying existence although undoubtedly this must have been increasing and refining even while in his extraverted and practical life man went from battering pebbles to shaping a hand-axe. We can assume at the intellectual level a growing ability to categorize and to draw conclusions from the past for the benefit of the future. At the imaginative level there must have been mounting power to picture things (and particularly objects of desire such as game animals) when they were not before the eyes, comparable to the ability to visualize the completed tool within the unshaped block of stone. The beautiful shape of the hand-axe itself can, indeed, be used as a proof of the early emergence of an aesthetic sense . . . their satisfying proportions show that already a quarter of a million years ago the imaginative mind had its own sense of rightness in pure form which, whatever its source, still holds good for us today.

There was immense time lag between man's development of a full-sized brain and his significant progress in cultural evolution, i. e. in the creation of World 3. For the greater part of the immensely long Paleolithic age, some 2 million years, all we know is the slow development of stone tools – from flaked pebbles to the very gradually improved hand-axe. It is generally believed that this almost unimaginable slowness demonstrates that man was greatly handicapped by not yet having an effective communication by speech. It was not until the Upper Paleolithic era that man seemed to have achieved a new awareness and sense of purpose – as witness the remarkable progress in a few thousand years, relative to the virtual stagnation for the previous hundreds of thousands of years. As one can readily imagine, man was lifted to a new level of creativity by a language that gave clear identification of objects and descriptions of actions and even more importantly, the opportunity of discussing and arguing. We can presume that this linguistic stimulus resulted in the development of the large variety of stone tools with greatly improved design, which is the most important characteristic of the Upper Paleolithic age.

But the most fascinating insight into the artistic creativity of Upper Paleolithic man is given by the cave paintings of southern France and northern Spain. When I saw the marvellous paintings of Lascaux (Fig. 6-3), I was overwhelmed by the feeling that these artists had highly developed imagination and memory as well as a refined aesthetic sense. Undoubtedly they had a fully developed language so that they could discuss the techniques they employed and the ideas that inspired them. One has the impression that, at this period of about 15,000 B.C., man was very richly contributing to the

Fig. 6-3. Paintings from Lascaux, the Hall of the Bulls. Between the two bulls' heads at the sides there is a horse with a group of stags below

Fig. 6-5. Susa Goblet of 4th millennium B. C. Reprinted with permission of the Musée du ▶ Louvre

Fig. 6-4. Samarra pottery of 5th millennium B. C. showing figurative and abstract designs. Reprinted with permission of The State Antiquities Organization Baghdad

world of culture. At the same time there were carvings and modellings of animals and of archetypal female figures that probably are representative of mother goddesses. Many would achieve distinction in modern sculpture exhibitions!

In the subsequent *Mesolithic age* man developed and perfected hunting methods and also clothing and housing, but artistically it was disappointing after the great achievements of the later Paleolithic.

This technological Mesolithic period beginning at 10,000–8000 B.C. was relatively brief, at least in the spearhead areas of cultural advance, where it was succeeded by the Neolithic age.

6.2.2 The Neolithic Age

The Neolithic age was characterized by settled farming communities that were made possible by the domestication of animals and the planting of crops. The farmers lived in villages, and gradually, in specially favourable areas on trade routes towns were formed.

The first town was Jericho founded at about 8000 B.C. at the extreme south of the fertile crescent that curved up to Anatolia and then down towards Mesopotamia. It was probably the first walled town, and in subsequent millennia was rebuilt each time more securely with substantial houses and tombs for the dead. It was remarkable for the skulls with plaster superimposed to represent the face and head at 6000 B.C. It had probably no more than 2000–3000 inhabitants.

The recent discovery of Catal Huyuk on the Anatolian plateau is the next advance, being a larger town, up to 6000, that was founded at 6500 B.C. Again it was in a trading area with a rich agriculture – domesticated animals and crops of wheat, barley, vegetables, nuts and fruits. The closely apposed family houses were of two stories and there were numerous shrines with sculptures, and murals. The tombs gave evidence of a rich community with jewellery, finely woven textiles and stylish weapons. Here was perhaps the first cultured community, but we lack all documentary evidence of the social and religious organization of this small city that existed for some thousands of years.

Our attention must now move from these early tentative efforts in civilization to Mesopotamia, where from 5000 B.C. there was the first great flowering of a civilization that flourished for some 3000 years. So much of the culture we cherish today had its origin in that miraculous epoch. Initially the first settlements were in the river valleys to the north of Mesopotamia, such as Jarmo in 6500 B.C. The towns and villages soon became remarkable for their substantial houses and for the fine pottery and weaving. These developments were possible because of the prosperous farming with crops of barley and wheat and with domesticated animals, sheep, ox, goat, pig and dog. In addition the stone tools were finely made with polished surfaces. The pottery clearly reveals that Mesopotamian man was guided by an aesthetic sense. The decorative patterns of Hasuma and Jarmo were in part abstract, but also, as with the Samarra pottery of the 5th millennium B.C. (Fig. 6-4), there was a very sophisticated stylization of animal forms to give designs that display a high artistic sense. This Mesopotamian pottery is remarkable for the combination of utility and elegance. Already they had invented the potter's wheel. Cultural evolution was well advanced and the ceramics of Susa (Fig. 6-5) represent their highest artistic performance in this field in the 4th millennium B.C.

About 5000 B.C. Neolithic culture had spread from there to Egypt, so seeding the great periods of Egyptian civilization. Later there was a wide dispersal to Europe and to Asia (first to the Indus valley and later to China) of this central feature of the Neolithic culture, namely farming with settled communities.

6.2.3 The Rise of Cities and the Flowering of Culture (Woolley, 1961)

Mesopotamia itself could only start when irrigation was developed from 5000 B.C. onwards to bring into productivity the fabulously rich land along the rivers. This harvesting of river water demanded a skilled technology from large organized communities. For the first time Planet Earth had large centres of civilization. Mesopotamia undoubtedly led the world during the magnificent periods of Sumerian civilization for more than a millennium from 3500 B.C. The Neolithic age gave place to the Copper age about 3500 B.C. and that in turn to the Bronze age by 3000 B.C. Metallurgical technology was highly developed in the many workshops in the cities with empirical experimenting and the handing on of traditions. During the 3rd millennium B.C. gold, silver and bronze workmanship was of a high order.

At 3500 B.C. the Sumerians were replacing the Ubaidian civilization of Mesopotamia and soon there were magnificent developments in sculpture that desplayed power, self-confidence and elegance. The Warka head, or what I prefer to call the Lady of Erech, is dated at 3000 B.C. or even earlier. Here we have a display of an amazing sensitivity (Fig. 6-6). The eyes and eyebrows were originally inlaid with coloured substances. Por-

Fig. 6-6. Female head in alabaster marble from Uruk of about 3000 B. C. Reprinted with permission of The State Antiquities Organization Baghdad

trayed for the first time is the mystery of the eternal feminine. We can sense the human spirit in the perfection of the cheeks and lips. It is one of the high achievements of human culture with its haunting beauty. But they also made gods and goddesses with curious distortions and large eyes and small hands (Fig. 6-7). This is symbolic, but the figures are stately and impressive.

In the first half of the 3rd millennium B.C. these most sensitive and appealing human sculptures revealed that the artists had great skill and humanity. However as Malraux in Parrot (1960) comments:

> The purpose of early artists is not to imitate but to reveal form enabling man to enter into communion with their gods – and so transcendent is this purpose that the artist is as unaware of it as the saint is unaware of his own sainthood.

This Malraux quotation is introduced in order to warn against a modern 'arty' outlook on the craftsmen of ancient civilizations. They did not set out to make their style and to win their recognition, but rather to be immersed

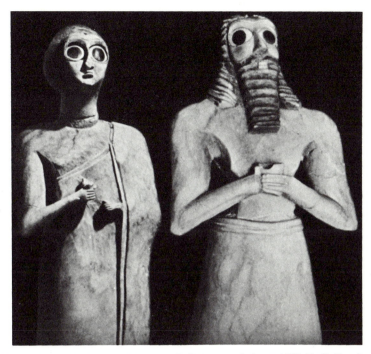

Fig. 6-7. Goddess and the God Abu from Tell Asmar of about 2700 B. C. Reprinted with permission of The State Antiquities Organization Baghdad

in the whole stream of their civilization, and to live with it and to create in harmony with it. This was the case even as recently as the Medieval civilization with the stone carvers, and the fresco and glass painters.

In this great era several sophisticated cities had grown up in Mesopotamia. The central Ziggurat towered above the city and was the temple of the god who 'owned' the city. It was also the seat of the priests and scribes who interpreted the will of the god and who administered the city for the common good, as also the whole of the productive farm land that belonged to the city through the god.

Woolley (1963) has estimated that the population of Ur was about 360,000 early in the 2nd millennium B.C. Architecture had flourished, but throughout an amazingly long period there was still no written language. The storage of all the information needed for the transactions and governance of the city was apparently in the memories of the officials, of the craftsmen, of the priests, and of course it was coded in the objects themselves – houses, pottery, sculptures and figurines, implements, weapons, and technical equipment, such as the potter's wheel and the metallurgical foundries.

It is hard for us to imagine how remembered tradition could cope with the complexities of such administrations. This dire need was the stimulus that caused Sumerians to make their greatest of all contributions to human culture – the development of a written language. Pictograms had been used to make records of numbers of objects – sheep, oxen, pigs, etc. However their purpose was to enumerate things, but they could not convey statements. As finely expressed by Woolley (1963):

> Pictorial representations ends and true writing begins at the moment when an indubitable linguistic element first comes in, and that can only happen when signs have acquired a phonetic value. The gap which divides the pictogram from the hieroglyph and ultimately from the phonetic sign is so great that for most peoples it has proved impassable. It is to the credit of the Sumerians that they were able to bridge that gap, and as soon as they had done so their neighbours were quick to adopt not necessarily the Sumerian system, but the Sumerian idea, and there arose a number of scripts which differed completely in form from the Sumerian but were indebted to it for the basic conception that a written sign might represent not a thing but a sound. All the archaeological evidence available seems to prove that true writing was first developed in southern Mesopotamia.

The earliest example of this occurs at about 3300 B.C., and by 3000 B.C. there had been developed a syllabary of up to 900 signs at Uruk – most of which were still ideograms of rather complex form. The usage was so complicated that it was restricted to a small body of specialists (the scribes). They progressively simplified the forms so that eventually it was completely abstract, consisting of various arrangements of tapered signs inscribed in soft clay tablets by a stylus made like a wedge, hence the name 'cuneiform' for the first written language that was fully developed by about 2800 B.C.

A written language must rank as one of the greatest discoveries in human history, for by means of it man could live beyond time. Thoughts, imaginings, ideas, understandings, and explanations experienced and developed by men living in one age can be written down for distribution in that age and also for recovery in later ages. A man's creative insights need no longer die with him, but, when encoded in written language, can be re-experienced by later men who have the ability to decode. And so we enter into the historical epochs where the different civilizations have left records of their economic and political activities, their myths and legends, their drama, poetry, history, philosophy and religion.

There is undoubtly a feeling of bathos in the uses to which this marvellous discovery was put initially. Mostly it was used for business documents, contracts, inventories, deeds of sale! But also it was used for royal inscriptions and at a later stage for recording religious texts. But even this limited usage gives us the first clear statements about an early civilization, so that history takes over from the proto-history of the preceding civilizations.

There is good evidence that the Sumerian idea – not the detailed scripts – was borrowed by other cultures so that they too developed their scripts, which in Egypt was the hieroglyphic script, and in China was essentially of an ideographic character. This borrowing must have occurred at the ideographic stage of Sumerian language before the stage of abstraction to the cuneiform script. Some authorities regard the Egyptian and Chinese as independent inventions without information from Sumer. But, when we

Fig. 6-8. Standard of Ur, about 2600 B. C. *Above:* detail of a war chariot; *below:* detail of a libation scene. Reproduced by courtesey of the Trustees of the British Museum

consider the long time man used a spoken language without essaying to convert it into a written form, it seems unlikely that there would be three independent discoveries, two a little later than the Sumerian. Certainly the close association between Sumer und Egypt would have facilitated the transfer of such a valuable idea.

6.2.4 Sumerian Technology

The Sumerians also invented the wheel, as can be seen in the 'Standard of Ur', 2600 B.C., in the British Museum, where we see the first armed vehicle (Fig. 6-8 *above*) and here in the same picture series we see the first portrayal of a cocktail party (Fig. 6-8 *below*)! And so we come to their great success with metals – copper, bronze and gold, as in the several representa-

Fig. 6-9. Statue in diorite of Gudea of Lagash 22nd century B. C. Reprinted with permission from The Metropolitan Museum of Art

tions of a goat poised on a flowering bush. The gold fluted vase in the University of Pennsylvania Museum has been described as the most beautiful metal object that man has ever made. The magnificent bronze head of the Semitic conqueror Sargon (2400 B.C.) was again beyond compare at that time. The perfect administrator of that time was Gudea (Fig. 6-9), Governor of Lagash, who ruled for at least 15 years around 2200 B.C. with a devotion to art and literature. He was a man of peace, justice and dedication. More than 30 statues of him are extant, there being a special Gudea room in the Louvre.

I have given a brief glimpse of cultural evolution in one of its greatest and most exciting periods. How rapidly the advance came when language was perfected and could be given an enduring form in the written records!

6.2.5 Sumerian Literature

It is more difficult to trace the development of literature than of the plastic arts because we are almost completely dependent on late copies for our knowledge of the original literature. But in Sumeria and Egypt there was fine poetry and prose as early as 3000 B.C. The greatest Sumerian literary achievement was undoubtedly the Epic of Gilgamesh (Sandars, 1973). Just as occurred with the Homeric epics more than 1500 years later, it probably had a long oral tradition before being written down at least in part on tablets from the late 3rd millennium. Most of it was written in the first centuries of the 2nd millennium. The epic is remarkable in that it portrays a great human hero who

> ... dominates the action of the poem. The Gods and their activities serve only as background and setting for the dramatic episodes of the hero's life. What gives these episodes lasting significance and universal appeal is their *human* quality. They revolve about forces and problems common to man everywhere through the ages – the need for friendship, the instinct for loyalty, the impelling urge for name and fame, the love of adventure and achievement, the all-absorbing fear of death, and the all-compelling longing for immortality. It is the varied interplay of these emotional and spiritual drives in man that constitutes the drama of the 'Epic of Gilgamesh' – drama which transcends the confines of time and space. (Kramer, 1959)

After 1800 B.C. all creativity in literature virtually ceased in both Mesopotamia and Egypt. As has happened with so many more recent civilizations, periods of great achievements come to an end. But cultural achievement survives in the preserved records, the scripts and the works in the plastic arts. In this way it was possible for the Medieval and Renaissance civilizations to recover so much of the forgotten Classical civilization. And in the last century there have been immensely successful efforts to discover the civilizations from more remote times, such as the Sumerian briefly referred to above. These efforts must rank as some of the glorious performances of man whereby he has recovered, organized and appreciated so much of the great creative achievements of earlier civilizations, and so has immeasurably added to the content and richness of our cultural world.

6.3 Cultural Evolution and World 3

I have chosen to focus on the achievement of the Sumerians in their great and lasting success in building World 3. The Egyptian civilization was a little later in onset, being seeded from Mesopotamia. There were magnificent achievements particularly in their great works in stone – the sculptures, temples and pyramids. With a complete subservience of all to the Pharaoh, the God King, Egypt was much more conservative and authoritarian than Sumer with its many city states. During much of the history of Sumer there was an amazingly open and tolerant society, where the rights of individuals were respected and even safeguarded by the first legal code, about 2100 B.C. (the Code of Ur-Nammu). It was unfortunately replaced in Babylonian times by the derivative, but much harsher, Code of Hammurabi (Hawkes, 1975).

The theme of my lectures is the human story to our present time, so I must keep to the main stream that led to our dominant Western civilization, and overlook the other great civilizations of Asia, India and Central America. The Sumerian achievement was continued in the Babylonian and then in the Assyrian civilizations. It spread widely in the Near East and so with the Egyptian legacy it led to the Minoan and Mycenean civilizations and so to Greece and thence to Rome. There was a fusion with the Hebrew civilization that had roots in Babylon and even in Sumer. Abraham is supposed to have been a citizen of Ur about 1800 B.C. And so we come through to Western Christianity and our own times.

We have been considering the material and the practical side of life in those great creative periods of human history. This is an important aspect of culture and it shows that something quite unique had appeared on Planet Earth. There were structures being created with purposive design and giving evidence of creative imagination. This evidence sharply separates cultural evolution from biological evolution, which in its official form cannot entertain purposiveness as a factor guiding evolution.

The immense developments of civilization during the last 2 millennia are part of our cultural heritage and there is no need to detail them. Suffice it to say that in each of the different ages there has been dominance of several forms of culture. We are the heirs not only of the cultural achievements of our age, but also of the cultural achievements of past ages that are available in some coded form (Fig. 6-1). Cultural evolution has given us an unimaginably rich World 3, so rich that in a whole lifetime only a minute fraction can be known by any one of us.

6.4 World 2: The World of Self-Consciousness

We must now return to consider the story of development of the other uniquely human world, the World 2 of subjective experience (Fig. 6-1). An important distinction must be made at the outset. I am not venturing into the controversial field of *consciousness,* which is so elusive to testing criteria. Presumably it is shared by all animals with highly developed brains, for example mammals and birds (see Fig. 5-4). By contrast in *self-consciousness* you know that you know and you are aware of your existence as an experiencing self. An alternative term is self-awareness. The many components of World 2 are diagrammatically illustrated in Figure 10-2, which will be considered in detail in the last lecture.

It might be thought that hominids came to selfhood as soon as they started on the creation of World 3 objects, e. g. finely designed hand axes. It may be that they did, but it must have been a dim and shadowy experience, and we have to go to more recent times for the first clear signs of self-consciousness. Paradoxically it comes not from the care of the living, but in the first instance from caring for the dead.

As described by Jacquetta Hawkes (1965):

> The first indication we have of our remote predecessors being troubled with metaphysical intuition (however little brought into consciousness) is in the careful disposal of the dead by Neanderthal man. Probably the earliest examples of such burial are those at the Wadi el Mughara in Palestine. Here the bodies of the Neanderthaloid inhabitants had been laid in trenches cut in the cave floor and joints of food and flint weapons put beside them – these interments, some of them elaborate enough to deserve their description as ceremonial burials, certainly indicate some form of a belief in a continued existence after death.

It can be safely inferred that Neanderthal man certainly had self-awareness of the kind experienced by us and had the feeling for other members of his community as beings like himself. Thus perhaps 100,000 years ago we could speak of our ancestors as being at the dawn of humanity and to have become self-conscious beings. Further archeological discoveries of ceremonial burials may push this period to the even earlier preneanderthal times.

Moreover it would seem that primitive man had progressed notably in purposiveness, imagination and perseverance, as is evidenced by the design and manufacture of tools. Thus the advance from Abbevillian to Acheulian hand axe design (Fig. 6-2) shows that at about 250,000 years ago the craftsman was envisaging the final form in the block of stone and was planning the flaking so that this form was achieved after much persevering effort. Surely man had attained to a remarkable level of consciousness at that time, though perhaps not yet the self-consciousness that is revealed by the ceremonial burials some 150,000 years later. However, the tool culture of some 250,000 years ago is at such a technological and aesthetic level that we must accord it World 3 status (*cf.* Fig. 6-2 A). I would suggest that already these preneanderthal men had achieved a level of conscious existence (World 2) to match their World 3 achievements. They had evolved far from their primate ancestry, for non-human primates have not even a rudimentary achievement in culture. I refer to their unaided performance, not to their performance when trained. There is much evidence (Popper and Eccles, 1977) to suggest that World 2 and World 3 develop together in some kind of symbiotic interaction. Unfortunately we can never know the developing linguistic performances of evolving man. This would give a far more reliable insight into his World 2 status than tool culture, but it seems probable that linguistic development matched the technological developments.

We can formulate the hypotheses that, as man's brain was developing both quantitatively and qualitatively from the level of the Australopithecine to that of *H. habilis* and *H. erectus,* as described in Lecture 5, he was achieving a further development of the conscious experiences that we have proposed for higher mammals. In particular there would be conscious recognition of an object by several sensory modalities, e. g. touch and vision. Jerison (1973) has stressed the important role of imagery in survival in stressful environments. This imagery would be dependent on auditory, tactile and kinaesthetic information integrated with the visual information that was already pre-eminent in anthropoids with their binocular vision. He states:

> . . . The hominids tended toward the construction of a perceptual world in which the information from the various sensory domains was bound together to provide a consistent picture of a spatially extended world, filled with objects that could move and emit sounds, be touched, smelled, and seen, and in which 'constancy' of objects over time was guaranteed. Furthermore it would have been a world in which time could be tremendously extended, to permit the integration of images over seconds, minutes, or even longer time periods. If time may be extended to retain events of the past, why not extend it into the

future as a projection of events to come? A perceptual world organized in this way is a world that is familiar to us. It is not only a world in which we can see and hear and touch, but a world in which we can imagine. And our images are not only of past events but of future events as well.

On this basis we come to the identification of objects in an external world and their naming. So descriptive language became possible and with it the experiences of conscious perception and of voluntary action. It appears that the dawning of self-consciousness may have been much later than the development of primitive language. Self-consciousness gives, as we know, experiences of wonders, beauties, excitements and enthusiasms, but it also has "... brought in its train somber companions – fear, anxiety, and death-awareness" (Dobzhansky, 1967). And at that stage of his ultimate concern man had to take refuge in primitive religions and rituals, and particularly at the time of death with ceremonial burial customs. Man had then evolved far from his primate progenitors. We may question, if this transcendent change was simply a result of the quantitative and qualitative developments of the brain. Certainly these developments of the brain were necessary; but, it may well be asked, were they sufficient (Eccles, 1970; Popper and Eccles, 1977)?

Related to this question is the concern that was expressed by Wallace, the co-discoverer with Darwin of natural selection in 1858. Wallace felt that human intelligence could only be explained by direct intervention of a cosmic intelligence. He pointed out that the mental requirements in the lives of primitive people were very low. Natural selection could have endowed a primitive man with a brain.

> ... but little superior to that of an ape, but he actually possesses one but little inferior to that of an average member of our learned societies.

Darwin let Wallace know that he was dreadfully disappointed at this heretical departure from his theory. Nevertheless Wallace returned to this theme repeatedly. I find myself in general sympathy with Wallace, who was more open-minded than Darwin.

It has been proposed above that, across the frontier in Figure 10-2, a unique part of World 1, the human liaison brain, is open to influences of a non-material character from World 2 (Popper and Eccles, 1977). By the evolutionary process creatures had been developed with brains that allowed them to transcend the hitherto unchallenged world of matter-energy. There was no longer a complete closedness of World 1, and this momentous change has resulted in an on-going progressive transformation of Planet Earth, as told in history. We have now come to an expression of the ultimate in the human mystery.

6.5 Relationship of Biological Evolution to Cultural Evolution

We have to recognize that it is the biological evolutionary process that has created the human brain in the manner outlined in Lectures 4 and 5. The building of a human brain is genetically coded, but cultural evolution is not. As well stated by Dobzhansky (1967):

> Genes make the origin of culture possible, and they are basic to its maintenance and evolution. But the genes do not determine what particular culture develops where, when, or how. An analogous situation is that of language and speech – genes make human language and speech possible, but they do not ordain what will be said . . . death awareness is not a primary irreducible, or unitary genetic or psychological entity . . . it is probably an out growth and a necessary concomitant of self-awareness. To say that self-awareness and death-awareness are genetically conditioned does not, however, imply that they are simple genetic units. There is no such thing as a gene for self-awareness, or for consciousness, or for ego, or for mind. These basic human capacities derive from the whole of the human genetic endowment, not from some kind of special genes.

Furthermore, in developing this theme, Dobzhansky goes on to state:

> Death-awareness became established in human evolution as a species trait. However this trait was not, and possibly is not, adaptive in itself. It is an integral part of the complex of human faculties, the core of which is constituted by self-awareness, capacity for abstract thought, symbol formation, and the use of language . . . Having become aware of the inevitability of death man has tasted the Forbidden Fruit. This awareness is one of the sources, possibly the prime source, of ultimate concern.

6.6 Values – Altruism

It is essential that we consider the developing World 2 experiences in relation to the coming of values. The guidance of a consciously planned life by some value system more than anything else sets man apart from animals. We have already noted the recognition of values in the story of cultural evolution. For example, the Epic of Gilgamesh is remarkable for the value system that is integral to the whole tragic story. Sherrington (1940) believed that the highest of all values was altruism, and furthermore that the continual practice of altruism is essential to our survival in a free and open society. With the records of totalitarianism from the Right and the Left, it should not be necessary today to warn that barbarism is an ever-present threat.

Altruism came very late in biological evolution. If we exclude instinctive behaviour patterns, the caring for others and the feeling for others (compassion) are not features even of higher animal life. With domesticated animals affectionate behaviour could be due to imitation and instruction. These animals in the wild behave quite differently. There are anecdotal accounts of apparently compassionate behaviour of dolphins to an injured companion, but according to Washburn (1969) primates in the wild display no trace of compassion. And we have the story of the indifference of the other chimpanzees of the colony to the sufferings of the gravely injured McGregor, as so poignantly told by Jane Goodall (1971). Aggression gives status, for example with respect to feeding priority. With the possible exception of chimpanzees, the stronger feed first with no thought of the weaker and the younger, who have to put up with what is left. In the social system of lions, there is no trace of compassion (Bertram, 1975).

Biological evolution is a process of ruthless struggle for survival, where the selection was effected by killing other animals competing for that ecological niche. As realistically to by Sherrington (1940, *Man on his Nature*, Chap. 12) for infrahuman life:

> Its world was under a rule of 'might-is-right' imposed by violence and pillared upon suffering. But yet the spell of 'urge-to-live' was over it all. Repicturing that life, so far as we can, we marvel and rejoice at our escape.
>
> The competition between lives which have mind is in origin one with that between the so-called mindless lives of which we were speaking. It overlaps and dovetails in with that and continues it on the new plane. It also, because a struggle to live, is essentially a struggle to the death.

There are no survivors of the hominids, our ancestors. Australopithecines and *H. habilis* were gone about 1 million years ago; *H. erectus* probably by 300,000 years ago; Neanderthal man by 40,000 years ago. Eventually, with growing self-consciousness, out of this purely aggressive relationship there developed co-operation between individuals that probably was based on an enriched linguistic communication which had become more than a signal system. Families and tribes were welded together for common good in hunting, in sharing of food and in resistance to enemies.

In human prehistory (60,000 years ago) the first evidence for compassionate behaviour has recently been discovered by Solecki (1971) in the skeletons of two Neanderthal men incapacitated by severe injuries. Yet the bones indicated that these incapacited creatures had been kept alive for up to 2 years, which could only have occurred if they had been cared for by other individuals of the tribe. Compassionate feelings can also be inferred from the remarkable discovery that burials at that time in the Shanidar cave were associated with floral tributes, as disclosed by pollen analysis (Solecki, 1977). We thus may date the earliest known signs of altruism in human prehistory at 60,000 years ago. One could hope that it could be earlier because Neanderthal men with brains as large as ours existed at least 100,000 years ago.

6.7 The Future for Biological and Cultural Evolution

With science and technology at his command man is now in a position to program and control biological change in animals and plants. Planned genetic manipulation now replaces the natural process of biological mutation by chance. And 'natural selection' or 'survival of the fittest' is no longer the arbiter judging the biological effectiveness of the mutations. Species that flourish too effectively bring upon themselves technological attack of a devastating kind. The enormous advances of the sciences, biology, chemistry and physics, are resulting in a technology that gives man progressively more power to control and exploit the biological world on the land surface. Only limited exploitation is yet possible for the oceans, but it can be doubted if any significant biological evolution can occur there before man effectively takes over with technologies for ruthlessly harvesting the oceans. Already we have witnessed the near extermination of some species of whales, and valuable species of fish are gravely threatened by over-harvesting.

It is important in any case to realise that the wonderful process of evolution may have come near to exhaustion in biological inventiveness. In the early eras of the evolutionary story there were large pools of relatively undifferentiated species, forming, as it were, a main stream from which differentiation could give evolutionary novelty. There is no way back in evolution. Differentiation results in living forms losing progressively more of their initially rich potentiality. For example in the evolutionary process the primitive five-toed mammal was differentiated to become the single- or double-toed herbivore. This toe loss is a one-way process. The herbivore can never evolve to recover those lost toes. We are endowed with that most wonderful structure, the human hand, because our mammalian forebears did not 'trade' the basic five-toed form for some immediate advantages in locomotion that was given by a hoof or a paw.

We may generalize by saying that man has taken over control of the biological processes of differentiation, multiplication and survival. Biology is not completely frozen at the end of the evolutionary era. Rather it is now enslaved for man's purposes so that useful species are deliberately changed by genetic engineering in order that they can be more useful for exploitation. What then can we predict for man as a biological organism? Will genetic engineering be effective in giving an on-going process of evolution to 'better' or 'more effective' human beings? No doubt this could be done, just as has been done with domesticated animals. If an enslaved population were to be ruthlessly treated as domesticated animals by a tyranny having a constant objective for centuries, a 'master-race' could be developed. But we may ask: What properties would such a 'master-race' be bred for? And would the succession of despotic rulers keep this objective fixed during the long periods required for significant change? I am happy to believe that we can dismiss this nightmarish plan for 'human cattle' as a science fiction in our present free society. Apart from this we must realize that the welfare state has brought human biological evolution to an end (see Lecture 5).

Let us look now at the future for cultural evolution. It is my thesis that this will provide man with virtually unlimited opportunities in the many rich fields of World 3. Even before the great and pioneering cultural achievements of Sumerian civilisation, we can assume that the cerebral potentiality of man had evolved to the level of modern man. From then on biological evolution had given place to cultural evolution. And if we survey the recent history of man, century by century, we can see that there have been tremendous achievements in one or other aspect of culture. Not all aspects advance continuously. Great creative discoveries and inspiring leadership by men of genius have led to a flourishing of now one great cultural discipline, now another. At one time it is in literature, at another in philosophy or in the plastic arts or in music or in science and technology. For example the classical age of Greece was remarkable for architecture, sculpture, literature and philosophy. In the Renaissance there were great developments in architecture, painting, sculpture and literature; later came music, philosophy, cosmology and science. It would be generally agreed that for more than a century the greatest cultural achievements of man have been in science and technology.

I will now recapitulate my thesis. It has been argued that man differs *radically in kind* from other animals. As a transcendence in the evolutionary process there appeared an animal differing fundamentally from other animals because he had attained to propositional speech, abstract thought and self-consciousness, which are all signs that a being of transcendent novelty had appeared in the world – creatures existing not only in World 1 but realizing their existence in the world of self-awareness (World 2) and so having in the religious concept, souls. And simultaneously these human beings began utilizing their World 2 experiences to create very effectively another world, the third world of the objective spirit. This World 3 provides the means whereby man's creative efforts live on as a heritage for all future men, so building the magnificent cultures and civilizations recorded in human history. Do not the mystery and the wonder of this story of our origin and nature surpass the myths whereby man in the past has attempted to explain his origin and destiny?

Are we to build further in this record of man's greatness in World 3? For that we require a free society, for only under such conditions can there be a free-flowering of man's creative powers in the sciences and the humanities. But how can we regard the future of human existence in the enormous time that Planet Earth will be in its present salubrious state – more than 1 billion years, as we have seen in Lecture 3? As told in this lecture our wonderful civilization started in Sumeria not much more than 5000 years ago, and only in the last 100 years has science been effectively used in technology, medicine, agriculture, communications – and warfare! It is difficult to imagine the scientific, technological and cultural performance even in 100 years. Extend that time to 1000, 10000, 100000, 1 million and we have still barely moved towards the more than 1 billion years that our sun will be providing a salubrious level of light and warmth to Planet Earth. The destiny and meaning of civilization (World 3) is a challenging theme for Natural Theology.

Lecture 7

From the General to the Particular: The Creation of a Self

Synopsis and Introduction

This lecture can be regarded as the climax of these lectures on the 'human mystery'. There will be a simplified account of the building of a human brain, which is almost completed at birth. Nevertheless a new-born baby is a very limited organism in its performance. An account will be given of the way in which motor control is learnt in the first few years. Special problems are concerned in learning movements in relation to the environment and in learning by visual and kinaesthetic experiences to sense the spatial relations and other features of the surrounding world. The most important learning is in communication by language. There will be an account of the cerebral mechanisms concerned in speech. The childhood learning of the first language is dependent on immersion in a continuous linguistic exchange. Evidence from deprivation will be given to show that the development of a human person is thwarted or even negated when this exchange is excluded by sensory deprivation or by extreme isolation. There are several anecdotal cases, but Helen Keller is a well-documented example of the former state, and Genie of the latter. In this recent case extreme isolation prevented human development until she was rescued when almost fourteen years old some seven years ago. She has recovered remarkably but not fully.

There will be a general account of the role of World 3 in producing the next generation of persons in a Society and in enabling those suitably endowed with creativity to contribute to the enrichment of World 3. The creation of a cultured person guided by values and with self-consciousness can thus be accomplished in a few years. Yet, when the brain had been fully developed by biological evolution, it took at least 50,000 years to create a high civilization. World 3 had to be continuously developed by human creative activity for thousands of generations, whereas we now have it ready-made. In the creation of the self it is completely mysterious how each of us is endowed with a unique selfhood, our own. It will be argued that there is no materialist explanation. It is a theme for Natural Theology.

We have now reached the climax of this story of the human mystery. We have traced the line of contingency that eventually led to us, first in cosmic terms, then in terms of Planet Earth; then in the origin of life and in the great evolutionary tree; then in the human origin from primate ancestry through the transitional hominid forms; and so finally to the marvellous cultural evolution which gave us the environmental influences that were ready to shape our growing up. All that has gone before is in a sense but background contingency. In materialist terms our existence began about

266 days befor our birth, when an ovum was fertilized by a spermatozoon. As I shall briefly describe in this lecture, the zygote so formed has been responsible for the building of our bodies and our brains. That is mystery enough. But still more wonderful and utterly mysterious is the coming-to-be of the unique selfhood that is what each of us is. I will quote briefly from Sherrington (1940) before considering various aspects of this story:

> The initial stage of each individual of us is a single cell. We have agreed that mind is not recognizable in any single cell we ever met with. And who shall discover it in the little mulberry-mass which for each of us is our all a little later than the one-cell stage; or even in Fernel's 40 day embryo? Yet who shall deny it in the child which in a few months' time that embryo becomes? Here again mind seems to emerge from no mind. So conversely at death it seems to re-emerge into no mind.

We shall be considering the coming-to-be of the self in terms of three disciplines – the structural, the functional and the cultural.

7.1 Building of the Structure

In the fertilization process about 266 days before our birth the $22 + X$ maternal and the $22 + X$ or Y paternal chromosomes combined to make the complement of the chromosomal genetic material that is uniquely ours, $44 + 2X$ for females, $44 + X + Y$ for males. As mentioned in Lecture 4 the information coded in these chromosomes is in the form of nucleotide sequences along the double strand of the total of 3.5×10^9 nucleotide pairs of the DNA. This DNA structure is so special for each of us that it will never be repeated and it has never existed in any human of the past or present, except if you have an identical twin. It is our evolutionary inheritance. It embodies in fact the entire creative endowment generated by the evolutionary process in the long line of contingency that led to each one of us. It contains the basic instructions for building our bodies and our brains.

The fertilized ovum embarks on an incessant process of subdivision. There are 2 cells at 30 h, 4 at 40 h, 8 at 55 h, 16 at 70 h, which is the little mulberry-mass referred to by Sherrington. Cell division continues relentlessly and by 6 days the cells are arranged as a hollow sphere, the *blastocyst*, one side of which is thickened and is destined to become the embryo. Figure 7-1 shows the growth and development from 14 days to 15 weeks. For the purpose of the story told in this lecture it is sufficient to concentrate on the development of the brain. In Figure 7-1 the human features can be recognized by 40 days, as Fernel noted. However it is still minute. At 60 days the foetus is only 3 cm long, at 90 days, 7.5 cm, and with a weight of only 14 g,

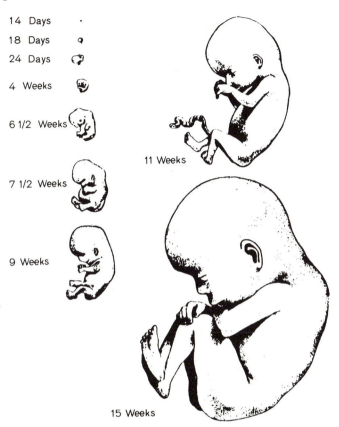

14 Days

18 Days

24 Days

4 Weeks

6 1/2 Weeks

11 Weeks

7 1/2 Weeks

9 Weeks

15 Weeks

Fig. 7-1. Human embryos of specified ages are shown on the same size scale. Reprinted from *Biology today,* 2nd ed., with permission of CRM Books, a Division of Random House, Inc.

and at 120 days about 19 cm and weight 150 g, which is the largest picture of Figure 7-1.

In the earliest stage the future central nervous system can be recognized on the surface of the blastocyst as an elongated neural plate, which is already differentiated from the surrounding ectoderm by its thickening due to elongation of the constituent neuroepithelial cells that extend right across the plate. Soon the rapid multiplication of these cells causes at 24 days the inward folding of the plate so that at 26 days it becomes the neural tube lying beneath the epidermis, which has united over it. The *neuroepithelial cells* thus extend between an inner ventricular attachment and an outer attachment to mesodermal tissue that eventually becomes the pia mater (Fig. 7-2 A). In the earlier stages the neuroepithelial cells multiply in a

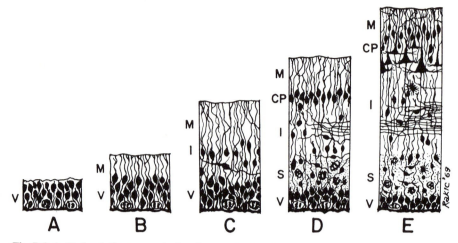

Fig. 7-2 A–E. Semi-diagrammatic drawings of the development of the basic embryonic zones and the cortical plate: *CP*, cortical plate; *I*, intermediate zone; *M*, marginal zone; *S*, subventricular zone; *V*, ventricular zone. Further description in text. Sidman, R. L., Rakic, P.: Neuronal migration with special reference to developing human brain: A review. Brain Res. *62*, *1–36 (1973)*

simple clonal manner with no differentiation, so producing an enormous population of these primitive germinal cells (Fig. 7-2 B). This clonal multiplication is soon replaced by what is called a *differentiating mitosis*. A germinal cell divides to give rise to primitive nerve cells that eventually become mature nerve cells.

The primitive nerve cells never divide again, but largely in their nuclei they carry the genetic instructions to develop into their appointed roles in the nervous system. They set about growing firstly an *axon* and then *dendrites*. These sprouts seem to know where they are going, as if guided by an 'intelligence' and a 'knowledge' of the ultimate design of the brain they are helping to build. It is a wonderful self-organizing, self-developing process. This biological performance in constructing a brain provides one of the most challenging scientific problems confronting us, not only now, but into the future. It was postulated in the 1930s that the brain was built as a more or less randomly organised structure, and then by use it was modelled so as to possess the appropriate connectivities. This hypothesis has been proved false by the many experimental demonstrations that the nervous system is already constructed in its detailed connectivity before it is used. But neither is it constructed by some programmer with a master plan and some detailed rigorous control. There is a simple self-organizing operation. Each stage leads to the next by virtue of its initial constitution, and of the environmental influences, e. g. by adjacent cells and by chemical inducing agents. At the present time we have no more than a general understanding of the principles of this sequential induction. I will now give a simplified account of the building of the cerebral cortex, because it is pre-eminently concerned in the phenomena of conscious selfhood, as has already been suggested in Lecture 5.

Figure 7-2 gives diagrammatically the early stages in the development of the human neocortex (Sidman and Rakic, 1973). A is just less than 6 weeks, and in B at 6–8 weeks some of the neuroepithelial cells (layer V) are undergoing a differentiating mitosis, becoming immature nerve cells. They migrate up to form the intermediate layer (*I*) in C at 8–10 weeks. In D at 10–11 weeks, the differentiating mitoses continue and the immature nerve cells so generated migrate to form the cortical plate (*CP*) that can be seen with its developing nerve cells in E at 11–12 weeks.

It is suggested by Sidman and Rakic (1973) that the final position of the neurones is dictated by interaction with processes of other neurones and even of afferent fibres that have already grown into the cortex, probably from the thalamus (*cf.* Lecture 8). The vertical migrations of the immature neurones to their final places in the cerebral cortex form the developmental basis of the columnar organization of the cerebral cortex that is illustrated in Figures 8-4, 8-7 and 8-8. The horizontal arrangements of dendrites and axonal branches develop at a much later stage.

Figure 7-3 A shows the cerebral end of the neural tube of a monkey foetus at an advanced stage of development. In this transverse section the wall of the neural tube is about 4 mm thick. The white strip between the arrowheads shows the piece that is cut out and displayed at a much higher magnification in B, where the outermost layer is at the top. This figure illustrates the vertical organization of the immature cortex that is attributable to the long glial fibres that act as guides for the migration of the nerve cells (Sidman and Rakic, 1973). Already the upper zone of the cortex is populated by an immense number of neurones, but there are still germinal cells in the deepest part (the ventricular layer as in Fig. 7-2 E), that are continuing the differentiating mitoses to generate more neurones.

After the immature neurones have taken up their final position there is a relatively long period of dendritic development to the fully mature form. The early stage of development of dendrites can be seen in Figure 7-2 E at 11–12 weeks, but the full structural development of the human cerebral cortex is not achieved until long after birth. The initial stages of dendritic

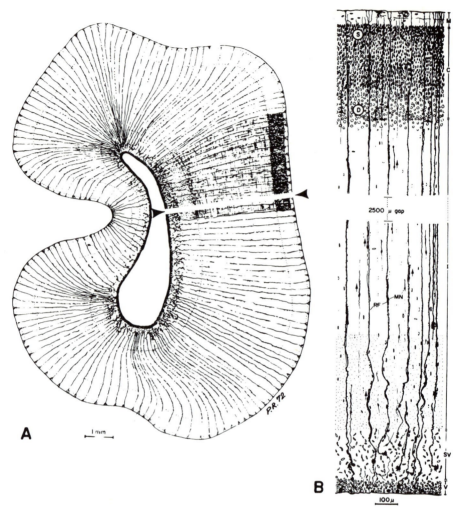

Fig. 7-3 A, B. Camera lucida drawings of a transverse section of the telencephalon of a 97-day monkey foetus. **A** At the parieto-occipital level. The area of the white strip between the *arrowheads* is drawn in **B** at a higher magnification, note scales. The middle 2500 μm is omitted; *M*, marginal layer; *C*, cortical plate; *I*, intermediate zone; *SV*, subventricular zone; *V*, ventricular zone; *S*, superficial cortical cells; *D*, deep cortical cells; *MN*, migrating cells; *RF*, radial glia fibres. Rakic, P.: Mode of cell migration to the superficial layers of fetal monkey neocortex. J. comp. Neurol. *145*, 61–84 (1972)

outgrowth are determined by factors internal to the neurone but, in later stages, the influence of the surrounding tissues (glial cells and other neurones) is paramount. There is need of a far more intensive and systemat-

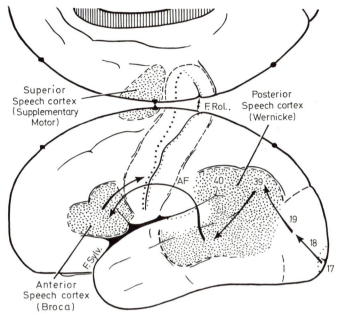

Fig. 7-4. Cortical speech areas of dominant (left) hemisphere. Note that the view is of left hemisphere from both lateral and medial aspects. *F. Rol.,* fissure of Rolando; *F. Sylv.,* fissure of Sylvius. Angular and supramarginal gyri are labelled as Brodmann areas 39 and 40 (*cf.* Fig. 5-10). Also shown by *arrows* is the pathway from area 17 to 18, 19 to 39 (angular gyrus) to the Wernicke speech area, thence by the arcuate fasciculus (*AF*) to Broca's area, and so to the motor cortex for speech. Modified from: Penfield, W., Roberts, L.: Speech and brain mechanisms. Princeton, N. J.: Princeton University Press 1959

ic study of the details of cortical development in the higher primates than has yet been carried out.

In Lecture 5 it was seen that, in the evolution from primate ancestors, the human brain had not only increased greatly in the area of the neocortex but also that large areas had arisen that were minimally represented in Brodmann maps even of an anthropoid ape (Fig. 5-12). These new areas, 39 and 40, are important constituents of the posterior speech area of Wernicke, as illustrated in Figure 7-4. In 95% of adult humans the speech area is on the left side, and correspondingly there is an enlargement of a central zone of the speech area, the planum temporale, on the left side in 65% of human brains (Geschwind, 1972), and this asymmetry is recognizable at birth and even in the 29-week-old foetus (Wada et al., 1975). So there is anatomical evidence that in the human brain speech areas are developed more than a year before they are used.

However, the actual story of speech representation in the brain is initially more tentative. As shown by studies of brain lesions in infants and children, both cerebral hemispheres participate in speech initially (Basser, 1962). Normally the left hemisphere gradually becomes dominant in speech performance, both in interpretation and in expression, presumably because of its superior neurological endowment. Meanwhile, the other hemisphere, usually the right, regresses in respect to speech production, but retains some competence in understanding. This process of speech transfer is usually complete by 4 or 5 years (Kimura, 1967).

As yet our understanding of the cerebral mechanisms of speech is at a very crude level. The arrows in Figure 7-4 show the neural pathways concerned in reading aloud. Presumably there must be very specialised patterns of neuronal connectivity in the speech areas, but as yet there have been only tentative studies of the structure and functioning of these areas. In Lecture 8 there will be an account of the microstructure of the primate neocortex. It cannot even be imagined what changes were evolved in order to provide the immensely complex neural mechanisms that are concerned in the linguistic performance of the human brain.

7.2 Development of the Functional Performance of the Human Brain

At birth a child is an extremely limited organism. It has a considerable reflex performance that is adequate for its survival when carefully tended and fed, and of course a wide range of autonomic responses. The brain is already highly developed with an almost full complement of neurones. However, the complexity of neuronal connectivities is far from being completely established.

My task is to give an account of the manner in which this almost helpless organism at birth becomes in a few years transformed into a human self. It is a route that each of us has traversed, but much of this transcendent adventure is lost beyond recall. At most we have vignettes of our first few years of life. The newborn baby with a consciousness presumably analogous to that of an animal undergoes a transformation into a fully self-conscious human being with its unique selfhood. Brief descriptions of the normal sequences of development will be analysed by reference to deprivation experiments. Human babies cannot of course be experimentally subjected to deprivation; but some studies have been made on the effects of enriched environments. With motor learning it is presumably sufficient to study deprivations in higher mammals such as cats or primates. Such studies may be valuable even in some kinds of cognitive learning. But the higher human functions illustrated in Worlds 2 and 3 of Figure 6-1 can be studied only in human beings. Tragic circumstances have provided examples of deprivations that will be described along with the remarkable recoveries that have been achieved.

7.2.1 Learning of Motor Control

White et al. (1964) have reported a detailed study of the learning of hand and arm movements during the first few months in 34 infants. In most respects their observations parallel earlier reports by Piaget (1953) on 3 infants. At 1–1.5 months a baby can follow a bright object with eye and head movement, but object-oriented arm movements do not occur until 2 months. From this time onwards the infant often fixes its gaze on its hand, and this 'hand-viewing' becomes very common and sustained during the next few months. Evidently there is an on-going learning of visual-kinaesthetic integration. At just over 2 months the first responses are crude swipes at the test object. By 5 months prehensile responses of the hand and arm are fully learnt. The infant can reach for and successfully grasp the test object in one quick direct motion of the hand in an adult-like reaction.

Testing of the hypothesis that motor learning requires visual guidance has been carried out on kittens (Hein and Held, 1967) and on infant monkeys (Held and Bauer, 1967). In both cases the animals were prevented from viewing their limbs and torso during the hours when they were in an illuminated environment. They were in darkness for the remainder of each day. The kittens were raised in darkness for 4 weeks, then for 12 days subsequently they moved freely in an illuminated patterned environment, but were unable to see their limbs or torso, because of a light plastic neck ruff. At the end of this period tests showed that with their forelimbs they were unable to carry out guided reaching for an object seen visually. Eighteen hours of normal freedom provided sufficient visual observations of the moving limbs for the learning of visually guided movements. In similar experiments infant monkeys were kept for 34 days after birth in an apparatus that prevented them from seeing their limbs or torso. On day 35 the monkey was allowed to see one arm during test periods of 1 h each day. Just as with young babies, hand-viewing dominated the test periods day by day, but gradually it declined and reaches for the test object became more frequent and better controlled. By 20 days of this testing both monkeys were proficient in visually guided reaching and grasping. The other forelimb was now exposed to vision, but the same slow procedure was necessary for the learning of its visually controlled movements.

These animal studies reveal that the visual experience of watching the moving limb is necessary for learning the control of its movements. Thus we can postulate that hand-viewing by the child is a necessary preliminary to the control of its arm movements in relation to objects that are visually observed. How then do blind children learn motor control? The answer is that they learn this control in relation to the tactually perceived world. This tactual guidance would of course also occur with normal children, but we may assume that it is overshadowed by the dominant visual input.

When the baby leaves the cot and moves about in the world, first by crawling, then by walking, an immense range of new sensory experiences flood into the brain by visual, tactual and proprioceptive channels. By this exploration the child builds up from the correlation of its movements with its visual experiences a three-dimensional construct of the surrounding world. Of greatest interest to it are the living bodies – persons or animals with their various movements – and of secondary interest are the more fixed structures such as toys, utensils, furniture, which usually move only when manipulated. It is important to recognize that the exploratory learning of a child is dependent on its active movements. For example a child in a perambulator learns nothing of the spatial relations of the world through which it is being pushed.

The most elegant and delightful example of the role of activity in visual learning is provided by the experiments of Held and Hein (1963). After being reared in darkness for 8–12 weeks, litter-mate kittens spend several hours a day in a contraption (Fig. 7-5) which allows one kitten fairly complete freedom to explore its environment actively just as a normal kitten. The other is suspended passively in a gondola, which by a simple mechanical arrangement is moved in all directions by the exploring litter mate so that the gondola passenger experiences the same play of visual imagery as the active kitten, but none of this activity is initiated by the passenger. Its visual world is provided for it just as it is for us on a TV screen. When not in this contraption both kittens are kept with their mother in darkness. After some weeks, tests show that the active kitten has learnt to utilize its visual fields for giving it a valid picture of the external world for the purpose of movement just as well as a normal kitten, whereas the gondola passenger has learnt nothing. One simple example of this difference is displayed by placing the kittens on a narrow shelf, which they can leave either on one side with a small drop, or on the other side with an intimidating fall. Actu-

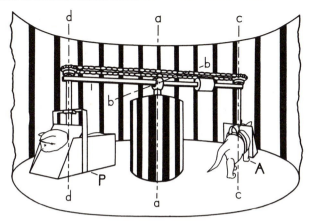

Fig. 7-5. Apparatus for equating motion and consequent visual feedback for an actively moving kitten (*A*) and a passively moved one (*P*). Held, R., Hein, A.: Movement-produced stimulation in the development of visually guided behaviour. J. comp. physiol. Psychol. *56*, 872–876 (1963)

ally a transparent shelf prevents any untoward damage in getting off on the dangerous side. The actively trained kitten always chooses the easy side, the passive chooses either in random manner.

7.2.2 Participation Learning

A wide variety of experimental tests on animals and man by Held and associates and by others corroborates the conclusion that movements must be actively generated if there is to be learning both of motor skills and of the topography of the surrounding world. There is a complete failure with passive movements, for example those generated by the investigator or by contraptions designed for the purpose, as with the gondola kitten (Fig. 7-5).

As a well-trained adult, it is difficult for me to realize that my earliest learning occurred in a cot with the movement of my limbs under visual observation; and thereafter, the field of kinaesthetic and visual education was extended by crawling, walking and still other modes of locomotion, so that my sphere of observation was progressively further enlarged. Thus I would know the dimensions of a visually observed room, because I have crawled, groped, walked and felt all round rooms like it at various stages of my life, and in this way have had my visual impressions built upon these kinaesthetic experiences; and this would be true also for you. I judge distance and space as distance and direction that could be travelled, if I so wish; and so I orientate the world around myself. Thus my three-dimensional perceptual world is essentially a 'kinaesthetic world'. It was initially bounded by the cot, but has thereafter been enormously extended in range and subtlety. The learning processes of early childhood are largely unremembered, but I can remember many early efforts to evaluate distance and size, as well as the errors of judgement that I made, when confronted by strange landscapes and seascapes where familiar clues were lacking.

Fortunately, I do not have to rely only on memories from infancy, for in his book *Space and Sight,* von Senden (1960) quotes well-documented accounts of adults who were given patterned vision for the first time by the removal of congenital cataracts from their eyes. They reported that their initial experiences were meaningless and quite unrelated to the spatial world that had been built up from touch and movement. It took many weeks, and even months, of continual effort to derive from visual experiences a perceptual world that was congruous with their kinaesthetic world, and in which, as a consequence, they could move with assurance.

A further illustration of the way in which learning can transform the interpretation of visual information is provided by Stratton's experiments (1897), in which a system of lenses was placed in front of one of his eyes (the other being covered), so that the image on the retina was inverted with respect to its usual orientation. For several days, the visual world was hopelessly disordered. Since it was inverted, it gave an impression of unreality and was useless for the purpose of apprehending or manipulating objects. But as a result of 8 days of continual effort, the visual world could again be sensed by him correctly, and then became a reliable guide for manipulation and movement. There have been several experimental confirmations of Stratton's remarkable findings, and many additional observations, particularly by Kohler (1951). Subjects with inverted retinal images have even learned to ski, which requires a very accurate correlation of visual with kinaesthetic experiences. These observations and many others of like kind establish that, as a consequence of active or trial-and-error learning, the brain events evoked by sensory information from the retina are interpreted so that they give a valid picture of the external world that is sensed by touch and movement, i. e. my world of visual perception becomes a world in which I can effectively move. Evidently the brain displays a remarkable plasticity in the processing of visual data.

I have considered motor learning at some length because it is of consuming interest to the growing child, which takes great delight in its motor skills. It is incessantly experimenting with new movements, and injoying all manner of vestibulo-kinaesthetic experiences.

Piaget (1973) reports his findings with children of 7–10 who have confused ideas about the volume and weight of different kinds of shapes made from a piece of clay, for example from ball to sausage. Only at 12 does he find that children have a clear idea of weight and volume. I suspect that these were naive children, and that they would have learnt such simple facts much earlier if they had participated by playing with clay and pressing it into all sorts of shapes. As another example of participation learning, I can cite the experiences we all have in learning to interpret the changing appearances of our surround when we experiment with a new kind of movement, e. g. from walking to cycling or to ski-ing or skating. It is essential for survival that correct judgements are made!

7.3 Participation in Culture: The Influence of World 3

7.3.1 Learning of Language

As we all know, even in the first months of life a baby is continually practising its vocal organs and is beginning so to learn this most complex of all motor co-ordinations. It is another variety of motor learning, but now the feedback is from hearing, not from vision. Of course hearing is also concerned in the learning of hand movements, as witness the delight of babies in toys that emit sounds when shaken. Hearing discrimination is developed very early, long before visual discrimination. A week-old baby can already recognize its mother's voice from other voices. Vocal learning is guided by hearing and is at first imitative of sounds heard, and this leads on to the simplest types of words of the type, dada, papa, mama that are produced at about 1 year. It is important to recognise that speech is dependent on the feedback from hearing the spoken words. The deaf are mute. In linguistic development recognition outstrips expression. A child has a veritable word hunger, asking for names and practising incessantly even when alone. It dares to make mistakes devolving from its own rules, as for example with the irregular plurals of nouns. Language does not come about by simple imitation. The child abstracts regularities and relations from what it hears and applies these principles in building up its linguistic expressions.

Lenneberg (1969) has made most interesting observations on 'hearing' children both of whose parents were congenitally deaf. The children heard no language from them and their own vocalizations had no effect in obtaining for them what they wanted. Yet these children began to speak at the usual time and showed normal speech development. Presumably this occurred because the chance encounters outside the home were sufficient guides to learning. From these and related observations Lenneberg (1969) concluded

> ... that language capacity follows its own natural history. The child can avail himself of this capacity if the environment provides a minimum of stimulation and opportunity. His engagement in language activity can be limited by his environmental circumstances, but the underlying capacity is not easily arrested.

To be able to speak given even minimal exposure to speech is part of our biological heritage. This endowment has a genetic foundation, but Lenneberg agrees with Dobzhansky (1967) that one cannot speak of genes for language. On the other hand the genes do provide the instructions for the building of the special areas of the cerebral cortex concerned with language as well as all the subsidiary structures concerned in verbalization. Table 7-1 (Lenneberg, 1969), shows the correlation of motor and language development during the early years of childhood.

It is not my task to present the immense intricacies involved in learning the correct syntactic construction of sentences. I am concerned with the manner in which linguistic communication plays a vital role in the development of the human person. It opens the way to participation in the immense riches of World 3, firstly in nursery stories and rhymes, then in books and pictures of progressively greater sophistication. The understanding of TV requires considerable linguistic competence and doubtless challenges linguistic learning in order to understand the pictures on the screen. However, the child is essentially a passive spectator, not a participant, so TV is a poor educator, lacking as it does the opportunities for participatory learning.

7.3.2 Effect of Deprivation of World 3 Inputs

This account of the factors involved in the normal development of language can be tested against the effects that various kinds and levels of deprivation have on linguistic development. As is well known, children that are deaf at birth or become deaf very early in life never learn to speak. If this deafness is not complete, compensation by specially designed deaf-aid appliances can be remarkably successful in giving language to otherwise deaf-mute children. In Australia N. E. Murray was thus able to save about 90% of the congenitally deaf children born after the rubella epidemic in Australia in 1940. There are anecdotal accounts, even legendary ones, of tests to discover if normal children will come to talk when hearing no speech. The alleged tests by the Egyptian Pharaoh, Psammetichus, by Frederick II of

Table 7-1. Correlation of motor and language development (Lenneberg, 1969)

Age (years)	Motor milestones	Language milestones
0.5	Sits using hands for support; unilateral reaching	Cooing sounds change to babbling by introduction of consonantal sounds
1	Stands; walks when held by one hand	Syllabic reduplication; signs of understanding some words; applies some sounds regularly to signify persons or objects, that is, the first words
1.5	Prehension and release fully developed; gait propulsive; creeps downstairs backward	Repertoire of 3 to 50 words not joined in phrases; trains of sounds and intonation patterns resembling discourse; good progress in understanding
2	Runs (with falls); walks stairs with one foot forward only	More than 50 words; two-word phrases most common; more interest in verbal communication; no more babbling
2.5	Jumps with both feet; stands on one foot for 1 second; builds tower of six cubes	Every day new words; utterances of three and more words; seems to understand almost everything said to him; still many grammatical deviations
3	Tiptoes 3 yards (2.7 meters); walks stairs with alternating feet; jumps 0.9 meter	Vocabulary of some 1000 words; about 80 percent intelligibility; grammar of utterances close approximation to colloquial adult; syntactic mistakes fewer in variety, systematic, predictable
4.5	Jumps over rope; hops on one foot; walks on line	Language well established; grammatical anomalies restricted either to unusual constructions or to the more literate aspects of discourse

Hohenstaufen, by James IV of Scotland and by the Emperor Akbar of India had a similar design, namely the isolation of young children with deaf-mute nurses or nurses forbidden to speak. In general the children did not speak, but made gestures, as would be expected from the similarly circumstanced congenitally deaf children. These children compensate for lack of speech by learning a sign language. It is remarkable how effectively deaf children learn to communicate by such signs, and they gain access to World 3 with the wonderful consequences we shall see later. It is important to recognize that all sign languages are handled in the speech centres exactly as are spoken or written languages. Inputs by hearing, vision and touch gain access to the speech centres by the well-known cortical association and commissural pathways that we shall be considering in the next lecture.

When affliction by blindness is added to deafness, both speech and visual sign language are excluded. There are well-documented accounts of the immense deprivation so suffered by two girls and of the heroic efforts made to overcome this tragic deficiency. Both Laura Bridgman and Helen Keller suffered from complete blindness and deafness before the age of 2, that is, before they had had more than a minimal linguistic experience. For example Helen Keller was stricken at the age of 20 months and could say a few words, which were soon lost in the silent darkness. She lived in the family, being tenderly cared for, but with sensory inputs restricted to touch, smell and taste. She was strong and high spirited but uncontrolled. No attempt was made to communicate with her in a subtle manner until Anne Sullivan came to teach her when she was 6 years and 9 months old. She taught words by tracing them on Helen's hand. The message got through to the young pupil when water was flowing over one hand and *'Water'* was traced on the other, first slowly then faster. It was a veritable revelation. She realized the mystery of language and immediately started to learn multitudes of words and their uses. With her superb enthusiasm and intelligence she became an accomplished scholar and writer and a wonderful human person. We are fortunate to have a detailed documentation by Anne Sullivan, her teacher, and by Helen herself (Keller, 1968). Thus despite linguistic deprivation until she was almost 7 years old Helen Keller was able to overcome the immense handicaps of her sensory deprivation and gain access to World 3, particularly to the literature. She read the classics in the originals and English, German and French literature were subjects for her arts degree. The great interest for our present theme is the transformation wrought in this child by participation in World 3.

There are anecdotal accounts of children brought up in the wild and apparently cared for by wild animals during a significant period of their development. The best authenticated are Caspar Hauser found near Hanover in 1723, Victor the 'wild-boy of Aveyron' found in Southern France in 1799, and Amala and Kamala found in Midnapur, India, in 1920. It appears from the records that these children had no language when rescued. Most were in very precarious health and soon died. The observations made on them are fragmentary and not of value for our present purpose. However, we can conclude that human beings develop normally only when immersed in a good human culture, World 3. Nurture is pre-eminent over Nature.

There are several recent cases of children virtually isolated from cultural contacts, but with one exception the periods were relatively short and the release occurred at a relatively young age. The exception is the girl Genie, who is unique in the whole field of child development (Fromkin et al., 1974; Curtiss, 1977). This last reference is to a comprehensive monograph in which linguistic studies are considered in depth, and also there is an account of the attempts by Dr. Curtiss to make Genie into a sociable human person.

On 4 November 1970, Genie was discovered and taken to a hospital for treatment. She was badly undernourished with a weight of only 25 kg and a height of 1.35 m. She was then 13 years and 7 months old and from the age of 20 months had been confined by her psychotic father to a small room under appalling conditions with no view of the outside world. She was harnessed to an infant's potty chair or in an infant's cot, was fed infant food and minimally cared for. She was punished if she made any noise and was never spoken to. On release she could not stand erect or chew food. She was emaciated and mute. Since release from her prison she has received every possible attention with tender loving care, and has been given the best possible chance to recover from the terrible privation for all those years during which normal children develop into fully formed human beings, both physically and mentally. Genie developed in a remarkable way after November 1970, when her human life began, but there remain tragic limitations in her performance, particularly in language, that probably will never be overcome.

The latest reports give summaries of the recovery during the first 4–5 years:

> She now expresses love, pleasure, and anger; she laughs and cries. She has learned many social skills; she can eat with utensils, chew her food, dress herself, brush her teeth, wash her hair, and tie her shoelaces. She rides a bus to school and sews on a sewing machine. She runs and jumps and throws basket-balls. And she speaks and understands – imperfectly, to be sure. This real life experiment is not finished. We do not yet know the extent of the damage which her isolation and sensory deprivation has wrought. She is still learning, still developing. (Curtiss et al., 1974)

> Genie's language is far from normal. More important however, over and above the specific similarities and differences that exist between Genie's language and the language of normal children, we must keep in mind that Genie's speech is rule-governed behaviour, and that from a finite set of arbitrary linguistic elements she can and does create novel utterances that theoretically know no upper bound. These are the aspects of human language that set it apart from all other animal communication systems. Therefore, abnormalities notwithstanding, in the most fundamental and critical respects, Genie has language. (Curtiss, 1977)

It is of great interest that though right handed, she uses the right hemisphere for speaking. As already stated, in very young children speech is bilaterally represented (Basser, 1962), but normally the left hemisphere gradually assumes dominance and by 4–5 years speech is fully lateralized (Kimura, 1967), being in the left hemisphere in about 95% of people. However, the right hemisphere still retains its competence in understanding, as can be recognized in recent studies on commissurotomy patients

(Zaidel, 1976). Presumably the speech centres of Genie's left hemisphere suffered from a functional atrophy when not used for all those years when they should have been attaining to full development. As a consequence, when Genie was taught language at the very late age of almost 14, the right hemisphere had to do what it could. But there is much syntactic deficiency. For example Genie has never asked one question in all those years, though she understands questions quite well and replies to them. Also during the first 3 years she had difficulty with the negatives 'no' or 'not', that were always placed at the beginning of a sentence. She speaks little and with difficulty, presumably because the extremely complex movements required for movement were not being practised for all those years of enforced mute isolation. For several years she displayed no interest in reading and writing lessons, but at last she has now a limited performance in these respects.

In contrast to her linguistic deficiencies Genie is extremely proficient in functions for which the right hemisphere is normally dominant, such as gestalt pattern recognition and spatial perception. For example on tests for facial recognition she scored far above normal children or adults. It would thus appear that Genie has an extremely efficient right cerebral hemisphere, while left-hemisphere functions are gravely depressed or absent. As Curtiss (1977) states:

> The fact that Genie has right-hemisphere language may be a direct result of the fact that she did not acquire language during the 'critical period' (before puberty). It suggests that after the critical period, the left hemisphere may no longer be able to function in language acquisition, leaving the right hemisphere to assume control. Thus Genie's case supports the 'critical period' hypothesis of Lenneberg (1967).

Figure 7-6 is a drawing that Curtiss (1977) comments on very movingly:

> This drawing is testimony to the importance and strength of the mother-child relationship for all human beings, and to Genie's need for a sense of her own history.
> Early in 1977, filled with loneliness and longing, Genie drew this picture (Fig. 7-6). At first she drew only the picture of her mother and then labelled it 'I miss Mama'. She then suddenly began to draw more. The moment she finished she took my hand, placed it next to what she had just drawn, motioning me to write, and said 'Baby Genie'. Then she pointed under her drawing and said 'Mama hand'. I dictated all the letters. Satisfied she sat back and stared at the picture. There she was, a baby in her mother's arms. She had created her own reality.

We can agree that Genie has become a sensitive human being, which is a wonderful transformation from the pathetic creature of November 1970. It is a most striking example of the creative influence of World 3, which could still be effective even after these many years of deprivation. It is a unique illustration of the resilience and plasticity of the human brain in its relation to the human spirit.

Fig. 7-6. Drawing made by Genie. Full description in text. Curtiss, S.: Genie: A psycholinguistic study of a modern-day "Wild-Child", p. 288. New York: Academic Press 1977

7.4 Interaction of Worlds 2 and 3 in the Creation of the Self

In the development of a human self from infancy, linguistic communication is of pre-eminent significance. In the absence of such communication even the highly gifted Helen Keller remained at a level scarcely human, and Genie was not a human self when discovered at almost 14 years of age. She had at most only one or two fragmentary memories of those long years. Yet linguistic communication transformed Helen Keller into a wonderfully rich and sensitive human being. Genie suffered a much longer and more severe deprivation of all World 3 inputs, including a complete absense of all linguistic experience. The consequent damage to her left hemisphere gravely handicaps her recovery, which probably will never be complete. Nevertheless, she has recovered in an amazing way to be a human self with a good range of emotions and skills. These well-documented cases of deprivation illustrate convincingly the necessity of input from an environment of World 3, and particularly by language, in the development of a normal human self.

Great importance attaches to the mother-baby interrelationship during the first months of infancy. However, I am now considering a later stage of development in which the child gradually learns to recognize what we may call its personal existence. This recognition grows out of an initial solipsism as the child begins to realise the existence of itself and of other selves like itself. At first the child will have an animistic tendency, endowing all sorts of inanimate objects with selfhood, especially dolls and animal toys. Animal pets play a special role in this regard, but eventually are recognized as being different from human beings. In this process of idealogical development language is of the greatest importance, resulting as it does in the growth of the imaginative and descriptive abilities, and later in argumentation with its logical basis.

Popper writes (Popper and Eccles, 1977, Part 1, Sect. 42):

> In all these matters it is the anchorage of the self in World 3 that makes the difference. The basis of it is human language which makes it possible for us to be not only subjects, centres of action, but also objects of our own critical thought, of our own critical judgement. This is made possible by the social character of language; by the fact, that we can speak about other people, and that we can understand them when they speak about ourselves.
>
> The social character of language together with the fact that we owe our status as selves – our humanity, our rationality – to language, and thus to others, seems to me important. As selves, as human beings, we are all products of World 3, which, in its turn, is a product of countless human minds.
>
> I have described World 3 as consisting of the products of the human mind. But human minds react, in their turn, to these products: there is a feedback. The mind of a painter, for example, or of an engineer, is greatly influenced by the very objects on which he is working. And he is also influenced by the work of others, predecessors as well as contemporaries. This influence is both conscious and unconscious. It bears upon expectations, upon preferences, upon programmes. In so far as we are the products of other minds, and of our own minds, we ourselves may be said to belong to World 3.

The emergence and development of self-consciousness (World 2) by continued interaction with World 3 is an utterly mysterious process. It can be likened to a double structure (Fig. 7-7) that ascends and grows by the effective cross-linkages. The vertical arrow shows the passage of time from the earliest experiences of the child up to the full human development. From each World 2 position an arrow leads through the World 3 at that level up to a higher, larger level, which illustrates symbolically a growth in the culture of that individual. Reciprocally the World 3 resources of the self act back to give a higher, expanded level of consciousness of that self (World 2). And so each of us has developed progressively in self-creation. The more the World 3 resources of the individual, the more does it gain in the self-consciousness of World 2. What we are is dependent on the World

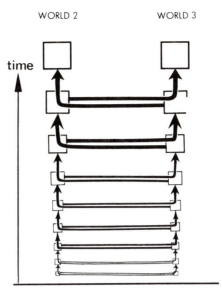

WORLD 2   WORLD 3

time

Fig. 7-7. Diagrammatic representation of the postulated interrelationship of the developments of self-consciousness (World 2) and of culture (World 3) in time as shown by the *arrows*. Full description in text

3 that we have been immersed in and how effectively we have utilized our opportunities to make the most of our brain potentialities.

The brain is necessary but not sufficient for World 2 existence and experience, as is indicated in Figure 10-2 (Popper and Eccles, 1977), which is a dualist-interactionist diagram showing by arrows the flow of information across the interface between the brain in World 1 and the conscious self in World 2. There will be a full treatment of this important diagram in Lecture 10.

The emergence of the self-consciousness of a human individual can be likened to the emergence of self-consciousness in the biological process by which man evolved. In that sense ontogeny recapitulates phylogeny. But in a few years the human infant can accomplish what took evolving man hundreds of millenia. The explanation lies to a large extent in the tremendously enriched World 3 environment. As we have seen with Genie, a human infant deprived of World 3 does not develop. And we do know that, in a greatly impoverished cultural environment, babies mature to become participants in the severe limitations of that culture without knowing of their privation. Yet if moved into a rich World 3 environment, children of primitive people can develop into full participation in that rich World 3 culture.

At this stage it is important to assess our progress in the theme of these lectures – the human mystery. How far have we been able to illuminate this deep problem? In Lectures 4 and 5, our concern was with the biological process of evolution by which chance (genetic mutation) and natural selection have resulted in all the marvellously developed and adapted forms of life. And, especially for our purpose, we were concerned with the evolutionary line through hominids to *H. sapiens* with its wonderful cerebral endowment. Because of this endowment *H. sapiens* was able to bring into existence something radically new and completely unpredictable, namely the world of culture and civilization that is collectively known as World 3, as described in Lecture 6.

Cultural evolution must be sharply distinguished from biological evolution. Biological evolution was necessary to develop brains with the cerebral performance required for culture. The skills deriving from culture such as in language and in tools and weapons were most important in the biological evolution of the hominid line, giving it overwhelming advantage over all other biological species. Yet the sharp distinction must be made. Biological evolution is genetically coded and so is inherited. Cultural evolution is not inherited even to the slightest degree. Each human child builds its own culture from zero, and, in turn it hands on zero to its progeny in the biological process of reproduction. There is no inheritance of acquired characters. Lamarkism is dead.

It may be thought that I have retreated to a purely materialistic position with biological evolution on the one hand and cultural evolution on the other giving a complete explanation of the human self. However, reference to Figure 7-7 shows that World 2, the world of states of consciousness, plays a key role in the formation of the self, and World 2 is the non-material world of the spirit, as is illustrated in Figure 6-1 and 10-2. The brain in World 1 and the world of culture in World 3 are necessary for the development of the conscious self in World 2, but they are not sufficient. Each of us knows the uniqueness of our personal self. The coming-to-be of each unique selfhood lies beyond the field of scientific enquiry (*cf.* Eccles, 1970, Chaps. V and X). It is my thesis that we have to recognize the unique selfhood as being the result of a supernatural creation of what in the religious sense is called a soul. There will be much more on this theme in the second series of lectures.

Lecture 8

Structure of the Neocortex –
Conscious Perception

Synopsis

It has been implicit in the reasoning of the three preceding lectures that the brain is central to the human mystery. We have seen that the brain was developed to its full size by biological evolution, and its development was associated with cultural evolution, with language, the arts and literature. More importantly the transcendental experience of self-consciousness came into existence when the brain had developed to the full human size in Neanderthal man. Hitherto we have considered the brain with little more attention to its structure than if it were a black box. It is now necessary to get inside the black box and to examine in some detail what goes on there in what we may call the neural machinery. Undoubtedly its properties derive from the structure with the connectivities of the ten billion neurones of the neocortex and from the principles of operation of this immensely complicated neuronal machine. The understanding of this machine is now so far advanced that it is possible to base upon it the hypotheses that will be formulated in this lecture and in the next two lectures.

What does conscious perception give us? Firstly it gives some symbolic image of the external world and of ourselves in relation to this world. Secondly it presents our inner states, our muscle contractions and body positions and inner sensations of pain, hunger and thirst. In vision we have the marvellous transmutation of electromagnetic waves or photons to sensations of light and colour. There will be an account of the comprehensive investigations of all stages from the inverted image on the retina to the coding by nerve impulse discharges and the sequential processing of this coded information in the higher centres of the brain. But the transmutation from these immensely complex neuronal happenings to the perceived image remains utterly mysterious. The conversion from neuronal events to the perceived picture has to be learnt not only in its spatial relations, as a flat picture, but also in features such as colour and depth perception, and in all the subtleties of experience that give aesthetic appreciation. This visual learning depends on correlation with other sensations, particularly with the somaesthetic (touch and movement). There is a unity of our perceptual experiences from moment to moment not only from sensory inputs, but also with overtones from emotions and memories.

8.1 Structure of the Neocortex

It has been implicit in the reasoning of the three preceding lectures that the brain is central to the human mystery. We have seen that the brain was developed to its full size by biological evolution, and in its later stages this development was associated with cultural evolution – with language, the arts, the sciences, literature and technology. More importantly the transcendental experience of self-consciousness came into existence when the brain was developed to its full human size in Neanderthal man. Hitherto we have considered the brain with little more attention to its structure than if it was a black box. It is now necessary to get inside the black box and to examine in some detail the neural machinery – both its structure and its operating performance. We shall be concentrating on the cerebral neocortex because it is generally agreed that it is paramount in giving the human mental qualities that will be the principal theme of these last three lectures.

The cerebral neocortex is a peculiarly mammalian structure and undoubtedly represents the highest evolutionary levels of the nervous system. There is good evidence that it developed in evolution from the external striatum that forms the highest level of the reptilian brain (Nauta and Karten, 1970). The special features of the neocortex result from a radical reorganization of nerve cells that are in origin comparable to the cells of the external striatum (*cf.* Fig. 7-3). That reorganization resulted in the laminated structure of the mammalian neocortex that is fairly standardized. The same general features can be observed in the cerebral cortices of all mammals from insectivores to primates. It might seem therefore that the human pre-eminence in mental functions is attributable to the quantity and not to the quality of the human neocortex. But this would be a mistake, as has been recognized already in Lecture 5, where there was seen to be a great development of special areas of the human neocortex, areas 39 and 40 for example, and also of the prefrontal lobes (*cf.* Figs. 5-10, 5-12). Correspondingly the primary sensory and motor cortices (Figs. 5-10 to 5-12) occupy a much smaller area of the neocortex.

8.1.1 General Anatomical Features

The principal anatomical features of the human brain are the two cerebral hemispheres, which are approximately symmetrical and that are linked together by a great commissural structure, the corpus callosum. The hemispheres are intimately connected by enormous tracts of nerve fibres to the next lower levels of the brain, the immense neuronal complexes of the thalamus and basal ganglia (diencephalon). Great ascending and descending pathways, composed of millions of nerve fibres, link the cerebral hemispheres and the thalamus to still lower levels, the mesencephalon, pons, cerebellum, medulla and spinal cord. A detailed description of these path-

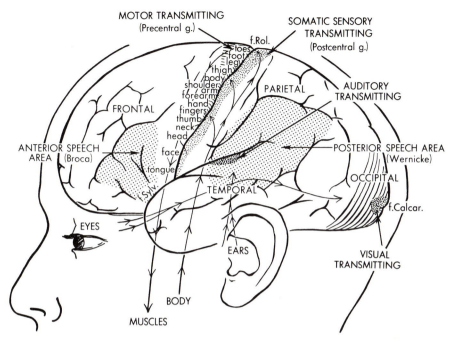

Fig. 8-1. Motor and sensory transmitting areas of the cerebral cortex. The approximate map of the motor transmitting areas is shown in the precentral gyrus, while the somatic sensory receiving areas (*cf.* Fig. 8-9) are in a similar map in the postcentral gyrus. Other primary sensory areas shown are the visual and auditory, but they are largely in areas screened from this lateral view. The frontal, parietal, occipital and temporal lobes are indicated. Also shown are the speech areas of Broca and Wernicke

ways would be out of place here, but there will be reference to some of them in the appropriate sections on perception and control of movement, later in this lecture and in Lecture 10 respectively.

The cerebral hemispheres are the most recently evolved part of the forebrain, hence the designation of the great covering cortex as the neocortex. As indicated in Figure 8-1, the neocortex of each hemisphere is rather arbitrarily subdivided into four lobes, frontal, parietal, temporal, occipital. Originally the older parts of the forebrain, the archicortex and paleocortex, were specifically related to the sense of smell. These older cortices have unique structural features and connections and there will be later reference to their special functions; for example there is the mnemonic role of the hippocampus (Lecture 9) that forms the principal part of the archicortex, and there is the role of other structures of the limbic system that are related to mood and emotion (Lecture 8). For the present, attention will be concen-

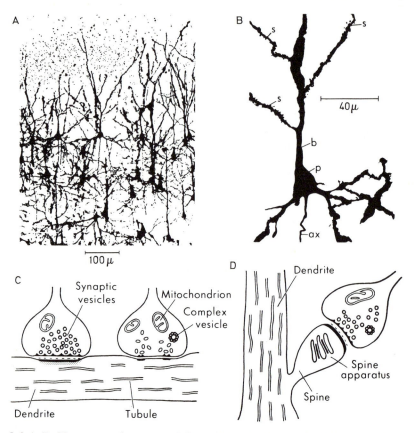

Fig. 8-2 A–D. Neurones and synapses. **A** Pyramidal and stellate cells of the cat visual cortex. **B** Golgi preparation of a neurone from cat cerebral cortex with spines (*s*) shown on apical and basal dendrites, but not on the soma (*p*), axon (*ax*) or dendritic stumps (*b*). **C** Type-1 and a type-2 synapse on a dendrite with the characteristic features described in the text. **D** Dendritic spine of a neocortical pyramidal cell with its spine apparatus and an associated type-1 synapse. Whittaker, V. P., Gray, E. G.: The synapse: Biology and Morphology. Br. Med. Bull. *18*, 223–228 (1962)

trated on the structure of the neocortex. The cerebral hemispheres are composed of the convoluted sheet of the cerebral cortex that covers the whole folded surface, so having the large total area of about 1200 cm² for each hemisphere. The neocortex is about 3 mm thick and is a massive assemblage of neurones, about 10,000 million. As can be seen in Figure 8-1, certain areas of the human neocortex are the specialized receiving sites for inputs from the receptor organs, and also outputs to the motor machinery. These areas make up a very small proportion of the total neocortex of the human brain – about 5%. The sensory inputs will be considered later in this lecture and the outputs in Lecture 10. Our present concern is with the remaining 95% of the neocortex.

The neurones of the cerebral cortex are so densely packed that the individual neurone can be recognized in histological sections only when it is picked out by the extraordinarily fortunate staining procedure discovered by Golgi. For example in Figure 8-2 A only about 1% of the neurones were stained, and several individuals can be recognized with the branching tree-like dendrites and the thin axon (nerve fibre) projecting downwards from the centre of the soma or body. In B there is shown one such pyramidal cell with short spines (s) on the dendrites, but not on the soma (p) or the axon (ax). The dendrites are truncated and are seen to be of two varieties, those arising from the apical dendrite (b) of the pyramidal cell, and those arising directly from the soma (p).

At the end of the nineteenth century it was first proposed by Ramón y Cajal, the great Spanish neuroanatomist, that the nervous system is made up of neurones which are isolated cells, not joined together in some syncytium, but each one independently living its own biological life. This concept is called the neurone theory. How then does a neurone receive information from other nerve cells? This happens by means of the fine branches of the axons of the other neurones that make contact with its surface and end in little knobs scattered all over its soma and dendrites, as indicated in Figure 8-2 C. It was Sherrington's concept also at the end of the nineteenth century that these contact areas are specialized sites of communication, which he labelled synapses from the Greek word *synapto*, which means to clasp tightly (Eccles, 1964, Chap. 1).

Electron microscopy has revealed that the neurone is completely separated from other neurones by its enveloping membrane. At the synapse there is the close contact illustrated in Figure 8-2 C, with separation by the synaptic cleft of about 200 Å. In electrically transmitting synapses the pre-synaptic and postsynaptic membranes are almost in direct contact; nevertheless the integrity of the neuronal membranes is maintained, there being no cytoplasmic fusion.

Transmission in the nervous system occurs by two quite distinct mechanisms. Firstly, there are the brief electrical waves called impulses that travel in an all-or-nothing manner along nerve fibres, often at high velocity. Secondly, there is transmission across synapses. (There is also a decremental transmission for short distances along nerve fibres by a cable-like spread.)

Impulses are generated by a neurone and discharged along its axon when it has been sufficiently excited synaptically. The impulse travels along the axon or nerve fibre and all its branches, eventually reaching synaptic

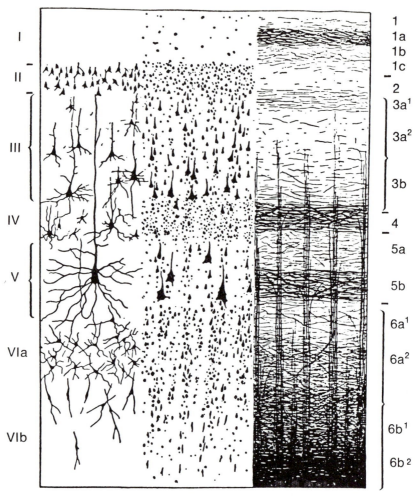

Fig. 8-3. Diagram of the structure of the cerebral cortex. To the left, from a Golgi preparation; centre, from a Nissl preparation; to the right, from a myelin sheath preparation. *I*, lamina zonalis; *II*, lamina granularis externa; *III*, lamina pyramidalis; *IV*, lamina granularis interna; *V*, lamina ganglionaris; *VI*, lamina multiformis. Brodman, K.: Vergleichende Lokalisations-lehre der Großhirnrinde. Leipzig: J. A. Barth 1909

knobs which are the axonal contacts with the somata and dendrites of other neurones. Figure 8-2 C shows the two varieties of synapses, excitatory to the left and inhibitory to the right (Whittaker and Gray, 1962). The former act by tending to cause the recipient neurone to fire an impulse down its axon, the latter act to inhibit this discharge. There are two kinds of neurones, those whose axons form excitatory synapses and those making inhibitory synapses. There are no ambivalent neurones. For a simple account of synaptic action reference is made to Chapter 3 of *The Understanding of the Brain* (Eccles, 1977). Figure 8-2 D shows a synapse formed on the dendritic spine of a pyramidal cell (*cf. s* in Fig. 8-2 B). There is now convincing evidence that all spine synapses are excitatory.

Another powerful technique for investigating synapses is the recording from the interior of nerve cells by fine microelectrodes, which has revealed not only the electrical independence of the neurones but also the mode of operation of synapses. Each neurone has hundreds or even thousands of synapses on its surface and it discharges impulses only when the synaptic excitation is much stronger than the inhibition.

Deep to the cerebral cortex is the white matter that is largely composed of the myelinated nerve fibres, which are the pathways to and from the cerebral cortices. They connect each area of the cerebral cortex to lower levels of the central nervous system, as listed above, or to other areas of the same hemisphere (the association fibres) and of the opposite hemisphere (the commissural fibres). There are about 200 million commissural fibres in the corpus callosum, which is by far the largest system connecting the two hemispheres. All parts of the neocortex have the same basic layered structure of neurones, usually six layers, as indicated in Figure 8-3, but there are structural differences which allow subdivision of the human cerebral hemisphere into over 40 discrete areas, the so-called Brodmann areas, which are depicted in Figures 5-10 A and B for the lateral and medial aspects respectively. Brodmann based his structural analysis on the features shown in the centre and right strips of Figure 8-3. There are many subdivisions of the six laminae and they vary greatly in the different Brodmann areas. This subdivision into Brodmann areas has a functional counterpart, many of the areas having specific physiological properties, as will appear in subsequent chapters. The limbic system can be recognized on the medial surface (Fig. 5-10 B). Areas 23–35 are classified either as in the limbic system or as paralimbic.

8.1.2 Columnar Arrangement and Modular Concept of the Cerebral Cortex

8.1.2.1 Modules Defined by Association and Callosal Fibres

In Figure 8-4 Szentágothai (1978 a) gives a diagrammatic display of the way in which the immense sheet of neocortex is subdivided into a "mosaic of quasi-discrete space units". These space units are the basic anatomical ele-

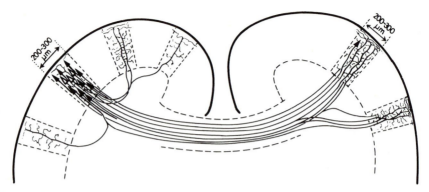

Fig. 8-4. The general principle of cortico-cortical connectivity shown diagrammatically in a non-convoluted brain. The connections are established in highly specific patterns between vertical columns of 200–300 μm diameter in both hemispheres. Ipsilateral connections are derived mainly from cells located in layer III (cells shown at left in *outlines*), while contralateral connections (cells shown in *full black*) derive from all layers II–VI. The diagram does not try to show the convergence from afferents originating from different parts of the cortex to the same columns, Szentágothai, J.: The neuron network of the cerebral cortex: A functional interpretation. Proc. R. Soc. (Lond.) B, *201*, 219–248 (1978a)

ments in the functional design of the neocortex. In the left of Figure 8-4 the closely packed pyramidal cells are shown in one such module or column, which has a width of about 250 μm. The axons from these pyramidal cells project to three other modules of that same hemisphere and, after traversing the corpus callosum, to two modules of the other hemisphere. Thus we have simply displayed the association and the callosal projections of the pyramidal cells of a module.

We should notice several important features of Figure 8-4, which is based on the beautiful radio-labelling experiments of Goldman and Nauta (1977). Firstly, several pyramidal cells of a module may project in a *completely overlapping manner* to other modules which are so defined and are again about 250 μm across. In Figure 8-4 this dimension is already represented by the branches of a single association fibre for two modules and the overlapping distribution is illustrated for two association fibres and for four and five callosal fibres. Secondly, the callosal projection is mostly, but not entirely, to symmetrical modules on the contralateral side. Thirdly, there is reciprocity of callosal connection between symmetrical modules.

In order to gain some insight into the manner of operation of this neuronal machine, we have to recognize that Figure 8-4 is greatly simplified. In the first place there are about 2500 neurones in a module 250 μm across, at least 1000 of which are pyramidal cells. On the basis of the fibre count for the corpus callosum, 200 million with 100 million in each direction, there would be about 50 pyramidal cells projecting from one module to make callosal afferents to the other side, instead of the 6 in Figure 8-4. On an estimate of 10 times as many association fibres as callosal fibres, there would be 500 pyramidal cells as association projectors instead of the 3 in Figure 8-4. Thus there would be a much more intense convergence of inputs from any one module than is represented in Figure 8-4, and also probably dispersion to many more modules.

But, even if this massive addition were made to Figure 8-4, the diagram would give the situation of connectivities for only a moment of time. If we assume a strong excitation of the primary module in Figure 8-4 with a powerful burst of impulse discharges from the constituent pyramidal cells, there will be within a few milliseconds strong excitatory inputs into many other modules by the association and callosal projections. Some of these secondary modules in turn will be excited sufficiently to discharge to tertiary modules, and these in turn to quaternary. So we have in effect a spreading pattern of excitation that is not random, but strictly specified by the sequential projections from the secondary, tertiary, etc. modules in this particular instance. There are approximately 4 million modules in the human neocortex, so there are immense possibilities for developing spatio-temporal patterns even on the simple assumption that each module operates as a unit in its reception and projection. However, there is certainly a gradation of the responses of the pyramidal cells in a module, which is exhibited by the wide range in their firing frequencies, as reported by many investigators.

8.1.2.2 Specific Afferent Fibres from the Thalamus

We now leave this attempt at an imaginative description of the sequential patterns of neocortical operation in response to one strongly excited module, and consider the much more investigated input of the specific (thalamic) afferents from some sensory system. In Figure 8-5 Szentágothai (1978b) presents a very simple diagram of a specific afferent fibre branching in lamina IV to make excitatory synaptic contacts on the basal dendrites of one pyramidal cell and on a spiny stellate cell. Cell Sst in turn makes a special type of powerful excitatory synapse on the apical dendrites of two pyramidal cells forming at the top of the figure a most interesting synaptic organ for powerful excitation, called a *cartridge*. There will be much reference to cartridge-type synapses in the next lecture (Fig. 9-8). Also shown in black are two inhibitory interneurones that will be illustrated more exten-

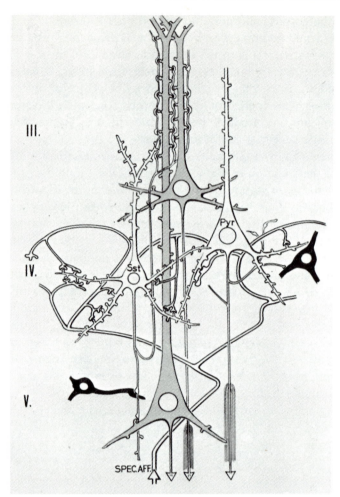

Fig. 8-5. The direct excitatory neurone circuit of the specific (sensory) afferents (*Spec. aff.*), as can be deduced from evidence that is, so far, available. Both spiny stellate (*Sst*, with ascending main axon) and true pyramid cells (*Pyr*) are monosynaptically contacted. Inhibitory inter-neurones (*black*) may be contacted only di-synaptically over the axon collaterals of the mono-synaptic target cells. Apical dendrites of both lamina III and V pyramidal cells (*stippled*) are probably the main targets (over multiple cartridge type synapses) of the ascending axons of the spiny stellate cartridge cells. Szentágothai, J.: Local neuron circuits of the neocortex. In: The Neurosciences: 4th Study Program. Cambridge (Mass.): MIT Press 1978b

sively in Figures 8-7 and 8-8. For our present purpose Figure 8-5 shows that the specific afferent fibre branches profusely in lamina IV to make many synapses, but not synapses on inhibitory interneurones.

In Figure 8-6 Szentágothai (1978a) contrasts the two types of input into the neocortex. There is firstly the ASSOC. CALL. AFF. (*cf.* Fig. 8-4) that branches in all laminae except IV, making many synaptic contacts within its module. Finally in lamina I it bifurcates to form a long fibre parallel to the surface that may go as far as 3 mm in each direction, making numerous synaptic contacts with the branching apical dendrites of pyramidal cells (*cf.* Figs. 8-8 and 9-8). In contrast the SPEC. AFF. branches profusely in lamina IV, making excitatory synapses on cell SS2 (like Sst in Fig. 8-5) that forms a cartridge 30 μm in diameter, which would embrace apical dendrites of pyramidal cells (Figs. 8-5, 9-8). In addition the SPEC. AFF. excites a neurone SS1, which in turn excites a cell CDB (*cellule á double bouquet*) also by a kind of cartridge and CDB gives a long double 'horsetail' set of fibres only about 10 μm in diameter. Another cell, MG (neurogliform type) also gives a descending bunch of fibres. Figure 8-6 is designed to show that the SPEC. AFF. synapses are in a disc in lamina IV, but, on the next synaptic relay, the SPEC. AFP. input is converted into powerful excitatory influences in a column or module extending right across the laminae, except for lamina I. Thus we have to regard the module as being designed for an amplification of the excitatory input, i. e. it is designed for power. Figure 8-6 further shows that the SPEC. AFF. disc in lamina IV may not be in register with the ASSOC. CALL. AFF. column. There is as yet no good evidence on this point. However, operational considerations would be simplified if in fact there were an approximate in-register relationship of the two kinds of cortical modules. They have much the same crosssectional area, though with the primary visual cortex the shape of the cortical unit for specific afferent input is a narrow slab, rather than a column (Fig. 8-13).

8.1.2.3 Cortical Inhibition

The connectivities that give the modular pattern of quasidiscrete space units are the synaptic excitatory actions. These may be induced either by the primary input to that element of the cortex, as with the association callosal modules (Fig. 8-4), or by the secondary and tertiary excitatory actions of the specific afferent input (Fig. 8-6). An important additional influence is exerted by the inhibitory interneurones that act to limit excitatory synaptic action. In part they are distributed to pyramidal cells of adjacent modules; hence they would have a sculpturing action, tending to sharpen the bound-

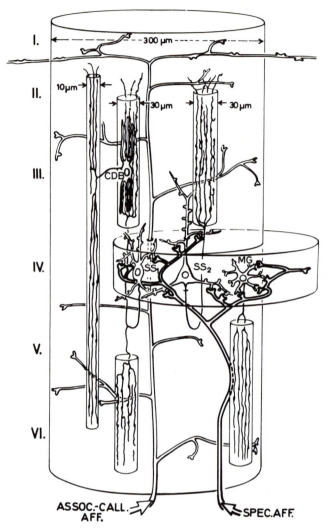

Fig. 8-6. Modular arrangement of excitatory connections and of assumed excitatory inter-neurones. The large cylinder of 300 μm diameter corresponds to the space of termination of a corticocortical (ipsilateral association or contralateral callosal) afferent, apart from lamina I, where the horizontal spread of the terminal branches may be considerably larger. The flat cylinder of the same diameter would correspond to the termination space of a specific (sensory) afferent. Two different types of spiny stellates are shown as monosynaptic target cells of the specific afferents: ss_1 has both an ascending and a descending axonal strand, while ss_2 has only one ascending strand. Neurogliform cells (*MG*) have more generally descending axon strands of similar diameter (around 30 μm). A typical "cellule a double bouquet" (*CDB*) of Ramón y Cajal is shown at upper left, giving rise to a long vertical axon strand of even smaller diameter. The diagram attempts to illustrate a possible mechanism for the selection of individual pyramidal cells, from the relatively widely distributed afferent input, over their apical dendrites embedded into the terminal axon strands of excitatory interneurones. Szentágothai, J.: The neuron network of the cerebral cortex: A functional interpretation. Proc. R. Soc. (Lond.) B, *201*, 219–248 (1978a)

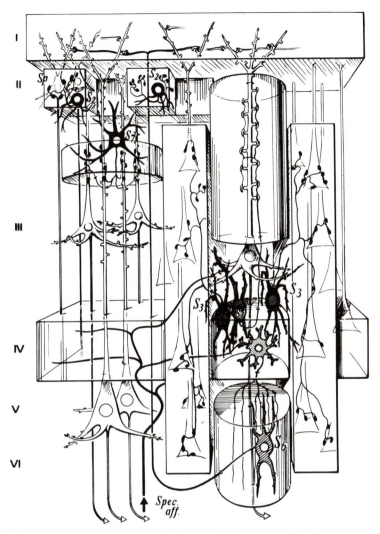

Fig. 8-7. Three-dimensional construct showing cortical neurones of various types and the endings of a specific afferent fibre as in Fig. 8-5. There are two pyramidal cells in lamina V and three in lamina III, one being shown in detail in a column. In this column there are two inhibitory cells (S_3) with axons making basket-like synapses on shadowy pyramidal cells in two adjacent cortical slabs that are shown in perspective. In lamina II there are two stellate-pyramidal cells (Sp) and two small inhibitory cells (S_2). S_1 is a spiny stellate cell whose axon forms a cartridge synapse around the apical dendrite of the pyramidal cell (*cf*. Fig. 8-5). Just below S_1 is a neurogliform cell (*MG* of Fig. 8-6) with a descending axon to the Martinotti cell (S_6) whose axon ascends to bifurcate in lamina I. S_7 is a chandelier cell with inhibitory endings on apical dendrites of pyramidal cells. Szentágothai, J.: The module-concept in cerebral cortex architecture. Brain Res. *95*, 475–496 (1975)

aries of a module. However, some have finer discriminative influences within the module. For example in Figure 8-7 the axons of two inhibitory neurones labelled S3 form synapses on the bodies of the pyramidal cells that are adjacent to that which is fully diagrammed with a cartridge assemblage on its apical dendrite from the spiny stellate cell S1. There are other inhibitory neurones, S2 in lamina II, that have a more localized action, perhaps giving a finer grain to the modular responses of the stellate pyramidal cells Sp of lamina II. Another interesting inhibitory interneurone is S7, whose axon terminates in a multitude of synapses on the apical dendrites of four pyramidal cells.

It should be noted in passing that the neurogliform cell of lamina IV has a profusely branched axon (*cf.* MG in Fig. 8-6), which gives multiple synapses to the Martinotti cell (S6), whose axon curves to ascend to lamina I, where it bifurcates. The two branches run parallel to the surface and give synapses to the bifurcated terminals of the apical dendrites of the pyramidal cells, exactly as is done by the bifurcated axons of the association and callosal fibres (Figs. 8-6, 8-8, 9-8).

8.1.3 Summary on Cortical Modules

Figure 8-8 provides a diagrammatic summary of the essential components of the neocortex together with the excitatory and inhibitory synaptic connections, the former being diagrammed in the right half, the latter in the left half. Centrally there is the module formed by the branches of the cortico-cortical (assoc. cal.) afferent that defines a columnar module of about 300 μm across (*cf.* Fig. 8-6). On either side are two discs in lamina IV formed by the terminals of the two specific afferent fibres that are not in register with the cortico-cortical module and that build up modules extending from laminae VI to II by secondary excitatory action, as is also illustrated in Figure 8-6.

In discussion of the functional operation of the neocortex there has been a tendency to neglect the dense meshwork of horizontal fibres in lamina I and the upper part of lamina II (*cf.* Mountcastle, 1978). As we have seen (*cf.* Fig. 9-8), these fibres have three origins; as the bifurcating terminals of the association fibres and of the commissural fibres (Figs. 8-6, 8-8) and of the Martinotti cell axons (Fig. 8-7). The former provide a wide range of inputs from both hemispheres, the latter an input from the local modules. Since the average length of these fibres is at least 5 mm, they will provide a mechanism for wide diffusion of the input to the apical dendrites of the

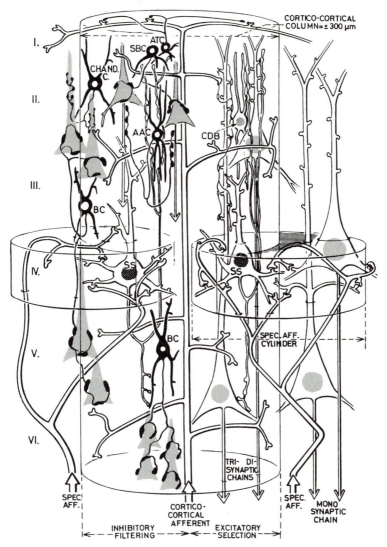

Fig. 8-8. Diagram illustrating a single cortico-cortical column and two specific subcortical afferent arborization cylinders. Lamination is indicated on the left margin. The right half of the diagram indicates impulse processing over excitatory neurone chains, while the left half shows various types of inhibitory interneurones (*full black*). Further explanation in the text. Szentágothai, J.: The local neuronal apparatus of the cerebral cortex. In: Cerebral correlates of conscious experience. Buser P., Buser, A. (eds.), pp. 131–138. Amsterdam: Elsevier Press 1978c

pyramidal cells of any one module. Admittedly the synaptic excitatory power will not be strong for synapses so remote from the impulse-generating sites, which are probably in the soma and main stem of the apical dendrite. However, there is opportunity for a large convergence onto the 2000 or so synapses in laminae I and II on a single pyramidal cell (Szentágothai, 1975), and in any case the function of these synapses is not to be impulse generators, but rather to act in a more subtle way as modulators of the discharge frequency of the pyramidal cell, as will be suggested in Lecture 10.

There has been speculation concerning the possible subdivision of the basic modules that are depicted in Figures 8-4, 8-6 and 8-8. For example Mountcastle (1978) postulates a much smaller unit, a mini-column of about 30 μm across, and Szentágothai (1978a) suggests that there is an ultimate refinement of a module by interaction of its internal excitatory and inhibitory interneurones to give a high degree of individuality in output, even to a single pyramidal cell. I prefer to consider the whole module as a processing unit with many output lines in parallel, so that there will be effective synaptic excitation on the modules to which it projects (*cf.* Fig. 8-4).

It has already been suggested that a module has to be regarded as a power unit. Its raison d'être is to build up power at the expense of its neighbours. We think the nervous system always works by conflict – in this case by conflicts between each module and the adjacent modules. Each one is trying to overcome the other one by building up its own power by all the vertical connections which Ramón y Cajal and Lorente de Nó first described and by the projection of inhibition out to the neighbouring modules (Szentágothai, 1969; Marin-Padilla, 1970). That functional discriminatory action is really what makes a module. A module is a unit because it has a system of internal power generation and around it is the delimitation secured by its inhibitory action on the adjacent modules. Of course each of these modules in turn has its own intrinsic power and it is fighting back with a counter-inhibition to its surrounding modules. Nowhere is there uncontrolled excitation. There is an immense power interaction of excitation and inhibition. It is in this continuous interaction that we have to think of the subtlety of the whole neuronal machine of the human cerebral cortex, composed perhaps of about 4 million modules each with about 2500 component neurones. We can only dimly imagine what is happening in the human cortex or indeed in the cortices of the higher mammals, but it is at a level of complexity, of dynamic complexity, immeasurably greater than anything else that has ever been discovered elsewhere in the universe or created in computer technology.

This conflict between the excitation and inhibition is actually giving all of the variation of performance from moment to moment; and superimposed on that at the level of laminae I and II there is the finer grain of inhibition (Fig. 8-7). It is of finer grain because the inhibitory cells have shorter axons, only inhibiting closely adjacent cells, not the more remote inhibitory action of the inhibitory cells of the deeper laminae that project to adjacent modules (Fig. 8-7). Besides this finer inhibitory grain the synaptic action is much more subtle, because in laminae I and II the synaptic excitatory power is very low, but on the other hand it is widely dispersed. There has to be a lot of convergence here because the excitatory synapses are scattered on the spines of the branching apical dendrites remote from the impulse-generating sites in the somata or in the adjacent dendrites and axon (*cf.* Szentágothai, 1972, 1974). There is not this powerful cartridge type of synapse along the apical dendrites of the pyramidal cell that is such a prominent feature of the deeper laminae. So we regard the synaptic influences of laminae I and II as exerting a more subtle and gentle modulating influence. It is of great interest that this proposed modulating influence is mostly exerted by the association and callosal afferent fibres. These afferents come from the pyramidal cells of other relatively remote modules (Fig. 8-4), and so you can think that other modules work upon this module at this gentle level and this module in turn is also working back on them at this same level (*cf.* Lecture 10).

It will be suggested in Lecture 10 that this gentle and subtle level of synaptic action in laminae I and II gives opportunity for the influence from the self-conscious mind to gain expression by bringing about slight changes in the impulse firing patterns of pyramidal cells. Meanwhile, we can marvel at the wonderful process of biological evolution that has built in the brain of *H. sapiens* a structure with such a fantastic sensitivity that the closedness of World 1 is transcended so that it is open to the world of conscious experience, as we shall propose in Lecture 10.

8.2 Conscious Perception

Let us start with the question: What does conscious perception give us? Firstly, it gives us some symbolic image of the external world and of ourselves in relation to this world. Such qualities as light, colour, distance, spatial relations, sounds and smells participate in this symbolic image. Secondly, it presents our inner states, our muscle contractions with joint positions and inner sensations such as pain, sex, hunger and thirst. In vision, we have the marvellous transmutation of electromagnetic waves or photons to sensations of light and colour. In hearing, pressure waves in the atmosphere are transmuted into sound with language and melody. It is proposed to give a general scientific account before entering upon the philosophical considerations relating to our theme, the human mystery.

There are certain principles relating to the neural events that lead to perceptions of the various sensory experiences. Touch and vision have been most thoroughly investigated, but there is good reason to believe that all other sensory experiences are dependent upon similar neuronal mechanisms. Necessarily the crucial experimental investigations of sensory experiences must be carried out on conscious human subjects, but both the design and interpretation of these experiments are dependent on the wonderful successes that have attended investigations on animal, and particularly monkey, sensory systems in the last few decades. The powerful techniques designed for precision and selectivity of stimulation have been matched by microelectrode recording from single neurones. But, just as importantly, there has been the success in defining by precise anatomical investigations the neural pathways from receptor organs to cerebral cortex and within the cerebral cortex.

There is a large variety of these receptor organs with built-in properties that enable them to encode in a highly selective manner some environmental change into a discharge of nerve impulses. In general it can be stated that intensity of stimulus is encoded as frequency of discharge of impulses. In this way there are transmitted to the higher levels of the central nervous system signals from receptor organs that result in the conscious experiences of vision, hearing and touch, for example. An introduction to the problem of conscious perception is best given in relation to cutaneous sensing. In the skin are receptor organs specialized for converting some mechanical stimulus, such as a touch or tap, into impulse discharges in nerve fibres.

The pathways from receptor organs to the brain are never direct. There are always synaptic linkages from neurone to neurone at each of several relay stations. Each of these stages gives the opportunity for modifying the coding of the 'messages' from the sensory receptors. Even the simplest stimuli such as a flash of light or a tap on the skin are signalled to the appropriate primary receiving area of the cerebral cortex in the form of a code of nerve impulses in various temporal sequences and in many fibres in parallel.

Our special interest is focussed on the neural events that are necessary for giving a conscious experience. It is now generally agreed that a conscious experience does not light up as soon as impulses in some sensory pathway reach the primary sensory areas in the cerebral hemisphere. In response to some brief peripheral stimulus the initial reaction is a sharp potential change, the evoked response, in the appropriate primary cortical area. Immediately afterwards there is a change in the background frequency of firing of numerous neurones in this area – an increase or a decrease, or some complex temporal sequence thereof. Our present problem is to gain some insight into the neural events that have a necessary relationship to conscious experiences.

8.2.1 Cutaneous Perception (Somaesthesis)

Figure 8-9 is a diagram of the simplest pathway from receptor organs in the skin up to the cerebral cortex. For example, a touch on the skin causes a receptor to fire impulses. These travel up the dorsal columns of the spinal cord (the cuneate tract for the hand and arm) and then, after a synaptic relay in the cuneate nucleus and another one in the thalamus, the pathway reaches the cerebral cortex. There are only two synapses on the way and you might say, why have any at all? Why not have a direct line? The point is that each one of these relays gives an opportunity for an inhibitory action that sharpens the neuronal signals by eliminating all the weaker excitatory actions, such as would occur when the skin touches an ill-defined edge. In this way a much more sharply defined signal eventually comes up to the cortex and there again there would be the same inhibitory sculpturing of the signal by the modular interaction (*cf.* Figs. 8-7, 8-8). As a consequence touch stimuli can be more precisely located and evaluated. In fact, because of this inhibition a strong cutaneous stimulus is often surrounded by a cutaneous area that has reduced sensitivity.

Also shown in Figure 8-9 are the pathways down from the cerebral cortex to both of these relays on the cutaneous pathway. In this way, by exerting presynaptic and postsynaptic inhibition, the cerebral cortex is able to block these synapses and so protect itself from being bothered by cutaneous stimuli that can be neglected. This is of course what happens when you are very intensely occupied, for example in carrying out some action or in experiencing or in thinking. In such situations you can be oblivious even of severe stimulation. For example, in the heat of combat severe injuries may be ignored. At a less severe level it has long been a practice to give counter-irritation to relieve pain. Presumably in this way there is produced inhibitory suppression of the pain pathway to the brain. Thus we can account for the afferent anaesthesias of hypnosis or of yoga or of acupuncture by the

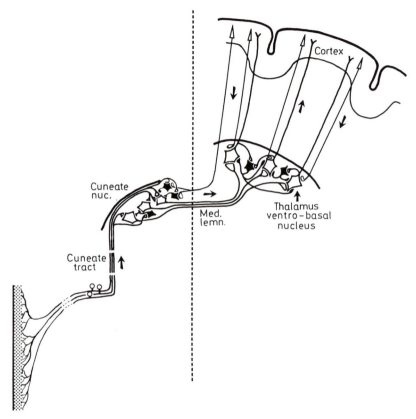

Fig. 8-9. Pathway to the sensorimotor cortex for cutaneous fibres from the forelimb. Note the inhibitory cells shown in black in both the cuneate nucleus and the ventro-basal nucleus of the thalamus. The inhibitory pathway in the cuneate nucleus is of the feed-forward type and in the thalamus it is the feed-back type. Also shown is one presynaptic inhibitory pathway to an excitatory synapse of a cuneate tract fibre. Efferent pathways from the sensorimotor cortex are shown exciting the thalamocortical relay cells and exciting both postsynaptic and presynaptic inhibitory neurones in the cuneate nucleus

cerebral and other pathways inhibiting the cutaneous pathways to the brain. In all these cases discharges from the cerebral cortex down the pyramidal tract and other pathways will exert an inhibitory blockage at the relays in the spinocortical pathways such as those diagrammed in Figure 8-9. This ability of the cerebral cortex is important because it is undesirable to have all receptor organ discharges from your body pouring into your brain all the time. The design pattern of successive synaptic relays each with various central and peripheral inhibitory inputs gives opportunity for turning off inputs according to the exigencies of situations.

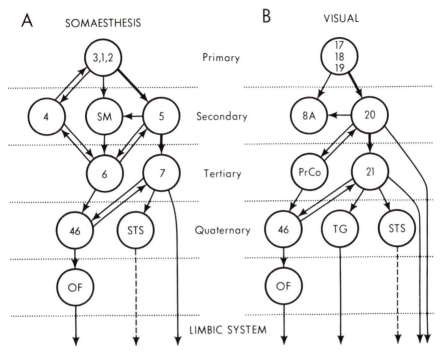

Fig. 8-10 A, B. Diagrammatic representation of cascade of connectivities for the somaesthetic (**A**) and visual (**B**) systems in the cerebrum. The numbers refer to the Brodmann areas (Fig. 5-10); the other areas are: *SM,* supplementary motor; *STS,* superior temporal sulcus; *PrCo,* precentral agranular; *TG,* temporal pole; *OF* orbital surface frontal lobe (*cf.* Jones and Powell, 1970)

Conventional studies on animals and man have defined the area of cortex that is primarily involved in responding to cutaneous sense, the somaesthetic area. As shown in Figure 8-1, the principal area is laid out as a long strip map in the postcentral gyrus, which is made up of three areas (Brodmann areas 3, 1, 2 in Fig. 5-10) distinguished by their different structures. All areas of the body surface from the extreme caudal to the extreme rostral lie in linear sequence along the postcentral gyrus from its dorsomedial end over the convex surface of the cerebral hemispheres. Area 3b is specialized for light touch and areas 1 and 2 for deep stimuli, skin pressure and joint movement, while area 3a is concerned with muscle sense (Jones and Powell, 1973).

So far we have considered the projection of the afferent fibres to the primary sensory cortex (Fig. 8-1), which would be by the specific afferents of Figures 8-5 to 8-8. The powerful excitatory amplification in the modules would result in the discharge of pyramidal cells that project to modules in other parts of the neocortex on the ipsilateral side, as indicated in Figure 8-4. With cutaneous inputs the first relay from the primary sensory cortex (Brodmann areas 3, 1, 2) is to area 5, and thence to area 7 (*cf.* Fig. 8-10), where more synthetic responses are generated (Mountcastle et al., 1975).

The responses of most neurones are related to the bringing about of movements in a holistic manner, the details of the movements being left to the motor areas, as will be described in Lecture 10. The neuronal machinery of area 5 contains a continually updated neuronal replicate of the position and movements of the limb in space. Complex stimulus patterns involving multiple joint and skin areas trigger responses of neurones that presumably are concerned in the synthetic sensing that occurs when an object is palpated. In palpation there is first the shaping of the hand for grasping an object, and secondly the moving of the hand over the surface of the object in an active exploration. In this way cutaneous sensing leads to feature detection that matches the visual feature detection in the inferotemporal lobe, as described below. Area 7 is also related to visual inputs (Mountcastle et al., 1975).

Figure 8-10 A shows diagrammatically the main sequential projection for the somatosensory system, where the numbers refer to the Brodmann areas of Figure 5-10. These projections would occur from module to module as in Figure 8-4. Thus a sensory input is widely distributed, giving specific patterns in the neocortex, which would also be transferred to the contralateral side by the callosal connectivities. The projections to the limbic system in Figure 8-10 A and to the prefrontal cortex (46 and OF) are of importance in memory, as will be described in Lecture 9.

8.2.2 Visual Perception

Highly complicated and exquisitely designed structures are involved in all steps of the visual pathways. The optic system of the human eye gives an image on the retina which is a sheet of closely packed receptors, some 10^7 cones and 10^8 rods, that feed into the complexly organized neuronal system of the retina. Thus the first stage in visual perception is a radical fragmentation of the retinal picture into the independent responses of a myriad of punctate elements, the rods and cones. In some quite mysterious way the retinal picture appears in conscious perception, but nowhere in the brain can there be found neurones that respond specifically to even a small zone

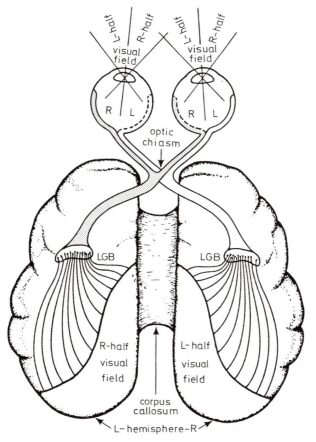

Fig. 8-11. Diagram of visual pathways showing the left-half and right-half visual fields with the retinal images and the partial crossing in the optic chiasma so that the right-half of the visual field of each eye goes to left visual cortex, after relay in the lateral geniculate body (*LGB*), and correspondingly for left visual field to right visual cortex

of the retinal image or the observed picture. The neuronal machinery of the visual system of the brain has been shown to accomplish a very inadequate reconstitution that can be traced in many sequences.

The initial stage of reconstitution of the picture occurs in the complex nervous system of the retina. As a consequence of this retinal synthetic mechanism the output in the million or so nerve fibres in each optic nerve is not a simple translation of the retinal image into a corresponding pattern of impulse discharges that travel to the primary visual centre of the brain, Brodmann area 17 (Figs. 5-10 and 8-11). Already in the nervous system of the retina there has begun the abstraction from the richly patterned mosaic of responses by the retinal receptor units into elements of pattern, which we may call features, and this abstraction continues in the many successive stages that have now been recognized in the visual centres of the brain (Fig. 8-10 B).

The complex interactions in the retinal nervous system eventually are expressed by the retinal ganglion cells that discharge impulses along the optic nerve fibres and so to the brain. These cells respond particularly to spatial and temporal changes in the luminosity of the retinal image by two neuronal subsystems signalling brightness and darkness respectively. The brightness contrasts of the retinal image are converted into contoured out-lines by several neuronal stages of information processing. One type of ganglion cell is excited by a spot of light applied to the retina over it and is inhibited by light on the surrounding retina. The other type gives the reverse response, inhibition by light shone into the centre and excitation by the surround. The combined responses of these two neuronal subsystems result in a contoured abstraction of the retinal image in the visual cortex. Hence what the eye tells the brain by the million fibres of the optic nerve is an abstraction of brightness and colour contrasts.

As illustrated in Figure 8-11, the optic nerves from each eye meet in the optic chiasma where there is a partial crossing. The hemi-retinas of both eyes (nasal of right and temporal of left) that receive the image from the right visual field (R) have their optic nerve projections rearranged in the chiasma so that they coalesce to form the pathway to the left visual cortex, and vice versa for the left visual field (L) projecting to the right visual cortex. Thus, with the exception of a narrow vertical (meridional) strip of the visual field that is directly in the line of vision, the visual imagery of the right and left fields comes to the left and to the right visual cortices respec-tively (Fig. 8-11) to form an ordered map, much as with the cortical map for cutaneous sensation (Fig. 8-1). There is of course topographic distortion. The fine visual sensing in the centre of the visual field results from a much more amplified cortical projection area than for the retina concerned with peripheral vision.

The visual systems of mammals such as cat and monkey have been subjected to a multitude of refined electrophysiological and behavioural studies during the last two decades. A brief description of these findings is essential before we undertake the task of trying to understand the way in which our brains give us visual experiences.

In the lateral geniculate body (LGB in Fig. 8-11), there is but little further sorting or synthesis. For example, a bright line in the visual field is

Orientational responses of neurone visual cortex

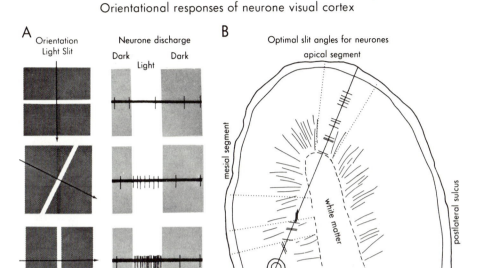

Fig. 8-12 A, B. Orientational responses of neurones in primary visual cortex of cat. Full description in text. Hubel, D. H., Wiesel, T. N.: Receptive fields, binocular interaction and functional architecture in the cat's visual cortex. J. Physiol. (Lond.) *160*, 106–154 (1962)

coded as a linear arrangement of excited neurones that project onto the stellate cells in lamina IV of the primary receiving area of the visual cortex (area 17). These neurones (called simple cells) are the first cortical stage in reassembly of the retinal image. They respond to a bright line in the retinal image and are selective to the orientation of this line. Moving bright lines are particularly effective.

In Figure 8-12 A there is a simple cell firing impulses, having been 'found' by a microelectrode inserted into the primary visual cortex of the cat. The track of insertion is shown for example in Figure 8-12 B as the sloping line with short transverse lines indicating the locations of many neurones along that track. With the microelectrode you can record extracellularly the impulse discharges of a single cell if you position it carefully. The cell has a slow background discharge (upper trace of Fig. 8-12 A), but, if the retina is swept with a band of light, as illustrated in the diagram to the left, there is an intense discharge of that cell when light sweeps across a certain zone of the retina, and there is immediate cessation of the discharge as the light band leaves the zone (lowest trace of Fig. 8-12 A). If you rotate the orientation of sweep, the cell discharges just a little, as in the middle trace.

Finally, if the sweep is at right angles to the most favourable orientation, it has no effect whatever (uppermost trace). It is a sign that this particular cell is most sensitive for movements of the light strip in one orientation and is quite insensitive for movements at right angles thereto. As illustrated by the direction of the lines drawn across the microelectrode track in Figure 8-12B, all cells along that track have the same orientational sensitivity. This is found when the track runs down a column of cells that is orthogonal to the surface, as in the upper group of 12 cells. However, in Figure 8-12B, the track continued on across the central white matter and then proceeded to pass through three groups of cells with quite different orientation sensitivities.

In the visual cortex, neurones with similar orientation sensitivity tend to be arranged in columns that run orthogonally from the cortical surface. Thus it can be envisaged that, in the large area of the human primary visual cortex, the population of about 400 million neurones is arranged as a mosaic of columns, each with some thousands of neurones that have the same orientation sensitivity (Hubel and Wiesel, 1963; Hubel, 1963). This arrangement can be regarded as the first stage of reconstitution of the retinal image. It will of course be recognized that this orientation map is superimposed on the retinal field map, each zone of this field being composed of columns that collectively represent all orientations of bright lines or of edges between light and dark.

It has already been shown in Figure 8-11 that both the ipsilateral and contralateral eyes project to the LGB on the way to the visual cortex. However in the primate these projections are relayed in separate laminae, three for the ipsilateral (2i, 3i, 5i) and three for the contralateral eye (1c, 4c, 6c) (Fig. 8-13). The projection to the columns of area 17 is illustrated in highly diagrammatic form in Figure 8-13 (Hubel and Wiesel, 1972, 1974). The ipsilateral and contralateral laminae of the LGB are shown projecting to alternating columns, the ocular dominance columns. Orthogonally the columns are defined by the orientation specificities as indicated in Figure 8-12 and these can be seen to have a rotational sequence in Figure 8-13 on the upper surface of the cortex. The actual columnar elements are of course much less strictly arranged than is shown in this diagram for the monkey cortex.

At the next stage of image reconstitution are neurones at other levels in area 17 and in the surrounding secondary and tertiary visual areas (Brodmann areas 18 and 19, Fig. 5-10A, B). Here there are neurones that are specially sensitive to the length and thickness of bright or dark lines as well as to their orientation and even to two lines meeting at an angle. These so-

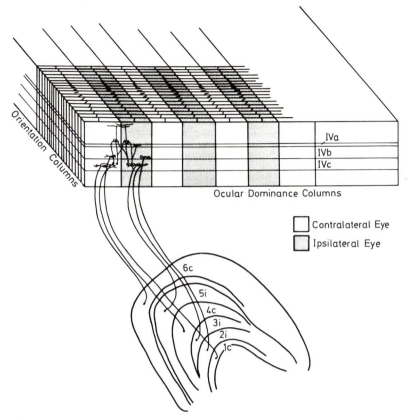

Fig. 8-13. Idealized diagram showing for the monkey the projection from the lateral geniculate body (*LGB*) to the visual cortex (area 17). The six layers of the lateral geniculate body are labelled according as they are associated with the ipsilateral (*i*) or contralateral (*c*) eye. These i and c layers project to specific areas so forming the ocular dominance columns for the ipsilateral and contralateral eyes. The stacked slab-like columns of the visual cortex are defined by the criteria of ocular dominance in one direction and orientation (shown on upper surface, *cf.* Fig. 8-12 in the other direction). Hubel, D. H., Wiesel, T. N.: Sequence regularity and geometry of orientation columns in the monkey striate cortex. J. Comp. Neurol. *158*, 267–294 (1974)

called complex and hypercomplex neurones (Hubel and Wiesel, 1963, 1965) constitute a further stage of feature recognition. It is believed that these 'complex' and 'hypercomplex' neurones acquire their specific properties by means of a synthesis of the neuronal circuits that are activated by 'simple' cells, these circuits containing inhibitory as well as excitatory components as in Figures 8-7 and 8-8 (Hubel and Wiesel, 1965; Hubel, 1971). In Figure 8-13 there are examples of two complex cells in the upper lamina that each receive from two simple cells of different ocular dominance columns.

So far we have a relatively clear story and there is identification in the visual cortex of neurones requisite for the various integrational tasks. This account is of course greatly oversimplified. For example, there has been neglect of the neural events responsible for the various contrast phenomena and for dark recognition that form the basis of many visual illusions. Colour recognition is dependent on coding by a three-colour process in the retina, beginning with red, green and blue cones that feed into relatively independent lines to the primary visual cortex (De Valois, 1973). At this stage there are various synthetic mechanisms, but we are far from understanding the neuronal mechanisms involved in colour recognition.

Since the complex and hypercomplex cells receive their inputs from various assemblages of simple cells, it would be expected that they would have inputs from a more extensive visual field. This is indeed the case, but the loss of field specificity is more than would be expected. It prompts the as yet unanswered question: how can the field specificity be recovered in the further stages of reconstitution of the visual field?

One further stage of synthesis of visual information has recently been studied physiologically (Gross, 1973). The main projection from visual areas 17, 18 and 19 is to areas 20 and 21 in the inferotemporal lobe (Fig. 8-10B, *cf.* Fig. 5-10). Many neurones in areas 20 and 21 have more exacting stimulus requirements than the lines and angles that were adequate for the complex and hypercomplex neurones of areas 17, 18 and 19. For example, neurones may be fired by rectangles in the visual field and not by discs, or by stars and not by circles. Evidently some of the neurones have a remarkable feature-recognition propensity. In these neurones of areas 20 and 21, visual mapping is sacrificed to feature recognition even more than with neurones of areas 18 and 19. Large areas of the visual field can effectively influence one neurone, and the topography for each 'feature-detection neurone' always includes the centre of vision. Again it can be envisaged that this specific response to geometrical forms such as squares, rectangles, triangles, stars, is dependent on the ordered projection onto these feature-detection neurones from complex and hypercomplex neurones sensitive to bright or dark lines or edges of a particular orientation and length and meeting at particular angles. For example, the feature-detection of a triangle would be the property of a neurone receiving inputs from neurones in the extra-striate visual cortex that are responsive to the angles and line orientations for composing the triangle.

Weiskrantz (1974) has demonstrated the manner in which monkeys can build up a remembered three-dimensional model of an object that is repeatedly examined from only one angle. This ability is impaired by lesions of the infero-temporal lobe (areas 20, 21). Hence Weiskrantz postulates that this lobe is concerned in building models and categories, and so is importantly involved in visual thinking and imagination.

Each stage of the processing of visual information from the retina to cortical areas 20 and 21 can be regarded as having a hierarchical order with features in sequential array:

1. The visual field becomes progressively less specific. This increasing generalization results in a foveal representation for all neurones of areas 20 and 21. Furthermore at this stage all neurones receive from both visual half-fields including the fovea through inputs to both occipital lobes via the splenium of the corpus callosum.
2. There is an increasing specificity of the adequate stimulus from a spot to a bright line or edge of particular orientation, then to lines of specified width and length and often with specificity for direction of movement, and finally to the more complex feature detection of some neurones of areas 20 and 21.
3. There is also evidence that neurones of areas 20 and 21 have an additional response feature, namely the significance of the response to the animal, exactly as has been discovered for neurones of areas 5 and 7 of the somaesthetic system (Mountcastle, 1975; Mountcastle et al., 1975).

8.2.3 The Perceived Visual Image

Wonderful as it is, this animal experimentation still gives no clue as to how a whole visual picture can be reconstituted by the neuronal machinery of the brain. Mountcastle (1978) suggests that the modular activities are linked together in echeloned parallel and serial arrangement to form a distributed system that could provide an objective mechanism for giving conscious awareness. But he does not provide any clue as to how this could come about. Such distributed systems have long been recognized and even diagrammed (Eccles, 1977, Fig. 6-6; Popper and Eccles, 1977, Figs. E7-3 and E7-4). Still there is no suggestion as to how the activities of the modules of a distributed system can be assembled in consciousness to give the whole visual picture. Presumably Mountcastle is basing his suggestion on the psychophysical identity theory of Feigl (1967). However, this theory has been subjected to severe criticism (Polten, 1973; Popper and Eccles, 1977), so it should be used only if these criticisms are answered or at least recognized.

In Lecture 10 there will be an account of a radical hypothesis (*cf.* Popper and Eccles, 1977, Chap. E7) of the brain-mind interaction. In terms of that hypothesis the reconstitution of the perceived image is due to the self-conscious mind that scans and reads out from the appropriate feature-recognition modules of the visual areas. These modules reconstitute the visual picture only in a fragmentary manner, but their distributed system is instrumental to the read-out by the self-conscious mind. It has to be recognized that the picture focussed on the retina never reappears in the brain. It is converted into the coded form of impulse discharges in the visual pathways and the visual centres. There is some reconstitution as described above in the feature-detection cells, but there is no hope that cells will be found to be so specialized that any one will be selectively responsive to a whole picture. This is the mythical situation ironically referred to as 'grandmother cells'. So the reconstitution of the retinal image as a perceived picture requires some synthetic operation that reads out from the modules and rebuilds the picture. This picture is perceived in the mind. It is a mistake to think that it can therefore be discovered in the brain, where instead there is only the coded information in countless neuronal discharges.

8.2.4 Auditory Perception

There is a highly specialized transduction mechanism in the cochlea where, by a beautifully designed resonance mechanism, there is a frequency analysis of the complex patterns of sound waves and conversion into the discharges of neurones that project into the brain. After several synaptic relays the coded information reaches the primary auditory area (Heschl's gyrus) in the superior temporal gyrus (*cf.* Fig. 8-1). The right cochlea projects mostly to the left primary auditory area, and vice versa for the left cochlea. There is a linear somatotopic distribution, the highest auditory frequencies being most medial in Heschl's gyrus and the lowest most lateral. It remains quite mysterious how a sequence of tones gives rise to a new synthesis, a melody. There are parallels with the connections in cascade that are shown in Figure 8-10 for somaesthesis and vision. The projections of all three systems both to the prefrontal lobe and the limbic system will be discussed in a later section.

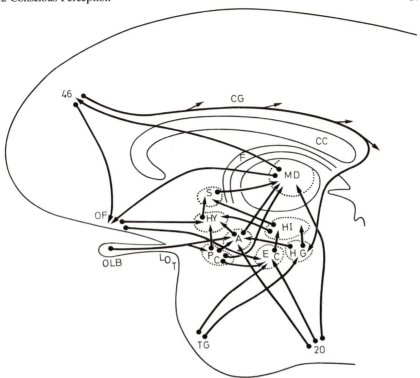

Fig. 8-14. Schematic drawing to show connectivities from the neocortex to and from the medio-dorsal thalamus (*MD*) and the limbic system. *OF,* orbital surface of prefrontal cortex; *TG,* temporal pole; *HG,* gyrus hippocampi; *HI,* hippocampus; *S,* septum; *F,* fornix; *CC,* corpus callosum; *OLB,* olfactory bulb; *LOT,* lateral olfactory tract; *PC,* piriform cortex; *EC,* entorhinal cortex; *A,* amygdala; *HY,* hypothalamus; *CG,* cingulate gyrus

8.2.5 Olfactory Perception

In most lower mammals olfaction (smell) is the dominant sensory input into the forebrain but, in the evolution of primates to man, olfaction became subordinated to vision and hearing, and even to somaesthesis, particularly when this became vital in manual skills. Chemical sensing in the olfactory mucosa is by receptor cells that are specialized neurones with axons that pass to the olfactory bulb, where there is a processing of information by a complex nervous system, much as in the retina. From the olfactory bulb the lateral olfactory tract passes to the brain where it has a complex distribution, only part of which is shown in Figure 8-14. The principal termination is in the piriform cortex, a primitive cerebral cortex. Thence there are connections to many structures of the limbic lobe, some of which are indicated in Figure 8-14. Connection to the primary receiving area of the neocortex (the orbito-frontal area) is effected only after several relays in the limbic system and is only in part via the medio-dorsal (MD) thalamus (Tanabe et al., 1975). Thus the olfactory connections are quite different from the somaesthetic, visual and auditory systems, where the connections are firstly to the neocortex and after several relays reach the limbic system (Fig. 8-10).

8.2.6 Pain

The sensation of pain is remarkable because, in contrast to the senses considered above, it has no material counterpart. It cannot be objectified. Yet intersubjective communication establishes for each of us that the pain which we uniquely feel is real and not an illusion. All others have similar experiences. There is a large scientific literature on pain of which there are many varieties: the sharp cutaneous pain of a needle prick; the throbbing pain of an inflammation; the agonizing pain of a visceral disorder of which colic is a severe example; dental pain that needs no description; and so on. The receptor organs are usually bare nerve fibres without special structural modifications. The information is coded in repetitive impulse discharges just as with other senses. Most diverse pathways relay the information to higher centres, the thalamus, the hypothalamus and the neocortex. Pain sensations are often blended with other sensations to give pleasurable experiences: the sensation of hotness as distinct from warmth is due to pain plus warmth; the tang of condiments is due to pain plus taste; and scratching and brushing excite pain plus touch receptors.

8.2.7 Emotional Colouring of Conscious Perceptions

It is a common experience that the conscious perception derived from some common sensory input is greatly modified by emotions, feeling, and appetitive drives. For example, when hungry the sight of food gives an experience deeply coloured by an appetitive drive! Nauta (1971) conjectures that the state of the organism's internal milieu (hunger, thirst, sex, fear, rage, pleasure) is signalled to the prefrontal lobes from the hypothalamus, the septal nuclei and various components of the limbic system such as the hippocampus and the amygdala. The pathways would be mainly through the MD thalamus to the prefrontal lobes (Fig. 8-14). Thus, by their projections to the prefrontal lobes, the hypothalamus and the limbic system modify and colour with emotion the conscious perceptions derived from sensory inputs and superimpose on them motivational drives. No other part of the neocortex has this intimate relationship with the hypothalamus.

Figure 8-10 shows for the somaesthetic and visual systems the many projections to the prefrontal lobes from the primary sensory and the principal secondary and tertiary areas. Simultaneously these areas project to the limbic system, and in Figure 8-14 there are also projections from the prefrontal lobe (areas 46 and OF) to the limbic system. So there are pathways for complicated circuitry from the various sensory inputs to the limbic system and back to the prefrontal lobe, with further circuits from that lobe to the limbic system and back again (Nauta, 1971). From the connectivities of Figure 8-14, it can be seen that the prefrontal and limbic systems are in reciprocal relationship and have the potentiality for continuously looping interaction. Thus by means of the prefrontal cortex the subject may be able to exercise a controlling influence on the emotions generated by the limbic system. An additional sensory input (olfaction) comes directly into the limbic system for cross-modal transfer to the other senses and thus contributes to the richness and variety of the perceptual experience. For example, the neocortical sensory systems via areas 46, OF, 20 and TG project to the hypothalamus, the entorhinal cortex and the hippocampal gyrus and so to the hippocampus, to septal nuclei and to the MD thalamus, while, after relay in the piriform cortex and amygdala, the olfactory input also goes to the hypothalamus, septal nuclei and the MD thalamus. Thus the MD nucleus is the receiving station for all inputs and it projects to the orbital and convex surfaces of the prefrontal lobe. So one can think of the prefrontal cortex as being the area where all emotive information is synthesized with somaesthetic, visual and auditory to give conscious experiences to the subject and guidance to appropriate behaviour, as will be described in Lecture 10. There it will be conjectured that conscious experiences are derived from spatio-temporal patterns of neuronal activity in special modules of the neocortex.

8.2.8 Summary of Conscious Perception

In conscious perception we attempt to abstract from the total sensory input from moment to moment in order to gain some meaningful evaluation of the situation we are in, according to interest and attention. In particular, meaning is given by a synthesis not only within one modality, but also across

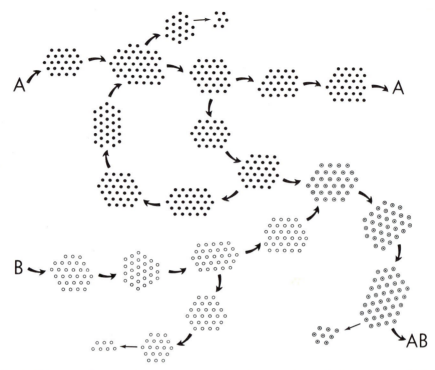

Fig. 8-15. In this schema of the cerebral cortex looked at from above, the large pyramidal cells are represented as *circles,* solid or open, that are arranged in clusters, each cluster corresponding to a module as diagrammed in Figures 8-4, and 8-8, where only four large projecting pyramidal cells are shown of the hundreds that would be in the module. The *large arrows* symbolize impulse discharges along hundreds of lines in parallel, which are the mode of excitatory communication from module to module as in Figure 8-4. Two inputs, *A* and *B,* and two outputs, *A* and *AB* are shown. Further description in text

several modalities: touch, vision and hearing for example. The sensory inputs from these three modalities project to the superior temporal sulcus (STS in Fig. 8-10) and this presumably gives opportunity for meaningful synthesis. It would be disastrous to attempt a synthesis of all the sensory information flooding into the brain by the millions of afferent fibres. In some way, not understood, we select from this overwhelming barrage in order to derive perceptions that are interesting and meaningful. Moreover there is a unity in the perceptual experience from moment to moment which gives what has been called a mental singleness (Bremer, 1966).

In Figure 8-4 there are shown the connectivities from module to module by association and commissural fibres. This is diagrammed in another convention in Figure 8-15, where the modules are shown by clumps of cells as observed from the cortical surface. The projections are greatly simplified to give at the most the bifurcation of one modular projection. One re-entrant loop is shown but, more importantly for our present purpose, there is convergence of two different modalities, A and B, onto modules that now signal sequentially A + B. This is the neural counterpart of cross-modal transfer. The cerebral basis of this happening is shown in Figure 8-10 A and B, where somaesthetic and visual projections converge onto the cortical areas STS and 46. We can regard such convergences as stages on the way to a synthesis of somaesthetic and visual inputs, as when we examine with our hands an object that is seen, the better to objectify it.

However, this study of the neural pathways does not advance our understanding of the mysterious transformation that occurs in the perceptual process. In Figure 10-2 there is shown diagrammatically a small element of the cerebral cortex with its modules. Arrows pointing up to the box labelled 'Perception' are assumed to convey information from many active modules of the neocortex, and we see above an array of perceptual experiences, light, colour, sound, pain, touch, smell, taste. There is no way in which a study of the neuronal performances in the modules can account for this transmutation to experiences of colour or touch, for example, though of course some modules are coded for one kind of perceptual experience, others for other kinds. There is no colour in the material world, only the emission of electromagnetic waves of various spectral composition. There is no colour as such in the brain, only modules responding selectively in their coded responses to visual inputs of various spectral characteristics (*cf.* Zeki, 1977). Colour is created by the reading out by the self-conscious mind of the responses of these 'colour-coded' modules. Colour is thus a purely subjective experience in the first place, but objectivity is attained by inter-subjective communication that is enlightened by a long learning process. Very interesting variants on colour recognition have been revealed by the study of subjects who have various kinds of colour blindness.

The human mystery is revealed by this extraordinary dichotomy between the coded performances of our cortical modules on the one hand and the perceptual experiences on the other. It has to be recognized that our recognition of the external world in all its manifestations is dependent on this transmutation from the activities of the cerebral cortex in World 1 to the experiences of World 2 (Fig. 10-2). Furthermore, this recognition is not only for the matter-energy world (World 1 of Fig. 6-1) but also for the world of culture (World 3 of Fig. 6-1) that is coded on material substrates and hence can come into consciousness only via sense organs and the modular activities generated thereby. We will return to this theme in Lecture 10.

Lecture 9

Learning and Memory

Synopsis and Introduction

Without memory there could not be a knowing of existence. It links our moment-to-moment experiences into a strand extending backwards in time to give that existential unity which is the self each of us knows. This storage of experiences for enactment or recall occurs in two modes. One is motor learning and memory, which is the learning of all skilled movements. The repertoire is immense! Secondly, there is what we may call cognitive learning and memory. At the simplest level there is the ability to recall some perceptual experience, but all levels can be involved, e. g. the remembrance of faces, names, scenes, events, pictures, musical themes. Then at a higher level there is the learning of language, and of stories, and of the contents of disciplines from the simplest technologies through to the most refined academic studies in the Humanities and in the Sciences. The two kinds of memory may be closely linked together, but different regions of the brain are concerned. For our present purpose motor memory is not of central interest in that it has no deep philosophical implications relating to the human mystery.

There will be concentration on the various aspects of cognitive learning and memory and on the neuronal machinery that is responsible for the laying down of memory traces, as they are called, and for their reading out when a memory is being recalled. A sharp distinction will be drawn between short-term memory – of a few seconds' duration – and long-term memory – minutes to a lifetime. It is generally agreed that short-term memory is due to the continuous circulation of impulses in neuronal circuits of reverberatory loops. Our knowledge of the neuronal machinery involved in long-term memory has been greatly advanced by the study of memory defects resulting from brain lesions. Special reference will be made to the role of the hippocampus and the prefrontal lobes of the neocortex and to the related neuronal pathways. However, much more is involved than the operation of neuronal machinery that carries in its modified connectivities the material substrate of the stored memory. The recall of a conscious memory involves a reciprocal transaction between the self-conscious mind on the one hand and the liaison areas of the brain on the other. We thus return again to the centrality of the brain-mind problem in our exploration of the human mystery.

Motivation plays a most important role in effecting the storage of memories. Moreover, in attempting to recover a memory, a deliberate mental effort is required, which may become quite severe and prolonged, as is revealed by the descriptive phrase, racking one's brains. Furthermore, a deliberate effort is demanded in mental concentration and in the selection from the immense congeries of neuronal happenings in the brain at any one instant those that give experiences of immediate interest or concern.

Without memory there could not be a knowing of existence. It links our moment-to-moment experiences into a strand extending backwards in time to give that existential unity which is the self each of us knows. Without conscious memory we could not know of the human mystery. Without memory we would just be reacting from moment to moment according to the input from the environment and in a standard, stereotyped way.

There is no more wonderful and necessary function of the brain than its ability to *learn* and to retrieve what is learnt in the *memory process*. For each of us the most precious activities throughout our lifetime are the storage of experiences, which in this way are made uniquely ours in that they are available for our *re-enactment* or *recall* in the memory process. These two words are chosen because there are two main kinds of learning and memory, though in many situations they are closely linked together. One is motor learning and memory, which is the learning of all skilled movements. The repertoire is immense: the playing of all musical instruments and games, as well as the learning of all arts, crafts and technologies. Furthermore there are all the expressive movements as in speaking, dancing, singing and writing. Secondly, there is what we may call cognitive learning and memory. At the simplest level there is the ability to recall some perceptual experience, but all levels can be involved, e. g. the remembrance of faces, names, scenes, events, pictures, musical themes. Then at a higher level there is the learning of language, and of stories, and of the contents of disciplines from the simplest technologies through to the most refined academic studies in the humanities and in the sciences.

It is a familiar observation that there may be an enduring cognitive memory of some single highly emotional experience. On the other hand motor memories require reinforcement by continual practice if they are to be retained at a high level of skill. Quite distinct parts of the brain are concerned in these two types of memory. Nevertheless, it appears likely that the same kind of neural mechanism is concerned.

In the last three decades there has been great progress in the understanding of many activities of the brain, both at the elemental level, such as the propagation of nerve impulses in nerve fibres and the generation of these impulses by synaptic action on neurones, and at more complex levels, such as the operation of neuronal pathways concerned in the many sensory systems, as mentioned in Lecture 8, and in the motor system. In all of these fields there is a large measure of agreement. By contrast, there are many divergent and even irreconcilable views on the nature of the neuronal mechanisms concerned in learning and memory. My task therefore is not to give an account of a well-established story of the mode of operation of the neuronal machinery in the learning and memory process but to meet the much more difficult and interesting challenge of building a coherent story from many diverse series of observations. I will limit my story to cognitive memory in the widest sense because it is of particular significance to the human mystery and also because it is possible to build up this story from observations on human subjects with only passing reference to experiments on non human primates.

I will attempt to answer the question: How can we recover or re-experience some events, or some simple test situation, as for example a number or word sequence? It will be recognized that two distinct problems are involved – storage and retrieval, or in relation to our present problem of conscious memory, learning and remembering. I propose to deal with these problems at two levels.

Firstly, it will be considered as a problem of neurobiology, namely the structural and functional changes which form the basis of memory. It is generally supposed that the recall of a memory involves the replay in an approximate manner of the neuronal events that were originally responsible for the experience that is being recalled. There is no specially difficult problem with short-term memories for a few seconds. It can be conjectured that this is effected by the neural events continuing during the verbal or pictorial rehearsal. The distinctive patterns of modular activity that are suggested in Figure 8–15 thus continue to recirculate for the whole duration of these brief memories and are available for read-out. On the other hand, with memories enduring for minutes to years, it has to be discovered how the neuronal connectivities are changed so that there tends to be stabilized some tendency for replay of the spatio-temporal patterns of modular activity that occurred in the initial experience, and that have meanwhile subsided.

Secondly, the role of the self-conscious mind has to be considered. It will be conjectured in Lecture 10 that a conscious experience arises when the self-conscious mind enters into an effective relationship with certain activated modules, 'open' modules, in the cerebral cortex. In the willed recall of a memory the self-conscious mind must again be in relationship to a pattern of modular responses resembling the original responses evoked by the event to be remembered, so that there is a reading out of approximately the same experience. We have to consider how the self-conscious mind is concerned in calling forth the modular events that give the remembered experience on demand, as it were. Furthermore the self-conscious mind acts as an arbiter or assessor with respect to the correctness or relevance of the memory that is delivered on demand. For example the name or number may be recognized as incorrect by the self-conscious mind, and a further recall process may be instituted, and so on. Thus the recall of a memory involves two distinct processes in the self-conscious mind: firstly that of initiating a recall from the data-banks in the brain; secondly the recognition memory that judges its correctness.

9.1 Structural and Functional Changes Possibly Related to Memory

In general terms following Sherrington, Adrian, Lashley and Szentágothai we have to suppose that long-term memories are somehow encoded in the neuronal connectivities of the brain. We are thus led to conjecture that the structural basis of memory lies in the enduring modifications of synapses. In mammals there is no evidence for growth or change of major neuronal pathways in the brain after their initial formation. It is not possible to construct or reconstruct major brain pathways at such a gross level. But it should be possible to secure the necessary changes in neuronal connectivity by microstructural changes in synapses. For example, they may be hypertrophied or they may bud additional synapses, or alternatively they may regress. Since it would be expected that the increased synaptic efficacy would arise because of a strong conditioning synaptic activation, experiments such as those illustrated in Figure 9-1 have been carried out on several types of synapses.

Figure 9-1 A shows the neural pathways in very recent investigations by Sarvey et al. (1978) on the effects of repetitive stimulation on synapses in a primitive part of the cerebrum, the hippocampus. Recording is by a microelectrode in the CA3 zone, where there are pyramidal cells which, as shown, receive synaptic excitation on their apical dendrites from two distinct afferent pathways and which also have axon collaterals projecting in close relation to these two afferent pathways. A stimulating electrode was inserted to excite selectively each of these pathways. One is labelled Sch because it excited the Schaffer collaterals from the axons of the CA3 pyramidal cells, the other mf because it excited the afferent pathway giving the mossy fibre synapses on these same cells. As shown, the mossy fibres are the axons of granule cells of the fascia dentata.

In Figure 9-1 B both the mf and Sch stimulations evoked in the extracellular recordings a double negative spike potential, the smaller earlier one (N_1) being due to the antidromic stimulation of CA3 cells, the larger second (N_2), to the synaptic excitation of these same cells. This interpretation is based on carefully designed control experiments. In C repetitive stimulation (300/s for 5 s) of the mf line to the CA3 cells resulted in a potentiation of

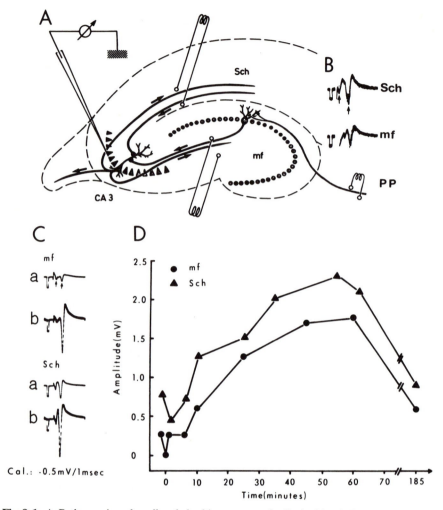

Fig. 9-1. A Pathways in a lamella of the hippocampus (a slice). Stimulating electrodes are shown for the Schaffer collaterals (*Sch*), the mossy fibres (*mf*), and on the perforating pathway (*PP*) from the entorhinal cortex. A recording electrode is shown for the CA3 pyramidal cells. **B** Extracellular records of population spike potentials generated by stimuli at *Sch* and *mf*. *Arrows* show the two negative spikes, the first antidromic, the second monosynaptic. **C** Initial control records (*a*) and the responses (*b*) 20 min after a conditioning tetanus through the *mf* electrode (300/s for 5 s). **D** Relative sizes of the N_2 spike before and after the conditioning tetanus. Sarvey, J. M., Misgeld, U., Klee, M. R.: Long-lasting heterosynaptic post-activation potentiation (PAP) of CA3 neurons in guinea pig hippocampal slice. Fed. Proc. 37, 251 (1978)

the synaptic response (N_2 spike) of those cells to both mf and Sch inputs when tested at 20 min after the stimulation. In D there is a plotting of the relative sizes of the responses observed at intervals up to 185 min after the conditioning tetanus. After an initial depression there was a potentiation that was increasing up to 60 min and that continued at a high level for many hours. With a less severe stimulation (for example 15/s for 10 s) the potentiation was smaller, but had a similar long duration for up to 5 h. A similar potentiation, both homosynaptic and heterosynaptic, was produced by repetitive Sch stimulation.

A remarkable feature was that the synapses not stimulated were potentiated as much and for as long a time as the synapses subjected to the conditioning stimulation (Fig. 9-1 D). This indicates that the effective changes were on the postsynaptic side of the synapses. It would be expected that, matching this potentiation, the postsynaptic elements would show an increased size.

Another synaptic pathway in the hippocampus is from the perforating pathway (PP) to synapses on the granule cells (Fig. 9-1 A). Repetitive stimulation of this pathway also gives a potentiation lasting for many hours (Bliss and Lømo, 1973). It has been shown by Fifková and van Harreveld (1977) that there is correspondingly a prolonged increase (for over 23 h) in the size of the spines (the postsynaptic elements, *cf.* Fig. 8-2 D) of these stimulated synapses. The larger size of the spines (S) can be seen in Figure 9-2 B relative to the control, unstimulated, size in Figure 9-2 A. Many thousands of the spines were measured. The mean increase was almost 40% and was highly significant. The presynaptic component of the synapse (Fig. 8-2 D) was also increased, but not significantly. It was of great interest that the prolonged time course of the synaptic swelling matched the prolonged potentiation observed in Figure 9-1 D and also by Bliss and Lømo (1973). Figures 9-1 and 9-2 provide the best evidence so far obtained in support of the conjecture that the prolonged potentiation following repetitive stimulation is due to a swelling of the synapses, which consequently may be called modifiable synapses.

Physiological experiments have thus indicated that the modifiable synapses which could be responsible for memory are excitatory and are specially prominent at the higher levels of the brain. In the cerebral cortex the great majority of excitatory synapses on pyramidal cells are on their dendritic spines, as illustrated in Figures 8-2 D and 8-5. There is also much evidence from Valverde (1968) and others that these spine synapses regress during disuse (*cf.* Eccles, 1970). Hence it is conjectured that these spine synapses on the dendrites of such neurones as the pyramidal cells of the

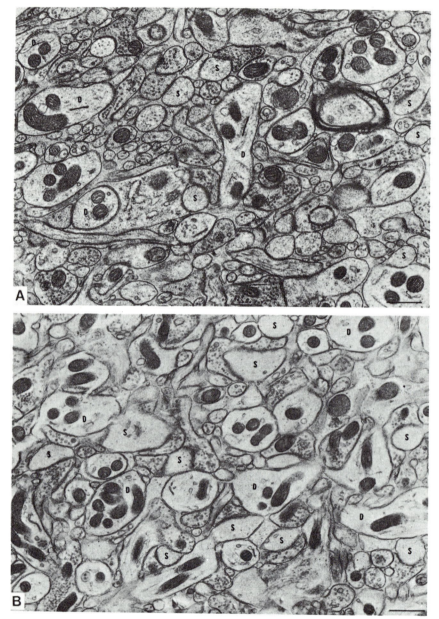

Fig. 9-2. A Electron micrograph of the distal third of the dentate molecular layer in a control preparation. **B** Electron micrograph at same magnification of the dentate molecular layer in a preparation in which entorhinal cortex was stimulated at 30/s for 30 s and then survived for 23 h before fixation. Bars represent 0.5 μm. *S*, spines; *D*, dendrites. Fifkova, E., van Harreveld, A.: Long-lasting morphological changes in dendritic spines of dentate granular cells following stimulation of the entorhinal area. J. Neurocytology *6*, 211–230 (1977). Reprinted with permission of Chapman & Hall Ltd.

cerebral cortex and the hippocampus are the modifiable synapses concerned in learning. These would be the synapses displaying the indefinitely prolonged potentiation illustrated in Figure 9-1 D. One can imagine that the superior performance by these synapses was indefinitely prolonged because a growth process had developed in the dendritic spines giving a structural change which could have great endurance. Moreover there is now a convincing demonstration of this growth in electron micrographs (Fig. 9-2; Fifková and van Harreveld, 1977). The changes are diagrammatically shown in Figure 9-3 where A represents the normal state and B and C the hypertrophied states. An alternative to the synaptic spine hypertrophy of Figure 9-2 B is shown in C, where an increase in synaptic potency has been secured by branching of the spines to form secondary spine synapses as reported by Szentágothai.

There is also histological evidence for the effects of disuse in causing a regression and depletion of spine synapses (Fig. 9-3 D). This has been beautifully demonstrated by Valverde (1967) on the dendrites of the pyramidal cells in the visual cortex of mice raised in visual deprivation, and indeed similar demonstrations have been made with other spine synapses. So it can be assumed that normal usage results in the maintenance of the dendritic spine synapses at the normal level depicted in Figure 9-3 A. It can be concluded that the excitatory spine synapses are probably the modifiable synapses concerned in memory.

If synaptic growth is required for learning, there must be an increase in brain metabolism of a special kind with the manufacture of proteins and other macromolecules required for the increases in membranes and in chemical transmission mechanisms. The specificities would be encoded in the structure particularly in the synaptic connections of the nerve cells, which are arranged in the unimaginably complex pattern that has already been formed in development. From then onward, all that seems to be required for the functional reorganization that is assumed to be the neuronal substrate of memory is merely the microgrowth of synaptic connections already in existence, as indicated in Figures 9-3 B and C, which can be regarded as models of the spine synapses on pyramidal cells.

The flow of impulses from receptor organs into the nervous system (*cf.* Lecture 8) will result in the activation of specific spatio-temporal patterns of modules linked by sequential impulse discharges (*cf.* Fig. 8–15). The synapses so activated will grow to an increased effectiveness and even sprout branches to form secondary synapses; hence, the more a particular spatio-temporal pattern of modular activity is replayed in the cortex, the more effective become its synapses relative to others. And, by virtue of this

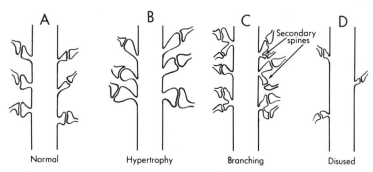

Fig. 9-3 A–D. Plasticity of dendritic spine synapses. The drawings are designed to convey the plastic changes in spine synapses that are postulated to occur with growth in **B** and **C** and with regression in **D.** Further description in text

synaptic efficacy, later similar sensory inputs will tend to traverse these same modular pathways and so evoke the same responses, both overt and psychic, as the original input.

9.2 Role of the Self-Conscious Mind in Short-Term Memory

Let us consider some simple and unique perceptual experience, for example the first sight of a bird or flower hitherto unknown to us or of a new model of a car. Firstly, there are the many stages of encoded transmission from retinal image to the various levels of the visual cortex, feature recognition being the highest interpretative level so far recognized, as described in Lecture 8. At a further stage we propose the activation of modules of the liaison brain that are 'open' to World 2 (Lecture 10), the consequent read-out by the self-conscious mind giving the perceptual experience with all its sensual richness. This read-out by the self-conscious mind involves the integration into a unified experience of the specific activities of many modules, an integration that gives the pictured uniqueness to the experience (Lecture 8). Furthermore, it is a two-way action, the self-conscious mind modifying the modular activity as well as receiving from it, and possibly evaluating it by testing procedures in an input-output manner. It must further be conjectured that there is an intense patterned interaction of open modules with each other and with closed modules, there being for this purpose the immense connectivities provided by association and commissural fibres as described in Lecture 8 (*cf.* Fig. 8-4).

Moreover we have to postulate closed self-re-exciting chains in these ongoing patterns of modular interaction (*cf.* Fig. 8–15). In this way there is a continuation of the dynamic patterned activity in time.

As long as the modular activities continue in this specific patterned interaction, we assume that the self-conscious mind is continuously able to read it out according to its interests and attention. We may say that in this way the new experience is kept in mind – as, for example, when we try to remember a telephone number between the time of looking it up and dialling.

We propose that the continued activity of the modules can be secured by continuous active intervention or reinforcement by the self-conscious mind, which in this way can hold memories by processes that we experience and refer to as either verbal or non-verbal (pictorial or musical, for example) rehearsal. As soon as the self-conscious mind engages in some other task, this reinforcement ceases, that specific pattern of neuronal activities subsides and the short-term memory is lost. Recall now becomes dependent on memory processes of longer duration.

9.3 Neural Pathways Concerned in Laying Down Long-Term Memories

It is not yet possible to investigate in any meaningful manner the actual neural events that are of crucial importance in the laying down of a memory. Experiments of the type illustrated in Figures 9-1 and 9-2 indicate the synaptic events that are likely to be concerned in long-term memory, but they do not define the neuronal circuitry. The most fruitful approach to this problem is to study the brains of patients who have largely lost their abilities to build new memories. The damaged regions should provide important clues to the neuronal circuitry.

9.3.1 Loss of Long-Term Memory

The clinical condition that is distinctively characterized by loss of memory, amnesia, is usually called Korsakoff's syndrome after its discoverer, who first described it in 1887. Such patients have good memories for their experiences before the onset of the disease and also memories for happenings in the previous few seconds, the short-term memory. In ordinary conversation they may not noticeably disclose their disability. However, they fail in the retention of memory as soon as they are distracted by a new situation. For example, a convenient clinical test is to ask the patient to remember simple bits of information such as the name of the doctor, the date and the time of day. The patient fails in such a test even though under instruction just before he had repeated the answers hundreds of times. But of course the defect applies to every new experience of the patient. He fails to remember names, objects, events, in fact anything he reads or sees or hears. However, memory for the remote past, years before the onset of the disease, is well retained. Nevertheless, the well-remembered past is not sharply separated from the later amnestic period. In between there are fragmentary memories that often are given incorrect time sequences and with varying degrees of inaccuracy. Strangely, the patients fail to realize the severity of their memory defect or even its existence. Often it is covered up by confabulation in which the patient invents experiences and happenings. For example, a bed-ridden patient may assert that he has just come back from a walk in the garden and give a description of his experiences there!

The classic amnestic syndrome as described by Korsakoff was due to alcoholism, but it is now recognized that it may be caused by many other illnesses. Perhaps the most frequent cases of memory defects of varying degrees of severity are a result of senile dementia.

There has been much dispute with respect to the site of the causal lesion. Victor and co-workers (1971) have given a comprehensive survey of the cerebral lesions that is based upon a careful study of a large series of brains. Unfortunately there was such a wide dispersal of the degenerated areas and such variability from one patient to another that no clear picture emerges of the cerebral regions concerned in learning and memory. However, it is important that the medio-dorsal nucleus of the thalamus was involved in every case, and the medial zone of the pulvinar and the mamillary bodies were much affected, as also was the hippocampus.

If we are to progress in understanding the manner in which memories are stored in the brain in the learning process, it is clear that even the most careful study of the cerebral lesions in Korsakoff's syndrome will be of little avail. Presumably many of the lesions are unrelated to the memory defect. The much more sharply defined lesions produced by surgical excisions would be of inestimable value, and it is to these that we now turn.

There is remarkable evidence (Milner, 1966, 1972) in support of the concept that the hippocampus plays a key role in human cognitive memory. It may arouse scepticism when I state that the really convincing evidence comes from investigations on one patient (H. M.) who in 1953 was subjected to an operative excision bilaterally of the hippocampus and the adjacent medial temporal lobe, as indicated in Figure 9-4. The operation was

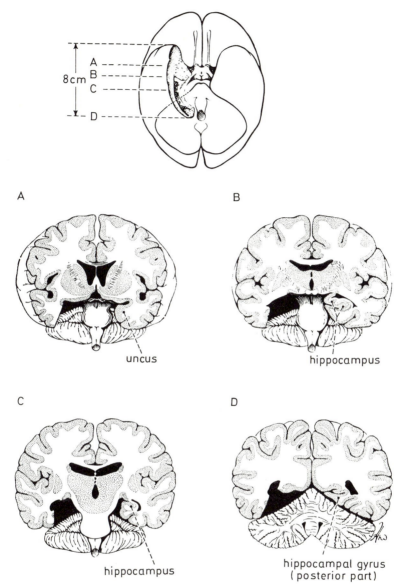

Fig. 9-4 A–D. Diagrammatic cross sections of the human brain, showing the estimated extent of removal in Scoville's medial temporal ablation in the case discussed in the text. The anterior-posterior extent of the hippocampus is shown in the upper drawings with **A, B, C** and **D** indicating the level of the transverse sections below. For illustrative purposes the removal is shown on the left side only, but the removal was made on both sides in a single operation. Milner, B.: The memory defect in bilateral hippocampal lesions. Psychiat. Res. Rep. Amer. Psychiat. Ass. *II*, 43-52 (1959)

designed to alleviate epileptic seizures of incapacitating severity that were uncontrolled by maximum anticonvulsant medication. Therapeutically the operation was a success in alleviating the seizures, but it produced an extreme amnestic syndrome, resembling Korsakoff's syndrome, only more severe. This operation will of course never be carried out again, so H.M. and three others will remain as unique cases for all time.

Despite his grave amnesia H. M. is a remarkably tolerant and co-operative person with a fairly good intelligence. In fact he has been an ideal subject for investigation for over 20 years, being perhaps more intensively investigated than any other neurological patient in history. Let us now look at some of the findings on this unique patient. H. M. lives entirely with short-term memories of a few seconds' duration and with the memories retained from before the operation. Milner (1966) gives a graphic account of his memory loss:

> His mother observes that he will do the same jigsaw puzzle day after day without showing any practice effect and read the same magazines over and over without ever finding their contents familiar. The same forgetfulness applies to people he has met since the operation. His initial emotional reaction may be intense, but it will be short-lived, since the incident provoking it is soon forgotten. Thus, when informed of the death of his uncle, of whom he was very fond, he became extremely upset, but then appeared to forget the whole matter and from time to time thereafter would ask when his uncle was coming to visit them; each time on hearing anew of the uncle's death, he would show the same intense dismay, with no sign of habituation.

He can keep current events in mind so long as he is not distracted. For example, he has succeeded in remembering a three-figure number sequence such as 584 for as long as 15 min by continually repeating it to himself. But distraction completely eliminates all trace of what he has been doing only a few seconds before. H. M. provides a unique example of short-term memory in its purest form. Milner (1966) sums this up by stating:

> Observations such as this suggest that the only way in which this patient can hold on to new information is by constant verbal rehearsal, and that forgetting occurs as soon as this rehearsal is prevented by some new activity claiming his attention. Since in daily life attention is of necessity constantly shifting, such a patient shows a continuous anterograde amnesia. One gets some idea of what such an amnestic state must be like from the patient's own comments, repeated at intervals during a recent examination. Between tests, he would suddenly look up and say, rather anxiously: "Right now, I'm wondering. Have I done or said something amiss? You see, at this moment everything looks clear to me, but what happened just before? That's what worries me. It's like waking from a dream; I just don't remember".

There are three other recorded cases where a comparable severe antero-grade amnesia (amnesia for all happenings after the operation) resulted from destruction of both hippocampi (Milner, 1966). There was almost no recovery, even after 11 years in these cases. However, the variable retrograde amnesia, i. e. the memory of events preceding the hippocampal destruction, showed a continued recovery in all cases, including that of H. M. There are two other reported cases (Penfield and Milner, 1958) where unilateral hippocampectomy resulted in a comparable anterograde amnesia, but there was evidence that the surviving hippocampus was severely damaged. We can conclude that the severe anterograde amnesia only occurs with grave bilateral hippocampal deficiency. Supporting evidence has been provided (Milner, 1966) with cases of unilateral hippocampectomy in which the remaining hippocampus and the cerebral hemisphere on that side were temporarily knocked out by the brief anaesthesia provided by sodium amytal injection into the carotid artery (the Wada test). A severe anterograde amnesia was produced that persisted after the transient anaesthesia. There is a limited amnesia following unilateral hippocampectomy, for words and numbers with the left and for patterns and shapes with the right; but, as this is not unduly incapacitating, this operation is frequently performed. However, it is essential to discover by the Wada test if the other hippocampus is normal. The ability of one hippocampus to prevent severe amnesia in activities of the contralateral cerebral cortex can be attributed to the cerebral commissures – the corpus callosum and the hippocampal commissure.

It is important to recognize that the hippocampus is not the seat of the memory traces. With the exception of the period of retrograde amnesia, memories from before the hippocampectomy are well retained and recalled. The hippocampus is merely the instrument responsible for the laying down of the memory trace or engram, which presumably is very largely located in the cerebral cortex in the appropriate areas. There is no obvious impairment of intellect or personality in these subjects despite the acute failure of memory. In fact, they live either in the immediate present or with remembered experiences from before the time of the operation. Recently, Marlen-Wilson and Teuber (1975) have shown by a testing procedure of prompting that a minimal storage of pictorial information even occurs for experiences after the operation, but it is of no use to the patient because he cannot himself provide the prompting.

There is one small relieving feature, namely that these patients still have the ability to learn motor acts. For example, they can build up skills in motor performances such as drawing a line in the narrow space between the double-line drawings of a five-pointed star, using for this purpose only the guidance provided by the view in a mirror of their hand and the double star; but they have no memory of how they learned the skill!

The surgical excision was not of course restricted to the hippocampus of H. M. As shown in Figure 9-4 the hippocampal gyrus was also excised and, as is usual, the uncus and amygdala. However, there is general agreement that bilateral excision of the uncus and the amygdala does not in itself bring about the amnestic syndrome. There is no doubt that the bilateral hippocampectomy is responsible for the anterograde amnesia and that, as stated above, the hippocampus is responsible for the laying down of memories, but is not itself the site of the storage. This conclusion is in general agreement with the findings in Korsakoff's syndrome, where memories of the remote past are much better retained than for recent events. When we come to consider the pathways whereby the hippocampus exerts its essential influence in the storage of memories, many of the neuronal lesions reported in Korsakoff's amnesia will be accounted for.

We can conclude this brief review of memory defects associated with hippocampal lesions by three statements, which are in accord with the concepts developed by Kornhuber (1973). (1) In retrieving the memory of an event that is not being continuously rehearsed in the short-term memory process, the self-conscious mind is dependent on some consolidation or storage process that is brought about by hippocampal activity. (2) The hippocampus is itself not the site of the storage. (3) We conjecture that the hippocampal participation in the consolidation process is dependent on neuronal pathways that transmit from the modules of the association cortex to the hippocampus and thence back to the prefrontal lobe.

9.3.2 Neural Pathways Concerned in Laying Down Long-Term Memories

In Lecture 8 there was a brief reference to the various pathways whereby the primary sensory areas for somaesthesis and vision projected to the limbic system, the major routes being diagrammed in Figure 8–10 on the basis of the sequential lesion studies by Jones and Powell (1970). In both cases there is a more direct route to the limbic system and a route through the prefrontal lobe via the orbital cortex (OF). In the limbic system these various inputs eventually can reach the hippocampus (HI in Fig. 8–14), which is a finding of great interest in view of the evidence presented above for its key role in the consolidation of memory traces. Similar pathways have been recognized also in the case of the less-studied auditory system. The olfactory system is specially privileged because it projects directly into the limbic system.

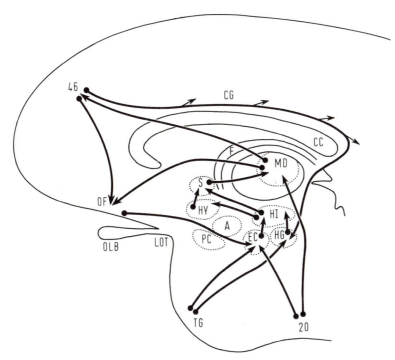

Fig. 9-5. Schematic drawing simplified from Figure 8-14 to show connectivities from the neocortex to and from the medio-dorsal thalamus (*MD*). *OF*, orbital surface of prefrontal cortex; *TG*, temporal pole; *HG*, gyrus hippocampi; *HI*, hippocampus; *S*, septum; *F*, fornix; *CC*, corpus callosum; *OLB*, olfactory bulb; *LOT*, lateral olfactory tract; *PC*, piriform cortex; *EC*, entorhinal cortex; *A*, amygdala; *HY*, hypothalamus; *CG*, cingulate gyrus

The postulated role of the hippocampus in consolidation of memory requires that there be also return circuits from the hippocampus to the neocortex. One well-known circuit is from the hippocampus to the MD thalamus and thence to the orbital surface (OF) and the convexity of the prefrontal lobe (Akert, 1964; Nauta, 1971; Fig. 9-5). Another major output line from the hippocampus is to the anterior thalamic nucleus (not shown in Fig. 9-5), thence via the cingulate gyrus (areas 24 and 23 in Fig. 5–10B) to the wide areas of the neocortex via association fibres (Brodal, 1969). There is need for a more detailed study of these pathways in Primates so that the clinical evidence on lesions of the hippocampus and related structures can be interpreted with confidence.

The theory here proposed for the role of the hippocampus in memory consolidation is based upon Kornhuber's theory, which is illustrated very schematically in Figure 9-6. All of the pathways shown have been anatomi-

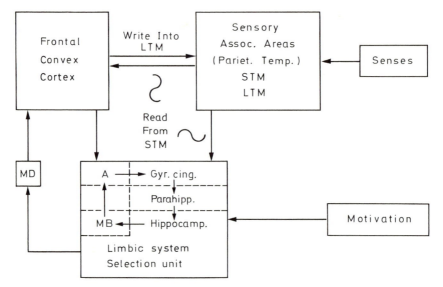

Fig. 9-6. Scheme of anatomical structures involved in selection of information between short-term memory (*STM*) and long-term memory (*LTM*). *MB,* mamillary body; *A,* anterior thalamic nucleus; *MD,* medio-dorsal thalamic nucleus. Kornhuber, H. H.: Neural control of input into long term memory: limbic system and amnestic syndrome in man. In: Memory and transfer of information. Zippel, H. P. (ed.), pp. 1–22. New York: Plenum Press 1973

cally identified. It must be appreciated that each of the pathways illustrated is constituted by hundreds of thousands or even millions of nerve fibres. To be the upper right there is shown a sensory input that goes in the conventional manner to the many sensory association areas, particularly in the parietal and temporal lobes. At that stage there is bifurcation, there being an association pathway to the prefrontal lobe and a pathway to the limbic system and hippocampus, largely via the cingulate gyrus. The hippocampal output is shown partly going to the prefrontal lobe via the medial dorsal thalamus and partly to a loop, the Papez loop, through which the hippo-campal output is returned to the hippocampus via such structures as the mammillary bodies, the anterior thalamus and the cingulate gyrus.

The box entitled 'sensory association areas' in Figure 9-6, together with the output paths to the frontal cortex and the limbic system can be expanded into the schematic diagram of Figure 9-7, which was developed by Kornhuber (1973) largely from data derived from degeneration studies on the monkey brain. This diagram shows very well the inputs from frontal, temporal and parietal cortical association areas to the hippocampus via the cingulate gyrus. The output from the hippocampus goes via the MD

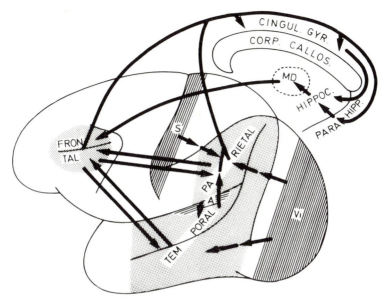

Fig. 9-7. Scheme of pathways in the monkey brain involved in the flow of information from primary sensory areas via the sensory association areas of the temporal and parietal lobe and the cortex of the frontal convexity to the limbic system and then the loop back via the medio-dorsal nucleus of the thalamus (*MD*) and the frontal cortex to the temporal and parietal areas for long-term storage. Primary sensory areas: *Vi*, visual; *A*, auditory; *S*, somatosensory; the vestibular area is in the lower part of S. Kornhuber, H. H.: Neural control of input into long term memory: limbic system and amnestic syndrome in man. In: Memory and transfer of information. Zippel, H. P. (ed.), pp. 1–22. New York: Plenum Press 1973

thalamus to the convexity of the frontal lobe, exactly as in Figure 9-5 and 9-6, as also are the reciprocal connections of the frontal convexity to the parietal and temporal lobes. Both these figures greatly simplify the connections, particularly in the limbic system (Pandya and Kuypers, 1969).

In Figures 9-6 and 9-7, two pathways are shown converging on the frontal cortex – that from the sensory association areas directly and that indirectly via a detour through the limbic system and the MD thalamus. In the frontal cortex we would propose that the indirect input would be via non-specific thalamic afferents from the MD thalamus that would excite the spiny stellate cells forming the *cartridge type* of synapse (*cf.* Figs. 8-5, 8-6 and 9-8), while the direct input would be the association fibres that terminate as *horizontal fibres* in laminae 1 and 2 and that are particularly well shown in Figure 9-8. On analogy with the learning theory for the cerebellum (Eccles, 1977), it is proposed that the cartridge-type synapse on a

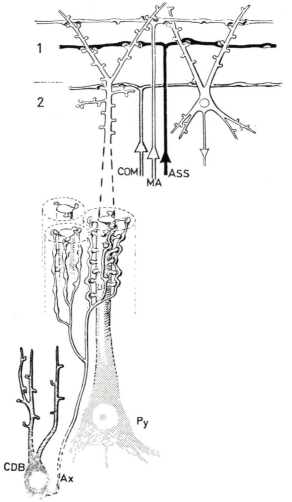

Fig. 9-8. Simplified diagram of connectivities in the neocortex (*cf.* Figs. 8-6 to 8-8). In laminae 1 and 2 there are shown horizontal fibres arising as bifurcating axons of commissural (*COM*) and association (*ASS*) fibres and also of Martinotti cells (*MA*). The horizontal fibres make synapses with the apical dendrites of a pyramidal and a stellate-pyramidal cell. Deeper there is shown a spiny stellate cell (*CDB*) with axon (*Ax*) making cartridge synapses with the shafts of apical dendrites of pyramidal cells. Szentágothai, J.: Les circuits neuronaux de l'écorce cérébrale. Bull. Acad. R. Med. Belg. *7, 10,* 475–492 (1970)

pyramidal cell acts similarly to the climbing fibres in selecting from the input of about 2000 horizontal fibres on the apical dendrites of that same pyramidal cell. This selection would be dependent on conjunction of the

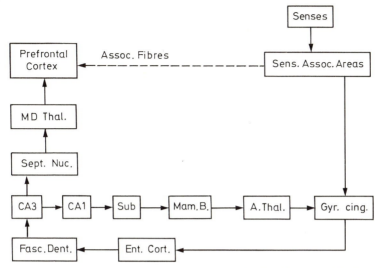

Fig. 9-9. Scheme of structures participating in the circuits involved in cerebral learning. Figure 9-6 is redrawn to show the two circuits emanating from the CA3 and CA1 hippocampal pyramidal cells. The connections within the hippocampus are as follows: entorhinal cortex by perforating pathway to fascia dentata; granule cells of fascia dentata by mossy fibres to CA3 pyramidal cells; axon collaterals of CA3 pyramidal cells (Schaffer collaterals) to CA1 pyramidal cells; CA1 to subiculum (*Sub*) to mamillary bodies; CA3 by fimbria to septal nucleus to mediodorsal thalamus

two inputs in some specific time relationship, as yet undefined, and would result in an enduring potentiation of the selected synapses on the apical dendrite. It is assumed that several association, commissural and Martinotti fibres would be selected from the 2000 as forming the context of the cartridge synaptic activity on that pyramidal cell (Marr, 1970; Eccles, 1978). Thus activity of the cartridge system is the *instruction* that *selects* for potentiation those horizontal fibre synapses that are activated in the appropriate temporal conjunction. As indicated in Figure 9-8, Szentágothai (1970) proposes that a single cartridge system comprises the apical dendrites of about three pyramidal cells, which thus form a unitary selection system. For further quantitative consideration see Eccles (1978). Possibly the Papez circuit (*cf.* Fig. 9-6) functions to provide the reverberatory activation of the hippocampus with its CA3 output through the septal nucleus to the MD thalamus, as is indicated in Figure 9-9.

Before we consider further the proposed mode of selective action of the hippocampal output on the immensely complex neuronal connectivities in the association cortex (*cf.* Fig. 8-4), we should enquire into the neuronal circuitry of the hippocampus in order to see if it is built so as to work in a highly selective manner with respect to the inputs it receives from the neocortex. This selectivity is necessary if the hippocampal inputs to the prefrontal neocortex are to act as 'teachers' selecting for hypertrophy a small fraction of the total excitatory synapses made by the horizontal fibres in laminae I and II. Recent investigations by Andersen and associates (1971, 1973) have shown to an amazing degree that the hippocampus is indeed organized in a series of narrow transverse lamellae which function independently through all the complex connectivity (*cf.* Fig. 9-1 A). This discrimination is maintained in the output line of the CA3 pyramidal cells by a strict segregation of the CA3 axons, according to location in the fimbria, the more rostral being medial and the more caudal, lateral. It can be presumed that this segregation leads on to a segregation in the septal nucleus. Andersen et al. (1971) sum up their findings:

> A point source of entorhinal activity projects its impulses through the four-membered pathway along a slice, or lamella, of hippocampal tissue oriented normally to the alvear surface and nearly sagittally in the dorsal part of the hippocampal formation.

The diagrammatic representation in Figure 9-9 gives deep meaning to the fundamental design feature discovered by Andersen et al. (1973), namely that the CA3 and CA1 pyramidal cells of the hippocampus are sharply discriminated by their distinctive projections, as indicated in Figure 9-9. One of the synaptic links in the circuits of Figure 9-9, the entorhinal cortex to the granule cells of the fascia dentata exhibits remarkable responses to repetitive stimulation, which would make it function very effectively in a reverberating loop such as that proposed for the Papez circuit in Figures 9-6 and 9-9. There is very large potentiation during repetitive stimulation at 10/ s (Bliss and Lømo, 1973), and with repeated short episodes there is a progressive build-up of a potentiation that is maintained for hours. It is of even more importance that the synapses on CA3 and CA1 pyramidal cells show this large and sustained potentiation (*cf.* Fig. 9-1). This synaptic transmission would operate with greatly increased potency during reverberating circuit action. As shown in Figure 9-9 this potentiation would also be on the circuit form CA3 neurones to the prefrontal lobe and so would be of importance in causing a progressive build-up in the activation of the cartridge synapses.

By the conjunction in the prefrontal cortex in Figures 9-6 and 9-9, it is proposed that there is an enduring potentiation of some of the synapses made on the pyramidal cells by the horizontal fibres stemming from the association and callosal afferents. Thus there would be a tendency for the same spatio-temporal pattern of modular activity to develop as with the original input. This modular replay would provide the neural basis for the memory that is experienced in the mind.

It is interesting that motivation comes into Kornhuber's circuit diagram (Fig. 9-6). This implies attention or interest in the experiences that are coded in the neuronal activities of the association cortex and that are to be stored. It implies a process of mind-brain interaction. We are all cognizant that we do not store memories of no interest to us and to which we do not pay attention. It is a familiar statement that a single sharp experience is remembered for a lifetime, but it overlooks the fact that the intense emotional involvement is re-experienced incessantly immediately after the original, highly charged emotional experience. Evidently there has been a long series of 'replays' of the patterns of cortical activity associated with the original experience, and this activity would particularly involve the limbic system as indicated by the strong emotional overtones. Thus there must be built into the neuronal machinery of the cortex the propensity for the reverberating circuit activity which would cause the synaptic potentiation giving the memory. In the further development of our hypotheses of long-term conscious memory we would propose that the self-conscious mind would enter into this transaction between the modules of the liaison brain and the hippocampus in two ways: firstly, in keeping up the modular activity by the general action of interest or attention (the motivation system of Kornhuber, 1973) so that the hippocampal circuit would be continuously reinforced; secondly, in a more concentrated manner by probing into the appropriate modules to read out their storage and if necessary to reinforce it or modify it by direct action on the modules concerned. Both of these proposed actions are from the self-conscious mind to those modules that have the special property of being open to it. However, as will be proposed in Lecture 10, by its direct action on open modules the self-conscious mind can exercise an indirect action on those closed modules to which the open modules project.

Although the conjunction theory has been developed in relation to the prefrontal cortex, it is not to be inferred that other regions of the neocortex do not also participate in learned responses. Further experimental evidence is needed, particularly on the circuits from the hippocampus. All that can be claimed is that the prefrontal lobes are probably the principal sites of memory storage. Over forty years ago Jacobson (1936) showed that a simple memory response, the delayed reaction test, was completely eliminated by bilateral excision of the frontal lobes of chimpanzees. Moreover several variants of this test have been developed and the memories also have been lost after prefrontal lobectomy (cf. Eccles, 1978).

9.3.3 Storage of Memories

At the conclusion of this rather complex story of the neural events that are related to the storage of memories, it is well to conclude with some simplified statements.

The learning story here presented is a special example of the generally accepted growth theory of learning, according to which some synapses are potentiated by activity. Thus some particular spatio-temporal pattern of neuronal activity comes to be stabilized by usage so that at some later time it can be caused to be replayed in the neuronal machinery of the cortex and thus remembered in the mind. It can be conjectured that literally millions of neurones participate in building up the specific pattern or engram that gives some particular memory to the mind. We are far from understanding how such patterns can be built up from elemental components such as would be represented in Figure 9-8 by the selective hypertrophy of the synapses formed by that association fibre on the apical dendrites of that pyramidal cell. But there is no rival theory of the neuronal mechanisms concerned in cognitive learning. There are only vague conjectures that have not been formulated in specific representations comparable to those in Figures 9-6 and 9-9.

It is important to recognize that the postulated synaptic hypertrophy would require a complex metabolic reaction with synthesis of an array of macromolecules concerned in building additional membranes and all the essential presynaptic and postsynaptic components such as synaptic vesicles and specific postsynaptic receptor sites. It is known that learning is prevented by poisoning the enzymes concerned in these metabolic processes. There is also the model discovered by Libet and co-workers (1975) for a conjunction operation in a sympathetic ganglion cell where input by dopaminergic synapses results in a prolonged enhancement of the cholinergic synapses on the same cell. This potentiation by conjunction is mediated by an intracellular metabolic system utilizing cyclic adenosine monophosphate (AMP).

In Figure 9–10 there is a diagrammatic representation of modules of the neocortex as seen from above (cf. Fig. 8–15). For diagrammatic convenience the modules are drawn well separated. The attempt is made to show how strong activation of a module causes it to excite scattered modules by means of the projections of its pyramidal cell axons (cf. Fig. 8–4). These modules in turn, if sufficiently excited, will excite other modules, and so on. The sequence of modular involvements is given by numbers, and the arrows indicate the excitatory pathways via pyramidal cell axons. All that can be

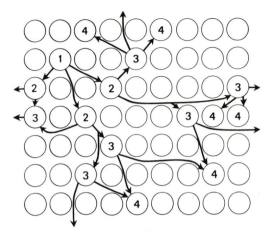

Fig. 9-10. Diagrammatic representation of cortical modules as seen from above as in Figure 8-15. In order to allow drawing of transmission pathways from module to module, the modules are drawn well separated and not in the actual close juxtaposition. Strong activation of module *1* as in Figure 8-4 leads to transmission effectively exciting modules labelled *2,* and these in turn to the modules (*3*) and then modules (*4*). Further description in text

shown in such a diagram is the serial manner in which a modular pattern is built up from one strongly excited module and from the projecting pathways from module to module. This diagram is a challenge to your imagination in several respects: to conceive that the total modular array is about 4 million instead of the 63 here represented; to conceive perhaps 100 modules initially active, not just the one here represented; to conceive of the pattern developing over as many as 100 modular relays with all manner of re-entry connectivities in the manner of the one shown in Figure 8–15.

9.4 Memory Retrieval

In retrieval of a memory we have further to conjecture that the self-conscious mind is continuously searching to recover memories, e. g. words, phrases, sentences, ideas, events, pictures, melodies, by actively scanning through the modular array (*cf.* Fig. 10-2 on the right-hand side) and that, by its action on the preferred open modules, it tries to evoke the full neural patterned operation that it can read out as a recognizable memory rich in emotional and/or intellectual content. Largely this could be by a trial-and-error process. We are all familiar with the ease or difficulty of recall of one or another memory, and of the strategies we learn in order to recover memories of names that for some unknown reason are refractory to recall. We can imagine that our self-conscious mind is under a continual challenge to recall the desired memory by discovering the appropriate entry into module operation that would by development give the appropriate patterned array of modules. Figure 10-2 is a most inadequate diagram. Even in a simple memory recall there probably would be hundreds of modules to be initially selected in defining the specificity of the memory together with thousands of modules in the response that delivers the fully fashioned memory.

It is proposed that there are two distinct kinds of conscious memory. Data-bank memory is stored in the brain and its retrieval from the brain is often by a deliberate mental act. Then another memory process comes into play – what we may call recognition memory. The retrieval from the data banks is critically scrutinized in the mind. It may be judged erroneous – perhaps a slight error in a name or in a number sequence. This leads to a renewed attempt at retrieval, which may again be judged faulty – and so on until the retrieval is judged to be correct, or until the attempt is abandoned. It is therefore conjectured that there are two distinct kinds of memory: (1) brain storage memory held in the data banks of the brain, especially in the cerebral cortex; (2) recognition memory that is applied by the self-conscious mind in its scrutiny of the retrievals from the brain storage memories. There is further discussion of memory retrieval in a recent book (Popper and Eccles, 1977).

Penfield and Perot (1963) gave a most illuminating account of the experiential responses evoked in 53 patients by stimulation of the cerebral hemispheres during operations performed under local anaesthesia. These responses differed from those produced by stimulation of the primary sensory areas, which were merely flashes of light or touches and paraesthesia (Lecture 8), in that the patients had experiences that resembled dreams, the so-called dreamy states. During the continued gentle electrical stimulation of sites on the exposed surface of their brains, the patients reported experiences that they often recognized as being recalls of long-forgotten memories. As Penfield states, it is as if a past stream of consciousness is recovered during this electrical stimulation. The most common experiences were visual or auditory, but there were also many cases of combined visual and auditory. The recall of music and song provided very striking experiences for both the patient and the neurosurgeon. All of these results were obtained from brains of patients with a history of epileptic seizures. Figure 9–11 shows the sites of stimulation that evoked experiential responses in

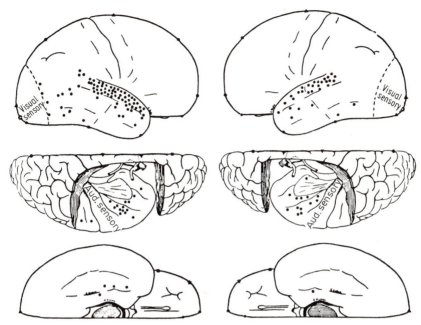

Fig. 9-11. Drawings of human brain to show sites from which experiental responses were produced by electrical stimulation in the total experimental series. In the upper row are the right and left hemispheres seen from the lateral aspect. In the middle row the view is from above and the parietal and frontal lobes are cut away to show the superior aspect of the temporal lobes. In the lowest rows the view is from below. Penfield, W., Perot, P.: The brain's record of auditory and visual experience. Brain *86*, 596–696 (1963)

the whole series of patients. It is noteworthy that the temporal lobes were the preferred sites, and that the minor hemisphere was more effective than the dominant. It also will be recognized that the primary sensory areas are excluded.

In summary of these most interesting investigations it is stated that the experiences are those in which the patient is an observer not a participator, just as in dreams.

The times that are summoned most frequently are briefly these: the times of watching or hearing the action and speech of others, and times of hearing music. Certain sorts of experience seem to be absent. For example, the times of making up one's mind to do this or that do not appear in the record. Times of carrying out skilled acts, times of speaking or saying this and that, or of writing messages and adding figures – these things are not recorded. Times of eating and tasting food, times of sexual excitement or experience – these things have been absent as well as periods of painful suffering or weeping. Modesty does not explain these silences. (Penfield and Perot, 1963)

It can be concluded that the stimulation acts as a mode of recall of past experiences. We may regard this as an instrumental means for a recovery of memories. It can be suggested that the storage of these memories is likely to be in cerebral areas close to the effective stimulation sites. However it is important to recognize that the experiential recall is evoked from areas in the region of the disordered cerebral function that is displayed by the epileptic seizures. Conceivably the effective sites are abnormal zones that are thereby able to act by association pathways to the much wider areas of the cerebral cortex which are the actual storage sites for memories.

9.5 Duration of Memories

An analysis of the durations of the various processes involved in memory provides evidence for three distinct memory processes (cf. McGaugh, 1969). We have already presented evidence for the short-term memory, usually of a few seconds, which can be attributed to the continual activity in neural circuits that holds the memory in a dynamic pattern of circulating impulses. The patients with bilateral hippocampectomy have almost no other memory. Secondly there is the long-term memory, which endures for days to years. According to the growth theory of learning, this memory (or memory trace) is encoded in the increased efficacy of synapses that have been hyperactive during and after the original episode that is being remembered. In the present context of conscious memory it can be conjectured that this synaptic growth would occur in multitudes of synapses in patterned array in the modules strongly reacting in response to the original episode that sets in train the operation of the reverberatory circuits through the hippocampus. As a consequence of this synaptic growth, the self-conscious mind would be able to develop strategies for causing the replay of modules in a pattern resembling that of the original episode, hence the memory experience. Moreover this replay would be accompanied by a renewed reverberatory activity through the hippocampus resembling the original, with a consequent strengthening of the memory trace.

However we are confronted with the urgent problem of filling in the temporal gap between the short-term memory of seconds and the hours required for the synaptic growth of long-term memory. Barondes (1970) reviews the experiments testing for the time course of action of substances, cycloheximide for example, that prevent protein synthesis in the brain, which at the same time is unable to learn. The approximate time of about 30 min to 3 h seems to be required for the synaptic growth giving long-term

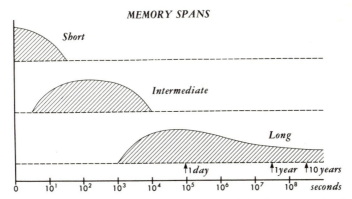

Fig. 9-12. Diagrammatic representation of the durations of the three memories described in the text. Note the logarithmic time scale and the conjectured rise and fall of the memories with time

memory. McGaugh (1969) has proposed an intermediate-term memory to bridge the gap of seconds to hours between the end of short-term memory and the full development of synaptic growth giving the long-term memory, as is diagrammed in Figure 9–12. We would propose that post-tetanic potentiation is exactly fitted for bridging this gap. It would be induced by the repetitive synaptic activations of short-term memory and would immediately follow those actions, utilizing the same hippocampal loop circuitry as for long-term memory. It would be restricted to the activated synapses and would be graded in accord with their action. In Figure 9-1 post-tetanic potentiations enduring for hours followed quite mild repetitive stimulation of hippocampal synapses. As that physiological process of synaptic potentiation declines, the metabolically induced synaptic growth (*cf.* Fig. 9-2) supervenes to provide an enduring basis for the strategic readout by the self-conscious mind.

9.6 Retrograde Amnesia

It is a common observation that loss of memory results from a severe trauma of the brain, as for example from mechanical damage giving unconsciousness (concussion) or from the convulsive seizures resulting from electroshock therapy. The retrograde amnesia is ususally complete for events immediately before the trauma, and becomes progressively less severe for memories of earlier and still earlier events. Depending on the severity of the trauma, retrograde amnesia may cover periods of minutes, hours or days.

Animal investigations have used the memory built up by training procedures to test for retrograde amnesia produced by trauma applied at various times after training. The trauma could be by electroshock or by various chemical agents. The experiments indicate that the memory storage process is consolidated during 6 h after the training period. With shorter times the memories are progressively more sensitive to trauma. It can be envisaged that the growing of synapses that results in long-term memory (*cf.* Figs. 9-2, 9-3B, C) is very sensitive to trauma for many hours, presumably until the whole growth process is completed (*cf.* McGaugh, 1969; Barondes, 1970).

Following hippocampectomy there was not only the severe anterograde amnesia for events following the operation but there was also a severe retrograde amnesia, i. e. for events preceding the operation by hours or days (Milner, 1972). Apparently the trauma of the operation caused this retrograde amnesia, which in the course of time became less severe, i. e. events preceding the operation were better remembered.

9.7 Conclusions

The ability to learn came very early in the evolution of the nervous system. There are remarkable studies on the learning processes of invertebrates and of lower vertebrates. Modifiable synapses have been identified in many nervous systems. As already mentioned motor learning involves quite different parts of the brain. Our concern in these lectures has been to trace the evolutionary process up to its pinnacle of achievement in the human brain. And cognitive memory must rank at the summit of the human memory processes because it concerns the storage and retrieval of conscious experiences.

Of course much of our memory is implicit, giving each of us our character in its widest sense. It is involved in our personal formation from the earliest childhood learning right up to the present time. For example we come to look at things differently and to react differently, but this is not consciously recognized by us, or only very dimly. There is a discussion on *implicit memory* in Popper and Eccles (1977).

This lecture has been on the much more recognizable *explicit memory*. In this memory *H. sapiens* is supreme. The range of memory is unbelievably large. We have immense 'data banks' with literally millions of stored memories. The difficulty is in retrieval, which becomes progressively more difficult with age, in part at least because of the progressively increasing storage.

I have also postulated another memory that is in World 2, not in the brain, as is shown in the box to the right of Figure 10-2. In the first place it functions in the attempt to recall a memory. This must be an active selection process exerted on cortical modules. In the second place it has a recognition role, judging the correctness of the retrieved memory, as experienced consciously, e. g. of a name or of a number. If the read-out from the data banks is judged as faulty, then it can reinstitute the search.

The cerebral mechanisms postulated for cognitive memory (Figs. 9-6, 9-8 and 9-9) must be regarded as an attempt to build up an explanatory hypothesis that is in accord with present knowledge and that challenges experimental testing. As has been pointed out (Eccles, 1978), this selection theory of cerebral memory is comparable with the cerebellar memory hypothesis for motor learning (Eccles, 1977) and both are derivative from Jerne's (1967) selection theory of immunity.

Undoubtedly the hypotheses developed for brain-mind interaction in memory storage and retrieval are still provisional. In particular the brain-mind problem is central to the problem of cognitive memory, and as we shall see in Lecture 10 the brain-mind problem is central to the human mystery. What is utterly mysterious is that the human brain was evolved for survival in a primitive community, yet it came to have immense and wonderful performances in cognitive memory. Contrast the poverty of the chimpanzee's abilities with the richness of the human performance.

The Mind-Brain Problem:
Experimental Evidence and Hypothesis

Synopsis and Introduction

There is a critical evaluation of the various hypotheses that have been developed in order to account for the conscious experiences that are associated with many cerebral activities. This leads on to the formulation of a strong dualist-interactionist hypothesis. Then follows an account of three lines of experimental evidence relating to this hypothesis.

Firstly there will be a description of experiments on the problem of voluntary action. These experiments raise very profound problems, for they establish that the willing of a movement activates neuronal systems of the brain. There has been an action across the interface between the self-conscious mind with its willing and the neuronal systems that are concerned in the eventual activation of the correct motor pyramidal cells for bringing about the desired movement. Secondly investigations on commissurotomized patients illuminate the brain-mind problem from many aspects. Thirdly investigation on the time relations of brain to mind in conscious experience also provide significant evidence.

On the basis of the experimental evidence given in this and the two preceding lectures there will be formulated in some detail a strong dualist-interactionist hypothesis which is built upon new insights into the working of the brain that derive from recent discoveries of its modular structure.

Thus I conclude this course of lectures by involvement in the most mysterious of all phenomena – the interaction of mental events, thoughts, desires, intentions, etc. with brain events. This interaction occurs in a two-way process of information flow across the frontier between the self-conscious mind on the one hand and the liaison areas of the brain on the other. Much of the second series of lectures will be concerned with these deep problems that are central to the human mystery.

In Chapter P3 of the recent book (Popper and Eccles, 1977), Popper gives a critical evaluation of the various materialist or physicalist theories of the mind. For our present purpose it is of value to clarify the issue by means of an explanatory diagram (Fig. 10-1) of the principal theories so that the materialist theories can be contrasted with the dualist-interactionist theory that is here being proposed. In Figure 10-1 World 1 and World 2 are defined in general terms, much as in Figure 6-1. For purposes of discussion and comparison World 1 can be divided into World 1p and World 1m. In general, materialist theories are those subscribing to the statement that mental events can have no *effective* action on the brain events in World 1. Thus the adopted notation leads to the formulation of the various types of materialist theories as expressed in Figure 10-1. Common to them all is the assertion that World 1 is closed. There is no violation of the first law of thermodynamics. There is no *effective* action on the World 1 events in the brain by any happenings outside World 1, such as is postulated by dualist-interactionism. This closedness of World 1 is ensured in four different ways as depicted in Figure 10-1.

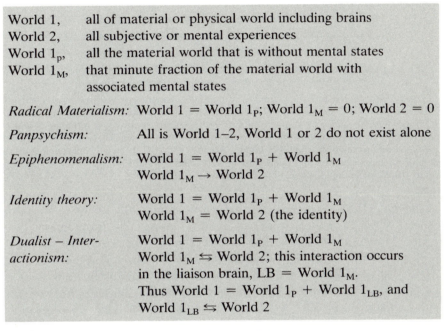

World 1, all of material or physical world including brains
World 2, all subjective or mental experiences
World 1_p, all the material world that is without mental states
World 1_M, that minute fraction of the material world with associated mental states

Radical Materialism: World 1 = World 1_p; World 1_M = 0; World 2 = 0

Panpsychism: All is World 1–2, World 1 or 2 do not exist alone

Epiphenomenalism: World 1 = World 1_p + World 1_M
World $1_M \rightarrow$ World 2

Identity theory: World 1 = World 1_p + World 1_M
World 1_M = World 2 (the identity)

Dualist – Interactionism: World 1 = World 1_p + World 1_M
World $1_M \leftrightarrows$ World 2; this interaction occurs in the liaison brain, LB = World 1_M.
Thus World 1 = World 1_p + World 1_{LB}, and World $1_{LB} \leftrightarrows$ World 2

Fig. 10-1. Diagrammatic representation of brain-mind theories

1. Radical materialism. It is asserted that all is World 1. There is a denial or repudiation of the existence of mental events. They are simply illusory. The mind-brain problem is a non-problem!

2. Panpsychism. It is asserted that all matter has an inside mental or proto-psychical state. Since this state is an integral part of matter, it can have no action on it. The closedness of World 1 is safeguarded.

3. Epiphenomenalism. Mental states exist in relation to some material happenings, but causally are completely irrelevant. Again the closedness of World 1 is safeguarded.

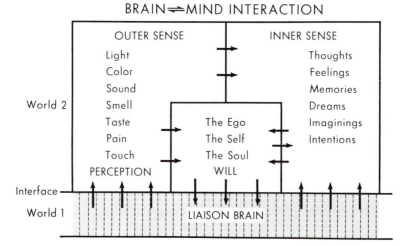

Fig. 10-2. Information flow diagram for brain-mind interaction. The three components of World 2: outer sense, inner sense and the ego or self are diagrammed with their connectivities. Also shown are the lines of communication across the interface between World 1 and World 2, that is from the liaison brain to and from these World 2 components. The liaison brain has the columnar arrangement indicated (*cf.* Figures 8-4, 8-6 and 8-8). It must be imagined that the area of the liaison brain is enormous with open modules (*cf.* Fig. 10-10) probably numbering up to 1 million and not just the 40 here depicted

4. Identity Theory or *Central State Theory*. Mental states exist as an inner aspect of some material structures that in present formulations are restricted to brain structures such as nerve cells. This postulated 'identity' may appear to give mental states an effective action, just as the 'identical' nerve cells have an effective action. However the result of the transaction is that the purely material events of neural action are themselves *sufficient* for all mind-brain responses, hence the closedness of World 1 is preserved.

In contrast to these materialist or parallelist theories are the *dualist-interaction* theories as diagrammed at the bottom of Figure 10-1. The essential feature of these theories is that mind and brain are independent entities, the brain being in World 1 and the mind in World 2 (Fig. 6-1), and that they somehow interact, as illustrated by the arrows in Figure 10-2. Thus there is a frontier, as diagrammed in Figure 10-2, and across this frontier there is interaction in both directions, which can be conceived as a flow of information, not of energy. Thus we have the extraordinary doctrine that the world of matter-energy (World 1) is not completely sealed, which is a fundamental tenet of physics, but that there are small 'crevices' in what is otherwise the completely closed World 1. On the contrary the closedness of World 1 has been safeguarded with great ingenuity in all materialist theories of the mind. Yet I shall argue that this is not their strength, but instead their fatal weakness (Popper and Eccles, 1977).

There are of course immense problems entailed in this postulate of an independent existence of mental events and their interaction with the brain. Their consideration will occupy much of this lecture.

Historically Descartes was the first to formulate clearly a dualist theory, but this suffered from the contemporary primitive and erroneous theories of nerve action. Sherrington (1940) developed a much more sophisticated dualist-interactionist theory, and recently Penfield (1975) has supported dualism on the basis of his life-long dedication, as a neurologist and a neurosurgeon, to the study of human persons and human brains, particularly when disordered.

Until 4 years ago my philosophical position could be described as equivalent to neo-Cartesian dualism. I believed that in its World 2 existence (*cf.* Fig. 10-2) the self-conscious mind was an immaterial entity distinct from the brain. However, if, as I then believed, the self-conscious mind was merely reading out from the spatio-temporal patterned operation of the brain, I came to realize that eventually there must be reduction of even the most esoteric thoughts and the most subtle decisions to the brain events from which they were derived. Parallelism would prevail. Brain events are entirely within the physical world (World 1 of Fig. 10-2), and, as we have seen, according to parallelism, the happenings in the neural machinery of the brain provide a necessary and sufficient explanation of the totality both of the performance and of the conscious experience of a human being. The subject is thus *completely determined* by the brain events. But as Popper (1972) states:

> According to determinism, any theory such as say determinism is held because of a certain physical structure of the holder – perhaps of his brain. Accordingly, we are deceiving ourselves and are physically so determined as to deceive ourselves whenever we believe that there are such things as arguments or reasons which make us accept determinism. In other words, physical determinism is a theory which, if it is true, is unarguable since it must explain all our reactions, including what appear to us as beliefs based on arguments, as due to purely physical conditions. Purely physical conditions, including our physical environment make us say or accept whatever we say or accept.

This is an effective *reductio ad absurdum*. This stricture applies to all of the parallelist theories including even my earlier formulation of dualism-interactionism (Eccles, 1970). This is the prohibitive price mentioned above. In the light of these considerations I was led to revise my dualist-interactionist hypotheses to the much more radical form that will later be developed *in extenso*, particularly in relation to the liaison brain and its mode of operation (*cf.* Chap. E7, Popper and Eccles, 1977).

10.1 Dualist-Interactionist Hypothesis

The essential feature of the hypothesis is the active role of the self-conscious mind in its relationship to the neuronal machinery of the brain. Recent experimental investigations provide evidence on important aspects of this relationship.

10.1.1 Relationship of Mind to Brain in Voluntary Action

A fundamental neurological problem is: How can willing of a muscular movement set in train neuronal events that lead to the discharge of pyramidal cells of the motor cortex and so to activation of the neuronal pathway that leads to the muscle contraction? We are now in a position to consider the experiements of Kornhuber (1974) on the electrical potential generated in the cerebral cortex prior to the carrying out of a willed action. There is an attractive parallelism between these beautifully simple experiments and those of Galileo in investigating the laws of motion of the universe by studying the movements of metal balls rolling down an inclined plane!

The problem is to have an elementally simple movement executed by the subject entirely on his own volition, and yet to have accurate timing in order to average the very small potentials recorded from the surface of the scalp. This has been solved by Kornhuber and his associates, who use the onset of muscle action potentials involved in the movement to trigger a reverse computation of the potentials up to 2 s before the onset of the movement. The movement illustrated was a rapid flexion of the right index finger. The subject initiates these movements 'at will' at irregular intervals of many seconds, and is scrupulously screened from all possible triggering stimuli. In this way it was possible to average from 250 to 800 records of the potentials evoked at each of several sites over the surface of the skull, especially the precentral and parietal regions, as shown in Figure 10-3 for the three upper traces. The slowly rising negative potential, called the *readiness potential,* was observed in all subjects as a negative wave with unipolar recording over a wide area of the cerebral surface (recorded by scalp leads), but there were small positive potentials of similar time course over the most anterior and basal regions of the cerebrum. Usually the readiness potential began almost as long as 800 ms before the onset of the muscle action potentials, and led on to a sharper potential, the *pre-motion positivity,* beginning at 80–90 ms. In the lowest trace there was bipolar leading from symmetrical zones over the motor cortex, that on the left being over the

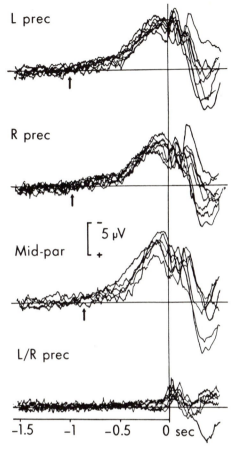

Fig. 10-3. Readiness potentials recorded at indicated sites from the scalp in response to voluntary movements of finger. Zero time is at the onset of the movement, the preceding potentials being derived by backwards computation, with averaging of 250 responses. *L prec,* left precentral; *R prec,* right precentral; *Mid-par,* mid-parietal; *L/R prec,* recording left precentral against right precentral. Further description in the text. Kornhuber, H. H.: Cerebral cortex, cerebellum and basal ganglia: An introduction to their motor functions. In: The neurosciences: third study program. Schmitt, F. O., Worden, F. G. (eds.), pp. 267–280. Cambridge (Mass.): MIT Press 1974

area concerned in the finger movement (*cf.* Fig. 8-1). There was no detectable asymmetry until a sharp negativity developed at 50 ms before the onset of the muscle action potentials.

We can assume that the readiness potential is generated by complex patterns of neuronal discharges that are originally symmetrical, but eventually project to the appropriate pyramidal cells of the motor cortex and

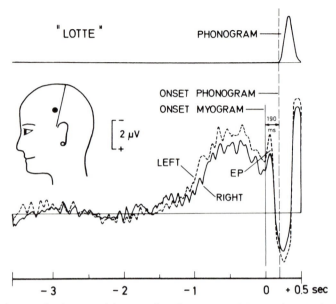

Fig. 10-4. Average brain potentials preceding the test word 'Lotte' (*N*=250). The latency between the onset of the mouth myogram and the phonogram is 190 ms. Evoked potentials occur during this interval. Left and right recordings were obtained from symmetrically placed electrodes at the site marked on the scalp. Grözinger, B., Kornhuber, H. H., Kriebel, J.: Methodological problems in the investigation of cerebral potentials preceding speech: Determining the onset and suppressing artefacts caused by speech. Neuropsychologia *13*, 263–270 (1975)

synaptically excite them to discharge, so generating this localized negative wave (the so-called *motor potential*) just preceding the motor pyramidal cell discharge that initiates the movement. With more complex movements the readiness potential was even longer, being for example about 1.5 s for articulating the word 'Lotte' (Fig. 10-4).

It is remarkable that initially the readiness potential is symmetrical and only at 150 ms before the movement is there a contralateral preponderance, which is of course related to that part of the motor cortex eventually generating the motor discharge (Deecke et al., 1976). There is a large discrepancy between the durations of the readiness potential and the reaction time. However, it must be recognized that reaction times are measured from a strong initiating stimulus that within a few milliseconds gives a massive cerebral excitation. By contrast, in the absence of any initiating stimulus, the voluntary command is very weak and requires hundreds of milliseconds to build up a cerebral excitation sufficiently intense for initiating a motor discharge, as is shown by the time course of the readiness potential.

These experiments at least provide a partial answer to the question: What is happening in my brain at a time when a willed action is in the process of being carried out? It can be presumed that during the readiness potential there is a developing specificity of the patterned impulse discharges in neurones so that eventually there are activated the pyramidal cells in the correct motor cortical areas for bringing about the required movement. The readiness potential can be regarded as the neuronal counterpart of the voluntary command. The surprising feature of the readiness potential is its wide extent and gradual build-up. Apparently, at the stage of willing a movement, there is very wide influence of the self-conscious mind on the patterns of module operation. Eventually this immense neuronal activity is moulded and directed so that it concentrates onto the pyramidal cells in the proper zones of the motor cortex (*cf.* Fig. 8-1) for carrying out the required movement. The duration of the readiness potential indicates that the sequential activity of large numbers of modules is involved in the long incubation time required for the self-conscious mind to evoke discharges from the motor pyramidal cells. Presumably this time is employed in building up the requisite spatio-temporal patterns in thousands of modules in the cerebral cortex. It is a sign that the action of the self-conscious mind on the brain is not of demanding strength. We may regard it as being more tentative and subtle, and as requiring time to build up patterns of activity that may be modified as they develop. It is important to recognize that during the readiness potential there probably would be activation of subcortical structures such as the cerebellum, the basal ganglia and the thalamus (Deecke et al., 1976), which are all of importance in ensuring that the movement will be well co-ordinated (Allen and Tsukahara, 1974).

In summary, the dualist-interactionist hypothesis helps to resolve and redefine the problem of accounting for the long duration of the readiness potential that precedes a voluntary action.

10.1.2 Mind-Brain Relationship as Studied in Commissurotomized Patients

The corpus callosum (Fig. 10-5) is a tract of about 200 million fibres that provides an immense commissural linkage in an approximately mirror-image manner between almost all regions of the cerebral hemispheres. The intense impulse traffic in the corpus callosum keeps the two hemispheres of

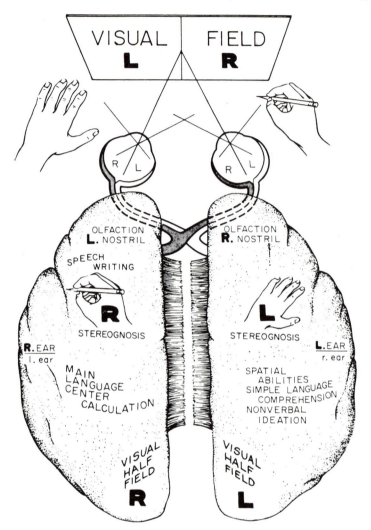

Fig. 10-5. Schema showing the way in which the left and right visual fields are projected onto the right and left visual cortices, respectively, due to the partial decussation in the optic chiasma (*cf.* Fig. 8-11). The schema also shows other sensory inputs from right limbs to the left hemisphere and that from left limbs to the right hemisphere. Similarly, hearing is largely crossed in its input, but olfaction is ipsilateral. The programming of the right hand in writing is shown pictorially to come from the left hemisphere. Sperry, R. W.: Lateral specialization in the surgically separated hemispheres. In: The neurosciences: third study program. Schmitt, F. O., Worden, F. G. (eds.), pp. 5–19. Cambridge (Mass.): MIT Press 1974

the brain working together. The corpus callosum has been completely severed in about 20 human subjects who were suffering from almost incessant epileptic seizures that could not be controlled even by heavy medication. It was surmised that seizures developed in one cerebral hemisphere and then excited the other via the corpus callosum so that the seizure rapidly became generalized. Hence it was proposed that section of the corpus callosum would at least keep one hemisphere free from the seizures. It turns out that the operation does better than predicted. There is a remarkable diminution of seizures in both hemispheres.

Sperry and associates (1974) have developed testing procedures in which information can be fed into one or the other hemisphere of these 'split-brain' patients and in which the responses of either hemisphere can be independently observed. All of the seven investigated subjects had the speech areas in the left hemisphere (*cf.* Fig. 8-1), which was thus always the dominant hemisphere. The most remarkable discovery of these experiments was that all the neural activities in the right hemisphere (the so-called minor hemisphere) are unknown to the speaking subject, who is only in liaison with the neuronal activities in the left hemisphere, the *dominant hemisphere*. Only through the dominant hemisphere can the subject communicate with language. Furthermore, in liaison with this hemisphere is the conscious being or self that is recognizably the same person as before the operation.

Figure 10-5 is a diagram drawn by Sperry several years ago. However, it is still valuable as a basis of discussion of the whole split-brain *(commissurotomy)* story. The diagram illustrates the right and left visual fields with their highly selective projection to the crossed visual cortices, as indicated by the letters R and L. Also shown in the diagram is the strictly unilateral projection of smell, and the predominantly crossed projection of hearing. The crossed representations of both motor and sensory innervation of the hands are indicated, and also the further finding that arithmetical calculation is predominant in the left hemisphere. Only very simple addition sums can be carried out by the right hemisphere.

We can say that the right hemisphere is a very highly developed brain except that it cannot express itself in language, so it is not able to disclose any experience of consciousness that we can recognize. Sperry postulates that there is another consciousness in the right hemisphere, but that its existence is obscured by its lack of expressive language. On the other hand, the left hemisphere has a normal linguistic performance, so it can be recognized as being associated with the prior existence of the ego or the self with all the memories of the past before the commissurotomy. In this view there

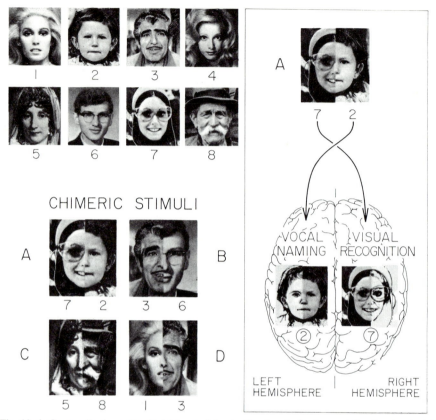

Fig. 10-6. Composite face stimuli (chimeras) for testing hemispheric specialization for facial recognition. Full explanation in text. Levy, J., Trevarthen, C., Sperry, R. W.: Perception of bilateral chimeric figures following hemispheric deconnexion. Brain *95*, 61–78 (1972)

has been split off from the talking self a non-talking self which cannot communicate by language, so it is there but mute, or aphasic. For the present we can say that we do not know if there is some inexpressible consciousness in the isolated right hemisphere, just as we do not know of any consciousness animals might have. We cannot discover it in any way, but we have to realize the limitations of our testing procedure both for higher animals and for the right hemisphere after section of the corpus callosum. It is important to distinguish between the self-consciousness associated with the left hemisphere, and the postulated consciousness associated with the right hemisphere.

In general, the dominant hemisphere is specialized in respect to fine imaginative details in all descriptions and reactions, i. e. it is analytic and sequential. Also it can add and subtract and multiply and carry out other computer-like operations. But of course its dominance derives from its verbal and ideational abilities and its liaison to self-consciousness (World 2). Because of its deficiencies in these respects the minor hemisphere deserves its title, but in many important properties it is pre-eminent, particularly in respect of its spatial abilities with a strongly developed pictorial and pattern sense. For example, the minor hemisphere programming the left hand is greatly superior in all kinds of geometrical and perspective drawings. This superiority is also evidenced by the ability to assemble coloured blocks so as to match a mosaic picture. The dominant hemisphere is unable to carry out even simple tasks of this kind and is almost illiterate in respect to pictorial and pattern sense, at least as displayed by its copying disability. It is an arithmetical hemisphere but not a geometrical hemisphere.

Remarkable examples of the complementary functions of the dominant and minor hemispheres have been revealed by the chimeric studies of Levy et al. (1972). Chimeric figures were formed by splitting pictures, for example of a face as in Figure 10-6. The faces are numbered 1–8 and chimeric stimuli are shown by four combinations in A, B, C, D. One of these combinations is flashed on the screen while the subject fixes the mid-point of the screen. For example, the chimeric ensemble A is formed from faces 7 and 2. The image in the left visual field (half of 7) is projected to the right hemisphere. Similarly the right visual field projects with half of image 2 to the left hemisphere. Because of the absence of commissural communication each hemisphere proceeds perceptually to complete the image, as shown by the images inscribed on each hemisphere. The chimeric nature of the total visual input is not recognized, but each hemisphere displays responses in accord with its specific functions. Thus if a verbal response is required, the vocal naming is in accord with the image, 2, completed in the left hemisphere. On the other hand, if there is a visual recognition response by pointing with the left hand to the array of 8 faces, face 7 is indicated. There have been many variants of this chimeric testing with various objects besides faces. Always the results illustrate the complete separation of the two hemispheres in their perceptual responses. If a verbal response is required, the left hemisphere dominates with its perception of the right visual field. The right hemisphere dominates if the required perception is for complex and nondescript patterns and when there is a manual readout, for example by pointing. Thus the chimeric testing confirms the distinctive functions of the two hemispheres as indicated in Figure 10-5 and 10-7.

Figure 10-7 shows that in their properties after commissurotomy the

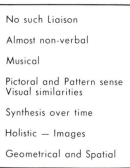

DOMINANT HEMISPHERE	MINOR HEMISPHERE
Liaison to consciousness	No such Liaison
Verbal	Almost non-verbal
Linguistic description	Musical
Ideational Conceptual similarities	Pictoral and Pattern sense Visual similarities
Analysis over time	Synthesis over time
Analysis of detail	Holistic — Images
Arithmetical and computer-like	Geometrical and Spatial

Fig. 10-7. Various specific performances of the dominant and minor hemispheres as suggested by the new conceptual developments of Levy-Agresti and Sperry (1968) and Levy (1973). There are some additions to their original list

two hemispheres are complementary. The minor is coherent and the dominant is detailed. Furthermore, not only is the minor hemisphere pictorial, but there is much recent evidence that it is musical. Music is essentially coherent and synthetic, being dependent on a sequential input of sounds. A coherent, synthetic, sequential imagery is made for us in some holistic manner by our musical sense. Furthermore, there is accumulating evidence by Milner (1967, 1974) that excision of the right temporal lobe does, in fact, seriously limit musical ability, as displayed in the Seashore tests.

The distinctiveness of the functions of the two hemisphere listed in Figure 10-7 is also indicated by the results of the dichotic technique. This is essentially a study of the subject's response to signals of a given modality that are applied so as to give competitive inputs into the two hemispheres. This new psychological technique of inter-hemisphere challenge has the great advantage that it can be applied to normal subjects, but on the other hand the results are not so discriminative as with studies of the effects of hemispheral lesions, both global and circumscribed.

It is an attractive hypothesis of Sperry's that the two hemispheres have complementary functions, which is an efficient arrangement because each can independently exercise its own peculiar abilities in developing and fashioning the neuronal input. Then, as illustrated in Figure 10-8 by commissural transfer the two complementary performances can be combined and integrated in the ideational, linguistic and liaison areas.

It is my thesis that the philosophical problem of brain and mind has been transformed by these investigations of the functions of the separated dominant and minor hemispheres in the split-brain subjects. Several years

MODES OF INTERACTION BETWEEN HEMISPHERES

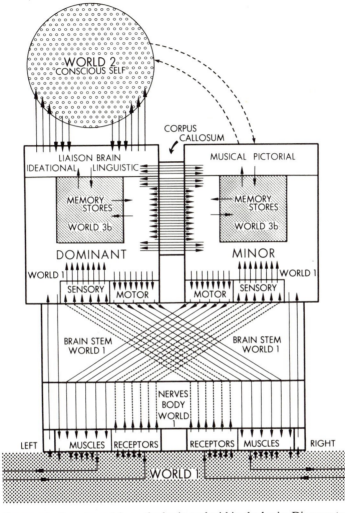

Fig. 10-8. Communications to and from the brain and within the brain. Diagram to show the principal lines of communication from peripheral receptors to the sensory cortices and so to the cerebral hemispheres. Similarly, the diagram shows the output from the cerebral hemispheres via the motor cortex and so to muscles. Both these systems of pathways are largely crossed as illustrated, but minor uncrossed pathways are also shown by the vertical lines in the brain stem. The dominant left hemisphere and minor right hemisphere are labelled, together with some of the properties of these hemispheres that are found displayed in Figure 10-7. The corpus callosum is shown as a powerful crosslinking of the two hemispheres and, in addition, the diagram displays the modes of interaction between Worlds 1 and 2, as described in the text, and also illustrated in Figure 6-1

ago (Eccles, 1970) I suggested that, even before splitting, the conscious self was in liaison only with the dominant hemisphere, and that the minor hemisphere was always an unconscious hemisphere per se, but in the ordinary situations its reactions achieved consciousness by communication with the dominant hemisphere by means of the massive impulse traffic through the corpus callosum. This hypothesis can be made quite specific in the diagrammatic illustration of the brain and its communications in Figure 10-8. The conscious self (the World 2 of Popper) is shown to be in direct liaison with specific linguistic and ideational zones of the dominant hemisphere.

In Figure 10-8 the corpus callosum is shown as an extremely strong communication system so that all happenings in the minor hemisphere can very quickly and effectively be transmitted to the liaison brain of the dominant hemisphere, and so to the conscious self. This occurs for the contribution of the minor hemisphere for all perceptions, all experiences and all memories, and in fact for the whole content of World 2 (cf. Fig. 10-2). When the corpus callosum was severed, I assumed that there was revealed what was there all the time, namely that the minor hemisphere is always per se an unconscious part of the brain and that linkage through the corpus callosum is necessary for it to receive information from and to give information to the conscious self. However, I now recognize that this conclusion must be challenged on the grounds that the removal of the immense interhemispheral communication by the commissurotomy may deplete the performance of the minor hemisphere; and that normally it may have some direct liaison with the self-conscious mind, as indicated by the broken arrows of Figure 10-8. The possible role of commissural support to the minor hemisphere will be referred to again later.

When I postulated many years ago (Eccles, 1953), following Sherrington (1940), that there was a special area of the brain in liaison with consciousness, I certainly did not imagine that any definite experimental test could be applied in a few years. But now we have this distinction between the dominant hemisphere in liaison with the conscious self, and the minor hemisphere with at the most a marginal liaison. It is this empirical discovery that I try to illustrate in Figure 10-8. In it are shown the communication lines going both ways; out to the muscles via the motor pathways; and receiving from the world – the receptors projecting to the sensory cortical areas. It will also be recognized that, in its communication to World 2, the minor hemisphere normally suffers no material disability relative to the dominant hemisphere from its necessity to transmit through the corpus callosum to the liaison areas of the dominant hemisphere. First, the corpus callosum is such an immense tract that in transmission through it the minor hemisphere would have no traffic problem. Second, as seen in Figure 10-8, the greater part of the dominant hemisphere presumably has also to transmit to the liaison areas.

10.1.3 Time Relationships of Brain to Mind in Conscious Perception

The experiments of Libet on the human brain show that direct repetitive stimulation of the somaesthetic cortex results in a conscious experience after a delay as long as 0.5 s for weak stimulation, and a similar delay is observed for a sharp, but weak, peripheral skin stimulus (Libet, 1973). Although there is this delay in the neuronal events that trigger the experience of a weak peripheral stimulus, the experience itself is actually judged by the subject to be much earlier, at about the time of cortical arrival of the afferent input. This *ante-dating procedure* is not explicable by any neurophysiological process per se. Presumably it is a strategy that has been learnt by the self-conscious mind (*cf.* Chap. E2, Popper and Eccles, 1977). Two comments may be made. In the first place these long recognition times of up to 0.5 s are attributable to the necessity for building up an immense and complex patterned modular activity before it is detectable by the scanning self-conscious mind. Secondly, the antedating of the sensory experience is attributable to the ability of the self-conscious mind to make slight temporal adjustments, i. e. to play tricks with time. The patterned neuronal acitivity is detectable by the scanning process of the self-conscious mind at the time that there is the requisite build-up of the neuronal activity. It is suggested that the antedating is effected by the self-conscious mind in compensation for the tardy development of weak neuronal spatio-temporal patterns up to the threshold level for conscious recognition. In this way all experienced events are corrected in time so that their time sequence corresponds to the initiating stimuli, whether they be strong or weak. We suggest that Libet has discovered a temporal adjustment attributable to the self-conscious mind. But for this adjustment, a sequence of weak and strong taps, as in playing a percussion instrument, would be experienced in a distorted time relationship.

We are all conscious that sometimes time seems to run slowly and sometimes quickly, depending on the circumstances we are in. There is one particular aspect of experienced time that is of great interest and that is known to everybody. When acute emergencies arise, time seems to run in slow motion. This occurs when the self-conscious mind is reading out from the modules that are under this acute input relating to the emergency. The self-conscious mind is now able to slow down the experience of time so that it apparently has more time to make decisions in the emergency.

10.2 Radical Dualist-Interactionist Theory of Brain and the Self-Conscious Mind

A brief initial statement is that the *self-conscious mind* is a *self-subsistent entity* that is actively engaged in reading out from the multifarious activities of the neuronal machinery of the cerebral cortex according to its attention and interest, and it integrates this selection to give the unity of conscious experience from moment to moment. It also acts back in a selective manner on the neuronal machinery. Thus it is proposed that the self-conscious mind exercises a superior interpretative and controlling role upon the neuronal events by virtue of a two-way interaction between World 1 and World 2, as is indicated by the arrows from and to the liaison brain in Figure 10-2.

In formulating a strong dualistic hypothesis I build upon the following six foundations.

1. I assume that the experiences of the self-conscious mind have a relationship with neural events in special areas of the neocortex that collectively are known as the *liaison brain,* there being a relationship of interaction giving a degree of correspondence, but not an identity. The postulated liaison areas are certainly very extensive, including as they do the speech areas and the prefrontal lobes (Fig. 8-1). Later there will be further references to the anatomical locations in the neocortex.

2. There is a *unitary character* about the experience of the self-conscious mind. We are able to concentrate now on this, now on that aspect of the cerebral performance at any one instant. This focussing is the phenomenon known as *attention.*

3. Information from sense organs is transmitted both to the brain and within the neuronal machinery of the brain as complex spatio-temporal patterns of modular responses, but on crossing the frontier (upward arrows in Fig. 10-2) there is a miraculous transformation into the manifold experiences that characterize our perceptual world and that are of a different order of existence from events in the neuronal machinery.

4. There is the continual experience that the self-conscious mind can effectively act on brain events (downward arrows across the frontier in Fig. 10-2). This is most overtly seen in voluntary action, as described above, but throughout our waking life we can evoke events in the neuronal machinery, as indicated by the EEG (electroencephalogram),

when we try to recall a memory or to carry out a mental calculation, or to discover a phrase appropriate for expressing a thought.

5. Interaction across the frontier of Figure 10-2 occurs only when there is a high level of diversified activity in the neuronal machinery of the liaison brain. With too low a level there is the unconsciousness of anaesthesia or coma. With the high driven levels of seizures there is also unconsciousness.

6. It is necessary to build up a hypothesis that recognizes the openness of World 1 to influences from the world of conscious experience, World 2. Popper (1973) expresses very well the necessity for some loophole in the apparent closedness of the world of matter and energy – that is of World 1 (*cf.* Fig. 6-1). It is not enough to have an indeterminacy provided by the probabilistic operation at the quantal level. He states that a closed indeterministic World 1

> would be a world ruled by chance. This indeterminism is *necessary but insufficient* to allow for human freedom and especially for creativity. What we really need is the thesis that *World 1 is incomplete;* that it can be influenced by World 2; that it can interact with World 2; or that it is causally *open* towards World 2, and hence, further, towards World 3. We thus come back to our central point; we must demand that World 1 is not self-contained or 'closed', but open towards World 2.

With this background I can now give a more complete statement of the strong dualist hypothesis. The self-conscious mind is actively engaged in reading out from the multitude of active modules at the highest levels of the brain, namely in the liaison areas that are largely in the dominant cerebral hemisphere (Figs. 10-2, 10-8). The self-conscious mind selects from these modules according to attention, and from moment to moment integrates its selection to give unity even to the most transient experience. Furthermore, the self-conscious mind acts upon these modules, modifying the dynamic spatio-temporal patterns of the neuronal events. Thus the self-conscious mind exercises a superior interpretative and controlling role upon the neuronal events both within the modules and between the modules.

A key component of the hypothesis is that the unity of conscious experience is provided by the self-conscious mind and not by the neuronal machinery of the liaison areas of the cerebral hemisphere. Hitherto it has been impossible to develop any neurophysiological theory that explains how a diversity of brain events comes to be synthesized so that there is a unified conscious experience of a global or gestalt character. The brain events remain disparate, being essentially the individual actions of countless neurones that are built into complex circuits (*cf.* Fig. 10-9) and so participate in the spatio-temporal patterns of activity. My present hypothesis

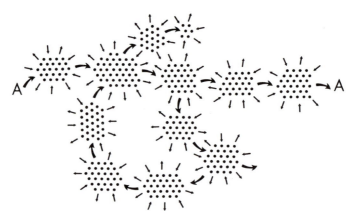

Fig. 10-9. In this schema of the cerebral cortex looked at from above, the large pyramidal cells are represented as dots that are arranged in clusters, each cluster corresponding to a column or module as diagrammed in Figures 8-4 and 8-8, where only four large projecting pyramidal cells are shown of the hundreds that would be in the column. The *arrows* symbolize impulse discharges along hundreds of lines in parallel, which are the mode of excitatory communication from column to column. Only a minimal system of serially excited columns is shown

regards the neuronal machinery as a multiplex of radiating and receiving structures (modules). *The experienced unity comes, not from a neurophysiological synthesis, but from the proposed integrating character of the self-conscious mind.* I conjecture that in the first place the *raison d' être* of the self-conscious mind is to give this unity of the self in all its conscious experiences and actions.

In developing the statement of the hypothesis I propose that in the liaison areas of the cerebral hemisphere some sensory input causes here and there an immense on-going dynamic pattern of neuronal activity. The different sensory modalities project from the primary sensory areas indicated in Figure 8-1 to common areas, the polymodal areas (Fig. 8–10). In these areas most varied and wide-ranging information is being processed in the unitary components, the modules of the cerebral cortex (Figs. 8-6 to 8-8). We may ask, how is this to be selected from and put together to give the unity and the relative simplicity of our perceptual experience from moment to moment? As an answer to this question it is proposed that the self-conscious mind plays through the whole liaison brain in a selective and unifying manner. An analogy is provided by a searchlight. Perhaps a better analogy would be some multiple scanning and probing device that reads out from and selects from the immense and diverse patterns of activity in the cerebral cortex and integrates these selected components, so organizing them into the unity of conscious experience. Figure 10-2 illustrates a fragment of a momentary 'fix' by the self-conscious mind. Thus I conjecture that the self-conscious mind is scanning the modular activities in the liaison areas of the cerebral cortex, as may be appreciated from the very inadequate diagram in Figure 10-2. From moment to moment it is selecting modules according to its interest, the phenomenon of attention, and is itself integrating from all this diversity to give the unified conscious experience.

This hypothesis may be considered to be just an elaborated version of parallelism – a kind of selective parallelism. However, this is a mistake. It differs radically in that *the selectional and integrational functions are conjectured to be attributes of the self-conscious mind,* which is thus given an active and dominant role. There is a complete contrast with the passivity postulated in parallelism (Fig. 10-1; *cf.* Feigl, 1967). Furthermore, the active role of the self-conscious mind is extended in this hypothesis to effect changes in the neuronal events. Thus not only does it read out selectively from the on-going activities of the neuronal machinery, but it also modifies these activities. For example, when following up a line of thought or trying to recapture a memory, it is proposed that the self-conscious mind is actively engaged in searching and in probing through specially selected zones of the neuronal machinery, and so is able to deflect and mould the dynamic patterned activities in accord with its desire or interest. A special aspect of this intervention of the self-conscious mind upon the operations of the neuronal machinery is exhibited in its ability to bring about movements in accord with some voluntary desired action, what we may call a motor command. The readiness potential (Figs. 10-3, 10-4) is a sign that this command brings about changes in the activity of the neuronal machinery.

10.3 Hypothesis of Cortical Modules and the Self-Conscious Mind

The question can now be asked: What neuronal events are in liaison with the self-conscious mind both for giving and receiving? The question concerns the World 1 side of the interface between World 1 and World 2 (*cf.* Fig. 10-2). I reject the hypothesis that the agent is the field potential generated by the neuronal events. The original postulate of the Gestalt school was based on the finding that a massive visual input such as a large illuminated circle resulted in some topologically equivalent field in the visual cortex, even a closed loop! This crude hypothesis need not be further considered. However, a more refined version has recently been proposed by Pribram (1971) in his postulate of micro-potential fields. It is assumed that these fields provide a more subtle cortical response than the impulse generation by neurones. However, this field potential theory involves a tremendous loss of information because hundreds of thousands of neurones would be contributing to a micro-potential field across a small zone of the cerebral cortex. All the finer grain of neuronal activity would be lost in this most inefficient task of generating a minute electrical potential by current flow in the ohmic resistance provided by the extracellular medium. In addition we have the further problem that there would have to be some homunculus to read out the potentials in all their patterned array! The assumed feed-back from micro-potential fields onto the firing frequencies of neurones would be of negligible influence because of the extremely small size of the currents.

We must believe that there are functional meanings in the discrete neuronal interactions in spatio-temporal patterns, otherwise there would be catastrophic losses of information. In this context, we must consider the organization of the cortical neurones in the anatomical and physiological entity that is called a module (Figs. 8-4, 8-7, 8-8). In the first place it is inconceivable that the self-conscious mind is in liaison with single nerve cells or single nerve fibres. These neuronal units as individuals are far too unreliable and ineffective. In our present understanding of the mode of operation of neuronal machinery I emphasize ensembles of neurones (many hundreds) acting in some collusive patterned array. Only in such assemblages can there be reliability and effectiveness. The modules of the cerebral cortex are such ensembles of neurones (*cf.* Lecture 8). The module has to some degree a collective life of its own with as many as 2500 neurones of diverse types and with a functional arrangement of feed-forward and feed-back excitation and inhibition (*cf.* Figs. 8-5 to 8-8). As yet we have little knowledge of the inner dynamic life of a module, but we may conjecture that, with its complexly organized and intensely active properties, it could be a component of the physical world (World 1) that is open to the self-conscious mind (World 2) both for receiving from and giving to. In Figure 10-2 the modules are indicated as vertical bands across the whole thickness of the cerebral cortex. I can further propose that not all modules in the cerebral cortex have this transcendent property of being open to World 2, and thus being the World 1 components of the interface. By definition there would be restriction to the modules of the liaison brain, and only then when they are in the correct level of activity.

Figure 10-10 gives a diagrammatic illustration of the conjectured relationship of open and closed modules as viewed by looking down at the surface of the cortex. A convenient diagrammatic liberty is to show the columns as separate discs, and not in the close contiguity that is the actual relationship (Fig. 8-8). Furthermore, it has to be recognized that the normal

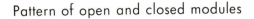

Pattern of open and closed modules

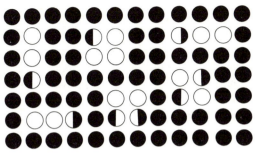

Fig. 10-10. Diagrammatic plan of cortical modules as seen from the surface. As described in the text the modules are shown as *circles* of three kinds, *open, closed (solid black)* and *half open.* Further description in text

intensely dynamic situation is frozen in time. The convention is that open modules are shown as open circles, closed as solid circles and that there are also partly open modules. It can be conjectured that the self-conscious mind scans this modular array, being able to receive from and give to only those modules that have some degree of openness. However, by its action on open modules, it can influence closed modules by means of impulse discharges along the association fibres from the open modules, as already described (Fig. 8-4) and may in this manner cause the opening of closed modules.

The complexity of the real situation can be appreciated when it is recognized that the modular assemblage of the liaison brain would be represented by increasing the dimensions of Figure 10-10, 100-fold in each direction. It can be conjectured that there is an intense dynamic interaction between modules. Interaction would be by inhibition of the immediately adjacent modules (Figs. 8-7 and 8-8) and by the excitatory actions of association and commissural fibres for the more remote modules (Fig. 8-4). Figure 10-9 shows in an extremely simplified form how sequential excitatory action by association fibres can result in some spatio-temporal patterns of modular interaction with even a closed loop. Since each module has some hundreds of pyramidal and stellate pyramidal cells with axons passing out of the module to other modules, the impulses discharged by a module would project to many other modules, and not just the one or two drawn in Figure 10-9. The number of projections is two or three in Figure 9–10. It may even be projecting to hundreds, altering their activity, and these in turn to hundreds of others. The complexity of the spreading pattern of activation is beyond all imagination, and would result in convulsive seizures were it not for the controlling inhibitory actions between modules as illustrated in Figures 8-7 and 8-8.

The simplest hypothesis of mind-brain interaction is that the self-conscious mind can scan the activity of each module of the liaison brain – or at least those modules tuned in to its present interests. I have already conjectured that the self-conscious mind has the function of integrating its selections from the immense patterned input it receives from the liaison brain – the modular activities in this present hypothesis – in order to build its experiences from moment to moment. The modules selected in this way constitute for the moment the World 1 side of the interface between World 1 and World 2, as diagrammatically shown in Figure 10-2. This interface is thus a constantly changing territory within the extensive area of the liaison brain. I have even presented evidence above that the self-conscious mind can make slight temporal adjustments in order to correct for perceptual delays, so that events in the external world come to be experienced in the correct temporal relationships regardless of their strength.

It has already been conjectured in Lecture 8 in relation to Figures 8-5 and 8-6 that only the afferents that have come in from the thalamic nuclei (*spec. aff.* in Figs. 8-5 and 8-6) preponderantly exert their influences at the power level (laminae 3, 4 and 5). So it is proposed that in the dynamic control and poise of the operating cerebral cortex there are all kinds of levels of subtlety and sensitivity in which activity is changed slightly, not with a 'bash'. Presumably the self-conscious mind does not act on the cortical modules with some bash operation, but rather with a slight deviation. A very gentle deviation up or down is all that is required. It may be conjectured that this effect builds up at the superficial laminae (1 and 2) and modulates and controls the discharges of pyramidal cells, which of course work on other modules. They are all playing this interacting game with one another. Furthermore I would conjecture that the self-conscious mind is weak relative to the power of the synaptic mechanisms in laminae 3 and 5 that are activated by the thalamic inputs. It is simply a deviator, and modifies the modular activity by its very slight influences that poetically we may call cognitive caresses!

We have to consider the arrangements for modular interaction through association and commissural fibres (Fig. 8-4) which are axons of the pyramidal cells of other modules. Thus each module is projecting to many others and they in turn to many others. So there are long and complex patterns of this mutual interaction. I conjecture that the self-conscious mind acts in modifying slightly some of these modules, presumably hundreds, and that the modules collectively react to these modifications, which are transmitted by the circuits of the association fibres and the callosal fibres. In addition the self-conscious mind is all the time reading out or perceiving the responses that it is making in this subtle manner. It is an essential feature of the hypothesis that the relations between modules and the self-conscious mind are reciprocal, the self-conscious mind being both an activator and a receiver.

As a consequence of the investigations on human brains with global (e. g. commissurotomy) or circumscribed lesions (Chaps. E5 and E6, Popper and Eccles, 1977), it may be conjectured that the liaison brain comprises a large part of the dominant hemisphere, particularly the linguistic areas and a large area of the prefrontal lobe. These extensive areas probably are composed of several large continuous sheets of cerebral cortex. However, the actual interface of open cortical modules of interest to the self-conscious mind at any moment would probably have a spotty or patchy character (Fig. 10-10). Presumably the reading out by the self-conscious mind would be concerned not with anatomical contiguity, but with the modules in functional communication by association or even by commissural fibres (Fig. 8-4). The integrational operation of the self-conscious mind in giving the unity of conscious experience would not be aided by the spatial proximity of modules. It is their functional interconnection that is important.

In further developing the hypothesis of some modules being open to World 2 in the guise of the self-conscious mind, it may be supposed that the self-conscious mind does not make a superficial pass over the module, as may be imagined if it merely sensed the micro-potential fields in the area. Rather it may be envisaged that it 'probes' into the module, reading out and influencing the dynamic patterns of neuronal performance. It can be assumed that this is done from moment to moment over the whole scattered assemblage of those modules processing information of immediate interest (attention) to the self-conscious mind for its integrational performance.

Another important feature of the interaction of self-conscious mind with modules is that, by its interaction with open modules, the self-conscious mind can indirectly interact with closed modules. Since the self-conscious mind is in liaison with open modules of the left hemisphere that project through the corpus callosum, I conjecture that there is a way into the right hemisphere for the self-conscious mind via open modules of the left hemisphere through the corpus callosum into all of the specialized but often closed modules of the right hemisphere (Fig. 10-8). These modules in turn will feed back into the open modules of the left hemisphere in a reciprocal operation. Thus the self-conscious mind can be engaged in the active processing of information in the right hemisphere, though it fails to do so after commissurotomy. There is a wealth of association and commissural connections whereby modules communicate very effectively both within a hemisphere and to the other hemisphere via the corpus callosum (*cf.* Fig. 8-4). There would be a very rich connectivity, and this is revealed by the losses of brain performance when the corpus callosum is sectioned, or when large areas of brain are ablated. For example both speech and verbal memory suffer after commissurotomy or after minor hemisphere lesions (Sperry, 1974; Milner, 1974).

10.4 Conclusions

The philosophy of a strong dualist interactionism as developed in this lecture has led me to build up conjectures upon the most advanced concepts at present available on the structure and functioning of the neocortex. I have endeavoured to keep the story as simple as possible, but I do realize that this lecture has been a long and arduous one. Yet how should we expect to have an easy solution of this greatest problem confronting us, namely the brain-mind problem? I do not claim to have offered a solution, but rather to have indicated in general outline the way the solution may come. In some mysterious manner the human brain evolved with properties of quite another order from anything else in nature. At the summit of these properties I would place initially the creative imagination that has built World 3, including all the values, and then pre-eminently there is the coming-to-be of self-consciousness. This is the climax of my story on the 'Human mystery', and here the mystery is furthest from comprehension.

Yet amazingly the human brain with these transcendental properties seems to differ from other mammalian brains merely by the size of the neocortex and by the evolution of special areas that have been distinguished in the Brodmann classification (Figs. 5–10 to 5–12). It is a measure of our ignorance that in the neocortex no special structural or physiological properties have been identified that distinguish sharply a human brain from the brain of an anthropoid ape. The tremendous difference in performance can hardly be attributable to a mere threefold increase in modules. We have no knowledge of any qualitative development that would account for the supreme performance of the human brain. Yet in Lectures 8 to 10 I have dared to build up hypotheses that relate to the brain-mind problem. The hope is that we may be challenged to enter on a new scientific era where the structure and function of the human neocortex will be studied by the most advanced techniques.

Epilogue

These lectures on the human mystery can be regarded as adventures or essays in ultimate concern. In the context of Natural Theology I have been inspired by Sherrington's challenge as cited in Lecture 1 to tell "the planet's story with what it has made and done".

We started in Lecture 2 from the Big Bang and followed the chain of contingency through to our galaxy with in Lecture 3, our solar system and that most unique and wonderful planet – our planet. Above every other attribute Planet Earth provided an environment fit for the origin and evolution of life (Lecture 4). After an immense delay at the stage of unicellular organisms for billions of years, our chain of contingency was traced in Lecture 4 through the strange vagaries of the evolutionary tree that led to us, a way that was quite unpredictable and also terribly hazardous. As I imagine back to that immensely long evolutionary process that was governed, we are dogmatically informed, solely by chance and necessity, I come to question a dogma that is so confidently asserted. As a scientist I recognize the necessity of criticism of scientific theories, particularly when the claim of scientific certitude is at issue. In these lectures, so far as it was possible, I have followed the materialist story of our origin – nay, of my origin. But I have grave misgivings. As an act of faith, scientific faith, it demands so much. The great French novelist Francois Mauriac whimsically said that it demanded an act of faith greater than for "what we poor Christians believe."

As I said at the outset, in the context of Natural Theology, I believe that there is a Divine Providence operating over and above the materialist happenings of biological evolution. That belief brands me as a *finalist*. We must not dogmatically assert that biological evolution in its present form is the ultimate truth. Rather we should believe that it is the main story and that in some mysterious way there is guidance in the chain of contingency that has led to us, as I have outlined in Lectures 4 and 5. With Lectures 6 and 7 we entered into the new age of human creativity, giving the world of culture (World 3). This advance was absolutely unpredictable. It was completely distinct from biological evolution though linked with it by reciprocal interaction. Furthermore cultural evolution had a quite distinct evolutionary logic of operation.

In Lecture 7 we saw that in some mysterious way World 3 was reciprocally linked with a new creation, the world of the spirit, World 2. And so the human self comes to exist, each self illuminated by its unique consciousness. Selfhood becomes an entity as discussed so imaginatively and poetically by Sherrington in his Gifford lectures.

In Lectures 8 to 10 we explored in depth the structure of the neocortex, so as to display its basic organization in modules by which any part of the neocortex communicates with a wide range of other parts. This new insight of Szentágothai in particular gives the basis for a much more meaningful theory on the spatio-temporal pattern of cortical activity, and on the manner of its interaction with the limbic system. In this basis there was consideration of the problems of perception, memory, motivation and voluntary action and ultimately of the conscious self in relation to the brain. A hypothesis of strong dualist-interactionism alone provided the hope of a satisfactory explanation of all these phenonema; however, in line with the theme of these lectures, it heightened the human mystery.

We can now recognize the relevance of those most startling ideas in Lecture 2, namely the anthropic principle according to which the universe was made for us. It is even implied in the title of Wheeler's (1973) memorable Copernican lecture: *'The universe as a home for man'.*

Overarching all the expression and argument of this lecture series is the insight that each of us is a participant in some great mysterious drama, as Sherrington and Schrödinger believed.

The profound tradgedy of our age is that this religious vision has become dimmed or rejected. As stated in the above quotations from Popper (1972, 1973), the strict dogma of science, in the conservation laws for example, leads to a philosophy of materialism and determinism with the closedness of World 1; and quantal indeterminacy provides not the slightest opening for the exercise of human freedom and creativity. Schopenhauer has wittily stated that materialism ... *'is the philosophy of the subject who has forgotten to take account of himself'.*

By contrast I attempt to build up a philosophy in which one's personal existence is central, but in which solipsism is rejected. There is recognition of the great mysteries in which we are immersed. Central to these mysteries is the fact of our personal existence as an experiencing and creating being, our coming-to-be in life and our apparent ceasing-to-be in death. I repudiate philosophies and political systems which recognize human beings as mere things with a material existence of value only as cogs in the great bureaucratic machine of the state, which thus becomes a slave state. The terrible and cynical slaveries depicted in Orwell's *1984* are engulfing more and more of our planet. Can we get the message of the recent rejection of human rights in the Belgrade conference of 1977 where cynicism replaced hypocrisy? The situation is so desperate that I prefer hypocrisy!

Is there yet time to rebuild a philosophy and a religion that can give us a renewed faith in this great spiritual adventure, which for each of us is a human life lived in freedom and dignity? My next series of Gifford lectures will be my humble effort to do what I can for humanity in this age of crisis and disillusionment.

References

[Numbers in square brackets at end of each entry indicate the pages on which it is cited.]

Abt, H. A.: The companions of sunlike stars. Sci. Amer. *236*, No. 4, 96–104 (1977) [43]

Akert, K.: Comparative Anatomy of the frontal cortex and thalamocortical connections. In: The frontal granular cortex and behaviour. Warren, J. M., Akert, K. (eds.), pp. 372–396. New York: McGraw-Hill 1964 [195]

Allen, G. I., Tsukahara, N.: Cerebrocerebellar communication systems. Physiol. Rev. *54*, 957–1006 (1974) [217]

Andersen, P., Bliss, T. V. P., Skrede, K. K.: Lamellar organization of hippocampal excitatory pathways. Exp. Brain Res. *13*, 222–238 (1971) [200]

Andersen, P., Bland, B. H., Dudar, J. D.: Organization of the hippocampal output. Exp. Brain Res. *17*, 152–168 (1973) [200]

Atkins, F. B.: Meteorites. In: Planet Earth. Hutchinson, P., Barnett, P. (eds.), pp. 24–27. Oxford: Elsevier Phaidon 1977 [42]

Bailey, P., Von Bonin, G., McCulloch, W. S.: The isocortex of the Chimpanzee. Urbana: University of Illinois Press 1950 [93]

Barondes, S. H.: Multiple steps in the biology of memory. In: Neurosciences, Vol. 2, pp. 272–278. Schmitt, F. O. (eds.), New York: Rockefeller University Press 1970 [207, 208]

Basser, L. S.: Hemiplegia of early onset and the faculty of speech with special reference to the effects of hemisherectomy. Brain *85*, 427–460 (1962) [130, 139]

Beloff, J.: The existence of mind. London: Macgibbon and Kee 1962 [4]

Bertram, B. C. R.: The social system of lions. Sci. Amer. *232*, No. 5, 54–65 (1975) [119]

Bliss, T. V. P., Lømo, T.: Long-lasting potentiation of synaptic transmission in the dentate area of the anaesthetized rabbit following stimulation of the perforant path. J. Physiol. *232*, 331–356 (1973) [185, 200]

Blum, H. F.: Time's arrow and evolution. Princeton: Princeton University Press 1968 [69, 72, 73]

Bok, B. J.: The births of stars. Sci. Amer. *227*, No. 2, 48–61 (1972) [25]

Brasier, M. D.: The fossil record. In: Planet earth. Hutchinson, P., Barnett, P. (eds.), pp. 240–244. Oxford: Elsevier Phaidon 1977 [53]

Bremer, F.: Neurophysiological correlates of mental unity. In: Brain and conscious experience. Eccles, J. C. (ed.). Berlin, Heidelberg, New York: Springer 1966 [178]

Brodal, A.: Neurological anatomy. In relation to clinical medicine. London: Oxford University Press 1969 [195]

Brodmann, K.: Vergleichende Lokalisationslehre der Großhirnrinde. Leipzig: J. A. Barth 1909 [89, 90, 93, 150]

Brodmann, K.: Neue Ergebnisse über die vergleichende histologische Lokalisation der Großhirnrinde. Anat. Anz. *41*, 157–216 (1912) [90]

Brown, G. M.: The moon. In: Planet earth. Hutchinson, P., Barnett, P. (eds.), pp. 14–18. Oxford: Elsevier Phaidon 1977 [42]

Brown, R. D.: Organic matter in interstellar space. In: In the beginning. Wild, J. P. (ed.), pp. 1–14. Canberra: Australian Academy of Science 1974 [60]

Calder, N.: Violent universe. p. 160. London: British Broadcasting Corporation 1969 [15, 16, 17, 18, 19, 20, 21, 22, 23, 24, 26]

Calvin, M.: Chemical evolution. Eugene (Oregon): University of Oregon Press 1961 [61]

Calvin, M.: Chemical evolution. London: Oxford University Press 1969 [61]

Cameron, A. G. W.: The origin and evolution of the solar system. Sci. Amer. *233*, No. 3, 32–41 (1975) [35]

Carter, B.: Large number coincidences and the anthropic principle in cosmology. In: Proceeding of extraordinary general assembly of International Astronomical Union (Krakov). Longair, M. S. (ed.). Boston: Reidel 1974 [30]

Curtiss, S.: Genie: A psycholinguistic study of a Modern-day "Wild Child". p. 288. New York: Academic Press 1977 [138, 139, 140, 141]

Curtiss, S., Fromkin, V., Krashen, S., Rigler, D., Rigler, M.: The linguistic development of Genie. Language *50*, 528–554 (1974) [139]

Deecke, L., Grözinger, B., Kornhuber, H. H.: Voluntary movements in man, Cerebral potentials and theory. Biol. Cybernet. *23*, 99–119 (1976) [216, 217]

De Valois, R. L.: Central mechanisms of color vision. In: Handbook of Sensory Physiology. Vol. VII/3 A. Jung, R. (ed.). Berlin, Heidelberg, New York: Springer 1973 [172]

Dicke, R. H.: Dirac's cosmology and Mach's Principle. Nature *192*, 440–441 (1961) [30]

Dobzhansky, T.: Mankind evolving: The evolution of the human species. New Haven: Yale University Press 1962 [101]

Dobzhansky, T.: The biology of ultimate concern. p. 152. New York: New American Library 1967 [6, 73, 97, 117, 118, 136]

Eccles, J. C.: The neurophysiological basis of mind. Oxford: Clarendon Press 1953 [224]

Eccles, J. C.: The physiology of synapses. Berlin, Heidelberg, New York: Springer 1964 [149]

Eccles, J. C.: Facing Reality: Philosophical adventures by a brain scientist. p. 210. Berlin, Heidelberg, New York: Springer 1970 [117, 144, 185, 213, 224]

Eccles, J. C.: The understanding of the brain. 2nd ed., p. 244. New York: McGraw-Hill 1977 [151, 173]

Eccles, J. C.: An instruction-selection theory of learning in the cerebellar cortex. Brain Res. *127*, 327–352 (1977) [197, 209]

Eccles, J. C.: An instruction-selection hypothesis of cerebral learning. In: Cerebral correlates of conscious experience. Buser, P., Buser, A. (eds.). Amsterdam: Elsevier 1978 [199, 201, 209]

Eigen, M.: Selforganization of matter and the evolution of biological macromolecules. Naturwissenschaften *58*, 465–522 (1971) [62, 63]

Eigen, M., Winkler, R.: Das Spiel. p. 404. München: Piper 1975 [62, 63]

Feigl, H.: The "mental" and the "physical". p. 179. Minneapolis: University of Minnesota Press 1967 [4, 173, 229]

Fifková, E., Van Harreveld, A.: Long-lasting morphological changes in dendritic spines of dentate granular cells following stimulation of the entorhinal area. J. Neurocytology *6*, 211–230 (1977) [185, 186, 187]

Forey, P.: Jawless fishes. In: Planet earth. Hutchinson, P., Barnett, P. (eds.) pp. 264–265. Oxford: Elsevier Phaidon 1977 [55, 56]

Fox, S. W.: Simulated natural experiments in spontaneous organization of morphological units from proteinoid. In: The origins of prebiological systems and of their molecular matrices. Fox, S. W. (ed.). New York: Academic Press 1964 [62]

Fromkin, V., Kraskin, S., Curtiss, S., Rigler, D., Rigler, M.: The development of language in Genie: A case of language acquisition beyond the critical period. Brain and Language *1*, 81–107 (1974) [138]

Geschwind, N.: Language and the brain. Sci. Amer. *226*, No. 4, 76–83 (1972) [129]

Geschwind, N.: The anatomical basis of hemispheric differentiation. In: Hemisphere function in the human brain. Dimond, S. J., Beaumont, J. G. (eds.), pp. 7–24. New York: John Wiley and Sons 1974 [90]

Goldman, P. S., Nauta, W. J. H.: Columnar distribution of corticocortical fibers in the frontal association, limbic and motor cortex of the developing rhesus monkey. Brain Res. *122*, 393–412 (1977) [152]

Goodall, J. Van L.: In the shadow of man. New York: Dell 1971 [119]

Gott, J. R., Gunn, J. E., Schramm, D. N., Tinsley, B. M.: Will the Universe expand forever? Sci. Amer. *234*, No. 3, 62–79 (1976) [15, 24]

Gross, C. G.: Visual functions of inferotemporal cortex. In: Handbook of Sensory Physiology, Vol. VII/3 B. Jung, R. (ed.), pp. 451–482. Berlin, Heidelberg, New York: Springer 1973 [172]

Grözinger, B., Kornhuber, H. H., Kriebel, J.: Methodological problems in the investigation of cerebral potentials preceding speech: Determining the onset and suppressing artefacts caused by speech. Neuropsychologia *13*, 263–270 (1975) [216]

Hartmann, W. K.: The smaller bodies of the solar system. Sci. Amer. *233*, No. 3, 142–159 (1975) [41]

Hawkes, J.: Prehistory in history of mankind. Cultural and scientific development, Vol. 1 Part 1. Unesco (London): New English Library 1965 [93, 101, 103, 115]

Hawkes, J.: The first great civilizations. London: Hutchinson 1975 [114]

Hawking, S. W.: The quantum mechanics of black holes. Sci. Amer. *236*, No. 1, 34–40 (1977) [24, 25]

Hein, A., Held, R.: Dissociation of the visual placing response into elicited and guided components. Science *158*, 390–392 (1967) [131]

Held, R., Bauer, J. A.: Visually guided reaching in infant monkey after restricted rearing. Science *155*, 718–720 (1967) [131]

Held, R., Hein, A.: Movement-produced stimulation in the development of visually guided behaviour. J. comp. physiol. Psychol. *56*, 872–876 (1963) [132, 133]

Henderson, L. J.: The fitness of the environment. New York: Macmillan 1913 [69, 72]

Henderson, L. J.: The order of nature. Cambridge (Mass.): Harvard University Press 1917 [72]

Holloway, R. L.: The casts of fossil hominid brains. Sci. Amer. 231 No. 1, 106–115 1974 [79, 93]

Hubel, D. H.: The Visual Cortex of the Brain. In: From cell to organism. pp. 54–62. San Francisco: W. H. Freeman 1963 [170]

Hubel, D. H.: Specificity of responses of cells in the visual cortex. J. psychiat. Res. *8*, 301–307 (1971) [170, 171]

Hubel, D. H., Wiesel, T. N.: Receptive fields, binocular interaction and functional architecture in the cat's visual cortex. J. Physiol. (Lond.) *160*, 106–154 (1962) [169]

Hubel, D. H., Wiesel, T. N.: Shape and arrangement of columns in the cat's striate cortex. J. Physiol. *165*, 559–568 (1963) [170, 171]

Hubel, D. H., Wiesel, T. N.: Receptive fields and functional architecture in two non-striate visual areas (18 and 19) of the cat. J. Neurophysiol. *28*, 229–289 (1965) [171]

Hubel, D. H. and Wiesel, T. N.: Laminar and columnar distribution of geniculo-cortical fibers in the Macaque monkey. J. Comp. Neurol. *146*, 421–450 (1972) [169, 170]

Hubel, D. H., Wiesel, T. N.: Sequence regularity and geometry of orientation columns in the monkey striate cortex. J. Comp. Neurol. *158*, 267–294 (1974) [170, 171]

Hunten, D. M.: The outer planets. Sci. Amer. *233*, No. 3, 130–141 (1975) [39]

Iben, I.: Globular-cluster stars. Sci. Amer. *223*, No. 1, 26–39 (1970) [19]

Jacobsen, C. F.: Studies on the cerebral function of primates: I. The functions of the cerebral association areas in monkeys. Comp. Psychol. Monogr. *13*, 3–60 (1936) [201]

Jansen, J.: The central nervous system in Cetacea. Nautilus (Basel) Documenta Geigy *14*, 7–8 (1973) [87]

Jasper, H. H., Ward, A. A., Pope, A. (eds.), pp. 13–28. New York: Little and Brown 1969 [160]

Jerison, H. J.: Evolution of the brain and intelligence. p. 482. New York, London: Academic Press 1973 [59, 60, 75, 81, 82, 83, 84, 85, 86, 87, 93, 94, 116, 117]

Jerison, H. J.: Paleoneurology and the evolution of mind. Sci. Amer. 234, No. 1, 90–101 (1976) [94]

Jerne, N. K.: Antibodies and learning: selection versus instruction. In: The Neurosciences. Quarton, G. C., Melnechuk, T., Schmitt, F. O. (eds.), pp. 200–205. New York: Rockefeller University Press 1967 [209]

Jones, E. G., Powell, T. P. S.: An anatomical study of converging sensory pathways within the cerebral cortex of the monkey. Brain 93, 793–820 (1970) [194]

Jones, E. G., Powell, T. P. S.: Anatomical organization of the somatosensory cortex. In: Handbook of Sensory Physiology, Vol. 2. Iggo, A. (ed.), Pp. 579–620. Berlin, Heidelberg, New York: Springer 1973 [165]

Keller, H.: The story of my life. New York: Magnum 1968 [138]

Kimura, D.: Functional asymmetry of the brain in dichotic listening. Cortex 3, 163–178 (1967) [130, 139]

Kimura, M.: Genetic codes and the laws of evolution as the bases for our understanding of the biological nature of man. In: The search for absolute values: harmony among the Sciences. 5th International conference on the Unity of the Sciences. pp. 621–630. New York: International Cultural Foundation 1977 [64, 72]

Kohler, I.: Über Aufbau und Wandlungen der Wahrnehmungswelt. SB Öst. Akad. Wiss. 227, 1–118 (1951) [134]

Kornhuber, H. H.: Neural control of input into long term memory: limbic system and amnestic syndrome in man. In: Memory and transfer of information. Zippel, H. P. (ed.), pp. 1–22. New York: Plenum Press 1973 [194, 195, 196, 197, 201]

Kornhuber, H. H.: Cerebral cortex, cerebellum and basal ganglia: An introduction to their motor functions. In: The neurosciences: third study program. Schmitt, F. O., Worden, F. G. (eds.), pp. 267–280. Cambridge (Mass): MIT Press 1974 [214, 215]

Kramer, N. K.: History begins at Sumer. New York: Doubleday 1959 [113]

Kumar, S. S.: Planetary systems. In: The emerging Universe. Saslaw, W., Jacobs, K. (eds.). Charlottesville: University Press of Virginia 1972 [43, 44]

Lenneberg, E. H.: Biological foundations of language. New York: John Wiley 1967 [140]

Lenneberg, E. H.: On explaining language. Science 164, 635–643 (1969) [135, 136, 137]

Leovy, C. B.: The atmosphere of Mars. Sci. Amer. 237, No. 1, 34–43 (1977) [44, 45]

Levy, J.: Psychobiological implications of bilateral asymmetry. In: Hemisphere function in the human brain. Dimond, S. J., Beaumont, J. G. (eds.). New York: John Wiley 1973 [222]

Levy, J., Trevarthen, C., Sperry, R. W.: Perception of bilateral chimeric figures following hemispheric deconnexion. Brain 95, 61–78 [220, 221]

Levy-Agresti, J., Sperry, R. W.: Differential perceptual capacities in major and minor hemispheres. Proc. Natl. Acad. Sci. 61, 1151 (1968) [222]

Lewis, J. S.: The chemistry of the solar system. Sci. Amer. 230, No. 3, 50–65 (1974) [36]

Libassi, P. T.: Early man, nearly man. The Sciences May 1975, 13–18 [76, 77, 78]

Libet, B.: Electrical stimulation of cortex in human subjects, and conscious memory aspects. In: Handbook of Sensory Physiology, Vol. 2. Iggo, A. (ed.), pp. 743–790. Berlin, Heidelberg, New York: Springer 1973 [225]

Libet, B., Kobayashi, H., Tanaka, T.: Synaptic coupling into the production and storage of a neuronal memory trace. Nature 258, 155–157 (1975) [202]

Margulis, L., Lovelock, J. E.: The view from Mars and Venus. The Sciences 17, No. 2, 10–13 (1977) [44, 45, 46]

Marin-Padilla, M.: Prenatal and early postnatal ontogenesis of the human motor cortex: A Golgi study. II. The basket pyramidal system Brain Res. 23, 185–191 (1970) [160]

Marlen-Wilson, W. D., Teuber, H. L.: Memory for remote events in anterograde amnesia: recognition of public figures from newsphotographs. Neuropsychologia 13, 353–364 (1975) [193]

Marr, D.: A theory for cerebral neocortex. Proc. R. Soc. (Lond.) B, *176*, 161–234 (1970) [199]

Mauss, T.: Die faserarchitektonische Gliederung der Grosshirnrinde bei den niederen Affen. J. Psychol. Neurol. *13*, 263–325 (1908) [90, 91]

Mauss, T.: Die faserarchitektonische Gliederung des Cortex cerebri der anthropomorphen Affen. J. Psychol. Neurol. *18*, [Suppl. 3] 410–467 (1911) [90, 92]

Mayr, E.: Descent of man and sexual selection. In: L'Origine dell' Uomo. pp. 33–61. Roma: Academia Nazionale dei Lincei 1973 [77, 80, 95, 96]

Mc Gaugh, J. L.: Facilitation of memory storage processes. In: The future of the brain sciences. Bogoch, S. (ed.), pp. 355–370. New York: Plenum 1969 [206, 207, 208]

Miller, S. L.: Production of some organic compounds under possible primitive Earth conditions. J. Am. Chem. Soc. *77*, 2351 (1955) [61]

Miller, S. L.: The mechanism of synthesis of amino acids by electric discharge. Biochim. biophys. Acta *23*, 488 (1957) [61]

Milner, B.: The memory defect in bilateral hippocampal lesions. Psychiat. Res. Rep. Amer. Psychiat. Ass. *II*, 43–52 (1969) [191]

Milner, B.: Amnesia following operation on the temporal lobes. In: Amnesia. Whitty, C. W. M., Zangwill, O. L. (eds.), pp. 109–133. London: Butterworths 1966 [190, 192,193]

Milner, B.: Brain mechanisms suggested by studies of temporal lobes. In: Brain mechanisms underlying speech and language. Millikan, C. H., Darley, F. L. (eds.), pp. 122–145. New York, London: Grune and Stratton 1967 [222]

Milner, B.: Disorders of learning and memory after temporal lobe lesions in man. Clin. Neurosurg. *19*, 421–446 (1972) [190, 208]

Milner, B.: Hemispheric specialization: scope and limits. In: The Neurosciences Third Study Program. Schmitt, F. O., Worden, F. G. (eds.), pp. 75–89. Cambridge, London: MIT Press 1974 [95, 222, 234]

Monod, J.: Chance and Necessity. New York: Knopf 1971 [5, 9]

Mountcastle, V. B.: The view from within: Pathways to the study of perception. Johns Hopkins Med. J. *136*, 109–131 (1975) [173]

Mountcastle, V. B.: An organizing principle for cerebral funcion: the unit module and the distributed system. In: The Neurosciences Fourth Study Program. MIT Press 1978 [158, 160, 173]

Mountcastle, V. B., Lynch, J. C., Georgopoulos, A., Sakata, H., Acuna, C.: Posterior parietal assoiation cortex of the monkey: Command functions for operations within extrapersonal space. J. Neurophysiol. *38*, 871–908 (1975) [166, 173]

Murray, B. C.: Mercury. Sci. Amer. *233*, No. 3, 58–69 (1975) [46]

Nauta, W. J. H.: The problem of the frontal lobe: a reinterpretation. J. Psychiat. Res. *8*, 167–187 (1971) [176, 177, 195]

Nauta, W. J. H., Karten, H. J.: A general profile of the vertebrate brain with sidelights on the ancestry of the cerebral cortex. In: The Neurosciences. Second Study Program. Schmitt, F. O. (ed.), pp. 7–26. New York: Rockefeller University Press 1970 [146]

Orgel, L. E.: The synthesis of life molecules. In: In the beginning. Wild, J. P. (ed.), pp. 85–101. Canberra (A.C.T.): Australian Academy of Science 1974 [61, 62]

Paecht-Horowitz, M., Berger, J., Katchalsky, A.: Nature *228*, 636 (1970) [62]

Pandya, D. N., Kuypers, H. G. J. M.: Cortico-cortical connexions in the rhesus monkey. Brain Res. *13*, 13–36 (1969) [197]

Parmentier, E. M.: Planet Earth. In: Planet Earth. Hutchins, P., Barnett, P. (eds.), pp. 9–13. Oxford: Elsevier Phaidon 1977 [47]

Parrot, A.: Sumer. Preface by A. Malraux. London: Thames and Hudson 1960 [108]

Penfield, W.: The Mystery of the Mind. pp. 123. Princeton (N. J.): Princeton University Press 1975 [213]

Penfield, W., Milner, B.: Memory deficit produced by bilateral lesions in the hippocampal zone. Arch. Neurol. Psychiat. *78*, 475–497 (1958) [193]

Penfield, W., Perot, P.: The brain's record of auditory and visual experience. Brain *86*, 596–696 (1963) [204, 205]

Penfield, W., Roberts, L.: Speech and brain mechanisms. Princeton (N. J.): Princeton University Press 1959 [90, 129]

Penrose, R.: Black holes. Sci. Amer. *226*, No. 5, 38–46 (1972) [24]

Piaget, J.: The origin of intelligence in the child. London: Routledge and Kegan Paul 1953 [131]

Piaget, J.: Operational Structures of the Intelligence and Organic Controls. In: Brain and Human Behaviour. Karczmar, A. G., Eccles, J. C. (eds.). Berlin, Heidelberg. New York: Springer 1973 [135]

Polanyi, M.: The tacit dimension. Garden City (N. J.): Doubleday 1966 [5, 6]

Pollack, J. B.: Mars. Sci. Amer. *233*, No. 3, 106–117 (1975) [44]

Polten, E. P.: A critique of the psycho-physical identity theory. pp. 290. The Hague: Mouton 1973 [4, 173]

Popper, K. R.: Objective knowledge: An evolutionary approach. Oxford: Clarendon Press 1972 [99, 213, 236]

Popper, K. R.: Indeterminism is not enough. Encounter *40*, 20–26 (1973) [227, 236]

Popper, K. R., Eccles, J. C.: The self and its brain. pp. 597. Berlin, Heidelberg, New York: Springer International 1977 [4, 9, 99, 100, 116, 117, 142, 143, 173, 174, 204, 208, 210, 213, 225, 233]

Prentice, A. J. R.: Formation of planetary systems. In: In the beginning. Wild, J. P. (ed.), pp. 15–47. Canberra (A. C. T.): Australian Academy of Science 1974 [34, 35, 36]

Pribram, K. H.: Languages of the Brain. pp. 432. Englewood Cliffs: Prentice-Hall 1971 [229]

Rakic, P.: Mode of cell migration to the superficial layers of fetal monkey neocortex. J. comp. Neurol. *145*, 61–84 (1972) [128]

Rees, M. J., Silk, J.: The origin of galaxies. Sci. Amer. *226*, No. 6, 26–35 (1970) [15, 17, 25]

Ringwood, A. E.: The early chemical evolution of planets. In: In the beginning. Wild, J. P. (ed.), pp. 48-84. Canberra (A. C. T.): Australian Academy of Science 1974 [37, 38, 39, 40, 41, 42, 47, 61]

Ryle, G.: The concept of mind. pp. 334. London: Hutchinson's University Library 1949 [4]

Sagan, C.: The solar system. Sci. Amer. *233*, No. 3, 22–31 (1975) [33]

Sagan, C., Drake, F.: The search for extraterrestrial intelligence. Sci. Amer. *232*, No. 5, 80–89 (1975) [73]

Sandars, N. K.: The epic of Gilgamesh. London: Penguin 1973 [113]

Sarvey, J. M., Misgeld, U., Klee, M. R.: Long-lasting heterosynaptic post-activation potentiation (PAP) of CA3 neurons in guinea pig hippocampal slice. Fed. Proc. *37*, 251 (1978) [183, 184]

Schramm, D. N.: The age of the elements. Sci. Amer. *230*, No. 1, 69–77 (1974) [22, 23]

Schrödinger, E.: Mind and matter. pp. 1–104. London: Cambridge University Press 1958 [4, 5, 31]

Schuster, P.: Models of selforganizing systems of biological macromolecules. In: The search for absolute values: harmony among the Sciences. 5th International conference on the Unity of the Sciences. pp. 565–602. New York: International Cultural Foundation 1977 [62, 63]

Senden, M. v.: Space and sight. Translated by P. Heath. London: Methuen 1960 [134]

Sherrington, C. S.: Man on his nature. pp. 413. Cambridge: Cambridge University Press 1940 [1, 2, 3, 7, 72, 118, 119, 124, 213, 224]

Sidman, R. L., Rakic, P.: Neuronal migration with special reference to developing human brain: a review. Brain Res. *62*, 1–36 (1973) [126, 127]

Siever, R.: The earth. Sci. Amer. *233*, No. 3, 82–91 (1975) [51]

Simons, E. L.: Ramapithecus. Sci. Amer. *236*, No. 5, 28–35 (1977) [60, 75]

Simpson, G. G.: This view of life: the world of an evolutionist. New York: Harcourt, Brace and World 1964 [73]

Simpson, G. G., Beck, W. S.: Life. An introduction to Biology. New York: Harcourt, Brace and World 1969 [66, 67, 68, 69]

Solecki, R. S.: Shanidar. New York: Knopf 1971 [119]

Solecki, R. S.: The implications of the Shanidar Cave. Neanderthal Flower Burial. Anm. N. Y. Acad. Sci. *293*, 114–124 (1977) [119]

Sperry, R. W.: Lateral specialization in the surgically separated hemispheres. In: The Neurosciences Third Study Program. Schmitt, F. O., Worden, F. G. (eds.), pp. 5–19. Cambridge, London: MIT Press 1974 [218, 219, 234]

Stephan, H., Andy, O. J.: Quantitative comparative neuroanatomy of primates: An attempt at a phylogenetic interpretation. Ann. N. Y. Acad. Sci. *167*, 370–387 (1969) [85, 87, 88]

Stratton, G. M.: Vision without inversion of retinal image. Psychol. Rev. *4*, 463–481 (1897) [134]

Sylvester Bradley, P. C.: The origin of Life. In: Planet Earth. Hutchinson, P., Barnett, P. (eds.), pp. 235–237. Oxford: Elsevier Phaidon 1977 [52]

Szentágothai, J.: Architecture of the Cerebral Cortex. In: Basic mechanisms of the Epilepsies.

Szentágothai, J.: Les circuits neuronaux de l'écorce cérébrale. Bull. Acad. R. Med. Belg. *7, 10*, 475–492 (1970) [198, 199]

Szentágothai, J.: The basic neuronal circuit of the neocortex. In: Synchronization of EEG Activity in Epilepsies. (Symposium of the Austrian Academy of Sciences). Petsche, H., Brazier, M. A. B. (eds.), pp. 9–24. Vienna: Springer 1972 [161]

Szentágothai, J.: A structural overview. In: Conceptual models of neural organization. Szentágothai, J., Arbib, M. (eds.). Neurosciences Res. Progr. Bull. *12*, 354–410 (1974) [161]

Szentágothai, J.: The module-concept in cerebral cortex architecture. Brain Res. *95*, 475–496 (1975) [157, 160]

Szentágothai, J.: The neuron network of the cerebral cortex: A functional interpretation. Proc. R. Soc. (Lond.) B, *201*, 219–248 (1978a) [151, 152, 153, 155, 156, 160]

Szentágothai, J.: Local neuron circuits of the neorcortex. In: The Neurosciences Fourth Study Program. 1978b [153, 154]

Szentágothai, J.: The local neuronal apparatus of the cerebral cortex. In: Cerebral correlates of conscious experience. Buser, P., Buser, A. (eds.), pp. 131–138. Amsterdam: Elsevier Press 1978c [159]

Tanabe, T., Yarita, H., Iino, M., Ooshima, Y., Takagi, S. F.: An olfactory projection area in orbiofrontal cortex of the monkey. J. Neurophysiol. *38*, 1269–1283 (1975) [176]

Thorne, K. S.: The search for black holes. Sci. Amer. *231*, No. 6, 32–43 (1974) [25]

Thorpe, W. H.: Biology, psychology and belief. London: Cambridge University Press 1961 [5]

Tillich, P.: Theology of culture. London: Oxford University Press 1959 [6]

Tobias, P. V.: The brain in hominid evolution. New York: Columbia University Press 1971 [97]

Tobias, P. V.: Darwin's prediction and the African Emergence of the Genus Homo. In: *D'Origine dell Uomo.* pp. 63–85. Roma: Academia Nazionale dei Lincei 1973 [77, 101]

Valverde, F.: Apical dendritic spines of the visual cortex and light deprivation in the mouse. Exp. Brain Res. *3*, 337–352 (1967) [187]

Valverde, F.: Structural changes in the area striata of the mouse after enucleation. Exp. Brain Res. *5*, 274–292 (1968) [185]

Victor, M., Adams, R. D., Collins, G. H.: The Wernicke-Korsakoff-Syndrome. pp. 1–206. Oxford: Blackwell Scientific 1971 [190]

Villee, C. A.: Biology. p. 915. Philadelphia. W. B. Saunders 1972 [53, 64, 65, 66, 68, 69, 74]

Wada, J. A., Clarke, R., Hamm, A.: Cerebral hemispheric asymmetry in Humans. Arch. Neurol. *32*, 239–246 (1975) [129]

Walker, A. E.: A cytoarchitectural study of the prefrontal area of the macaque monkey. J. comp. Neurol. *73*, 59–86 (1940) [92]

Washburn, S. L.: The evolution of human behaviour. In: The uniqueness of man. Roslansky, J. D. (ed.). Amsterdam: North Holland 1969 [119]

Weinberg, S.: The first three minutes. p. 188. London: André Deutsch 1977 [14]

Weiskrantz, L.: The interaction between occipital and temporal cortex in vision: an overview. In: The Neurosciences Third Study Program. Schmitt, F. O., Worden, F. G. (eds.), pp. 189–204. Cambridge (Mass.), London: MIT Press 1974 [173]

Wheeler, J. A.: The Universe as a home for man. Am. Scientist. 62, 683–691 (1974) [25, 27, 28, 29, 236]

Wheeler, J. A.: Genesis and observership. In: University of Western Ontario Series in the Philosophy of Science. Butts, R., Hintikka, J. (eds.). Boston (Mass.): Reidel 1977 [25, 28, 29, 30, 31]

White, B. L., Castle, P., Held, H.: Observations on the development of visually-directed reaching. Child Developm. 35, 349–364 (1964) [131]

Whittaker, V. P., Gray, E. G.: The synapse: Biology and Morphology. Br. Med. Bull. 18, 223–228 (1962) [148, 150]

Wigner, E. P.: Two kinds of reality. The Monist 48, 248–264 (1964) [4, 5]

Wilson, E. O.: Sociobiology: The new synthesis. Cambridge (Mass.): Belknap Press, Harvard University Press 1975 [87]

Woolley, L.: The art of the middle east including Persia, Mesopotamia and Palestine. New York: Crown 1961 [107]

Woolley, L.: The beginnings of civilization. New York: Mentor Book, New American Library 1963 [109, 110]

Wood, J. A.: The Moon. Sci. Amer. 233, No. 3, 92–105 (1975) [42]

Young, A., Young, L.: Venus. Sci. Amer. 233, No. 3, 70–81 (1975) [46]

Zaidel, E.: Auditory language comprehension in the right hemisphere following cerebral commissurotomy and hemispherectomy: A comparison with child language and aphasia. In: The acquisition and break-down of language: parallels and divergencies. Zurif, E., Caramazza, A. (eds.). Baltimore: Johns Hopkins University Press 1976 [140]

Zeki, S. M.: Colour coding in the superior temporal sulcus of rhesus monkey visual cortex. Proc. R. Soc. (Lond.) B, 197, 195–223 (1977) [179]

Subject Index

Karl R. Popper
Penn, Great Britain

John C. Eccles
Contra, Switzerland

The Self
and Its Brain

66 figures. XVI, 597 pages. 1977
Cloth DM 39,–; US $ 19.50; £ 9.40
ISBN 3-540-08307-3
Available from your bookseller

Contents:
Materialism Transcendens Itself. The Worlds 1, 2 and 3.
Materialism Criticized. Some Remarks on the Self.
Historical Comments on the Mind-Body-Problem.
Summary. – The Cerebral Cortex. Conscious Per-
ception. Voluntary Movement. The Language Centres
of the Human Brain. Global Lesions of the Human
Cerebrum. Circumscribed Cerebral Lesions. – The
Self-Conscious Mind and the Brain. Concious
Memory: The Cerebral Processes Concerned in
Storage and Retrieval. – Dialogues.

In Part I, Popper discusses the philosophical issue
between dualist or even pluralist interactionism on the
one side, and materialism and parallelism on the other.
There is also a historical review of these issues.

In Part II, Eccles examines the mind from the neurological standpoint: the structure of the brain and its
functional performance under normal as well as abnormal circumstances, for example when lesions
(especially those surgically induced) are present. The
result is a radical and intriguing hypothesis on the
interaction between mental events and detailed neurological occurrences in the cerebral cortex.

Part III, based on twelve recorded conversations,
reflects the exciting exchange between the authors as
they attempt to come to terms with their conflicting
opinions. This part preserves the intimate quality of the
dialogues, and shows how some of the authors' view-
points changed in the course of these daily discussions.

Prices are subject to change without notice

Springer
International

J. C. Eccles

Facing Reality

Philosophical Adventures by a
Brain Scientist

36 figures, XI, 210 pages. 1970
DM 25,–; US $ 11.00
(Heidelberg Science Libary, Volume 13)
ISBN 3-540-90014-4

Contents:
Introduction: Man, Brain and Science. –
The Neuronal Machinery of the Brain. –
Synaptic Mechanisms Possibly Concerned
in Learning and Memory. – The Experiencing Self. – The Brain and the Unity
of Conscious Experience. – Evolution and
the Conscious Self. – The Understanding
of Nature. – Man, Freedom and Creativity.–
The Necessity of Freedom for the Free
Flowering of Science. – The Brain and the
Soul. – Education and the World of Objective Knowledge. – Epilogue . – References.

From the reviews:
"This book is an account of the views of a
brain scientist of world renown on the life-
long interplay between the conscious self
and the external world. It is based on various lectures and papers written over the
last few years, including some unpublished
material...
The reality of which he speaks in the title of
his book is above all the realitiy of self
awareness and death awareness. These two
are at the heart of many present discon-
tents, and as a brain scientist Sir John
Eccles is distressed that the problems
should so often nowadays be treated with
irrationality and not with reason. Sir John
has often broken a lance with the philo-
sophers and has read widely. This is a
deeply interesting book."
Durrant's British Medical Journal

John C. Eccles, William C. Gibson

Sherrington – His Life and Thought

1979. 7 figures. Approx. 290 pages
Cloth DM 34,–; US $ 18.70
ISBN 3-540-09063-0

Contents:
The Early Years. – The Liverpool
Professor. – Oxford. – The Years of the Presi-
dency of the Royal Society 1920–1925. – The
Last Decade of Oxford 1925–1935. – Major
Correspondents in his Later Years (Oxford
and Thereafter). – Sherrington, the Philoso-
pher of the Nervous System. – Books and the
Man. – Sherrington the Poet. – Public
Service. – The Final Philosophical
Messages. – Epiloque. – Selected Referen-
ces. – Appendices.

Although several studies have been published on Sherrington's work, until now none
has dealt in depth with the man and his world.
Sir John Eccles and William C. Gibson
chronicle Sherrington's life from his under-
graduate days at Cambridge to the Brown
Institution in London, the University of
Liverpool and Oxford University, and finally
his election to the Presidency of the Royal
Society and his receipt of the Nobel Prize.

The authors draw on Sherrington's volumi-
nous correspondence, on little known papers,
speeches and poems, on his Gifford Lectures
(1937–1938) and his superb biography of
Jean Ferall (which he published at the age
of 89). The result is a rigorous appraisal of
Sherrington's philosophy and a portrait of the
man as compelling as it is complete. This
work will remain the definitive Sherrington
biography for many years to come.

Prices are subject to change without notice

 Springer-Verlag Berlin Heidelberg New York